David Lavery is Professor of English and Popular Culture at Middle Tennessee State University. He is author and editor of over 20 books, including *Joss Whedon: Conversations*, *The Essential Cult Television Reader*, *The Essential Sopranos Reader*, as well as *Reading The Sopranos* and *Reading Deadwood* (both I.B.Tauris). Dr Lavery is co-founder of the Whedon Studies Association, founding co-editor of its journal *Slayage*, and one of the founders of *Critical Studies in Television*. He has lectured around the world on the subject of television and taught at Brunel University in London from 2006 to 2008.

JOSS WHEDON, A CREATIVE PORTRAIT

From Buffy the Vampire Slayer to Marvel's The Avengers

David Lavery

I.B.TAURIS

LONDON · NEW YORK

Published in 2014 by I.B.Tauris & Co Ltd
6 Salem Road, London W2 4BU
175 Fifth Avenue, New York NY 10010
www.ibtauris.com

Distributed in the United States and Canada Exclusively by Palgrave Macmillan
175 Fifth Avenue, New York NY 10010

ISBN: 978 1 84885 030 9

A full CIP record for this book is available from the British Library
A full CIP record is available from the Library of Congress

Library of Congress Catalog Card Number: available

Typeset in Adobe Caslon Pro by www.freerangeproduction.com

Printed and bound in Great Britain by Page Bros, Norwich

CONTENTS

LIST OF FIGURES

LIST OF TABLES

ACKNOWLEDGEMENTS

On 5 October 1999, I was teaching a course on film history at Middle Tennessee State University. One of my students asked before class began if I would be watching the season premiere of *Buffy the Vampire Slayer* that evening. I responded with disdain. I had hated the movie and was barely cognizant of the TV show, although I had just noticed with surprise that my new copy of *Entertainment Weekly* featured "The Ultimate *Buffy* Viewer's Guide" as though it were worthy of careful attention. Two other students in the class chimed in, insisting that it would be a show I would love – that it was my "kind of show." I agreed to check it out and that evening watched "The Freshman" (4.1). I was instantly hooked, even though, in retrospect, it was not an especially strong episode. I was not aware then that Joss Whedon had written and directed, nor did I even know who Whedon was. Since one of my students had taped the first three seasons, I caught up quickly. Within a month, I had seen all of *Buffy the Vampire Slayer*. Soon thereafter I had begun working on a book on *Buffy* (*Fighting the Forces: What's at Stake in* Buffy the Vampire Slayer) with Rhonda Wilcox. The book you are about to read began that day as well.

Its road to publication has been long and winding. I wrote the original draft in a London flat while teaching in the UK. Originally, back when my subject was supposed to write and direct a Wonder Woman movie, it was to have been called *Wonder Boy* and would track Whedon's career arc from television writer to blockbuster filmmaker, but that never happened (as I chronicle in Chapter 12). Then it was revised to tell the new and very different story of a brilliant cult creator who aspired to become mainstream but failed to make the leap. But the spring of 2012 – which saw the release of the long-on-the-shelf, ingenious horror flick *The Cabin in the Woods* and, less than a month later, the record-setting, billion-dollar-grossing *The Avengers* – dramatically overwrote that story and demanded a new, happy ending, the present one, in which Whedon makes the leap and sticks the landing.

Without the worldwide community of Whedonians who have listened to and inspired many of the ideas in these pages, it could never have been written (I name but a few; they are legion): Gerry Bloustien, Angela Ndalianis, Trisha Pender, Patrick Porter, Katy Stevens and Sue Turnbull in Australia; Tuna Erdem and Selim Eyuboglu in Turkey; Stacey Abbott, Dee Amy-Chinn, Viv Burr, Bronwen Calvert, Janet Halfyard, Matt Hills, Christine Jarvis, Lorna Jowett, Roz Kaveney, Ewan Kirkland, Tanya Krzywinska, Matt Pateman, Zoe-Jane Playdon and Milly Williamson in the UK; Jes Battis, Stan Beeler, Michele Byers, Francis Early, Cynthea Masson, Erma Petrova, Douglas K. Rabb, J. Michael Richardson, Nikki Stafford and Sharon Sutherland in Canada; Barbara Maio and Giada da Ros in Italy; Marcus Recht in Germany; Michael Adams, David Bianculli, Alyson Buckman, Tamy Burnet, Jeff Bussolini, Tanya Cochran, AmJo Comeford, Agnes Curry, Kevin Durand, Lynne Edwards, Greg Erickson, James Francis, Sherry Ginn, Jonathan Gray, Dale and Ensley Guffey, Nancy Holder, Alysa Hornick, Linda Jencson, David Kociemba, Neil Lerner, Bill Lund, Gordon Melton, Joyce Millman, Mary Alice Money, Ananya Mukherjea, Deborah Overstreet, Beth Rambo, Jana Riess, Lawrence Rosenfeld, Suzie Siegel, Jim South, Sarah Swann, Greg Stevenson, Tamara and Jim Wilson, and Stephanie Zacharek in the USA.

I am indebted as well to many of my MTSU students: to Chris Peltier, Erin Gonzalez, Becky Short, and Brian Loggins, who originally introduced me to the Whedonverses; and to the wonderful seminarians in my 2005 and 2012 Joss Whedon courses: Byron Brown, Joe Gualtieri, Cindy O'Malley, Cynthia Burkhead, Hillary Yeager, Melissa Lamb, Becky Bobbitt, Nicholas Bush, Erica Marsh, Michelle Herr, Sara Hays, Sarah Gray-Panesi, Luke Patton, Tom Cruz, Dan Copp, Lisa Jass, Dawn Schock, Tori Warenik and Cori Mathis.

A special thanks to Nancy Holder for the Preface, Hillary Yeager for her tombstone, and Alison Raines for the index.

Jeanine Basinger and Richard Slotkin, Whedon's professors, were willing to answer some of my many questions.

Without the late Howard Gruber and his brilliant life's work on the nature of creativity, this book would have been a shallow endeavour indeed.

My debt to Philippa Brewster at I.B.Tauris is immense. She is the kindest and most astute of editors. Thanks, too, to my agent Uwe Stender for helping to make this book (and several others) a reality.

The Lavery women, my wife, Joyce, and daughters, Rachel and Sarah, have nurtured me and put up with my obsessions more than I deserve. And now we have Addy, our wonderful grandchild, as well. I love you all so much.

Most of all, my thanks to Rhonda Wilcox, mother of *Buffy* Studies, a critic and scholar whose brilliance constantly humbles (though she is herself the most modest person I know) and the finest of friends. This book is dedicated to her.

PREFACE

The first time I interviewed Joss Whedon (during the filming of the *Buffy the Vampire Slayer* season two finale), I asked him if he considered himself an auteur. He blinked and laughed, looking flattered, and told me no. But I think it's pretty clear to many of us that he is. In this fascinating book, David Lavery explores Joss's artistic development, juxtaposing his findings with the work of Harold Gruber, whose field is the nature of creativity. What were the forces and influences that informed Joss as an innovator capable of such a body of quirky, beloved work, versus those that produced a skilled, more "commercial" director such as Michael Bay? David begins at the beginning – Joss's boyhood – and tracks the elusive "X" factor with a keen scholar's eye. The result, this book, is a must-have for anyone who is interested either in the matter of Whedon or the artistic life, or both.

I met David Lavery and Rhonda Wilcox, the father and mother of Buffy Studies, at the first Slayage Conference in Nashville, in 2004. As one of the few attending non-academicians, I was moved to tears by the rigour and brilliance of hundreds of Buffy scholars presenting papers and holding erudite discussions of the show I loved above all others. David and Rhonda have become my friends, and through them, I have met many of the authors of the vast scholarly canon about Joss and his work. Because of our association, I have joined the ranks of academia and now teach at two universities. I look forward to presenting this book to my students. It's an irreverent and dead-on case study of a brilliant auteur who has changed the shape of the pop-culture landscape, And if that weren't enough, it's a great, fun read.

Astronauts, definitely.

Nancy Holder, author of *Buffy: The Making of a Slayer*, co-author of *The Watcher's Guides*, and Bram Stoker Award-winning novelist

What we will find, I think, is not some little component part here and there, like this person has photographic memory or some terrific inborn ability that nobody else has, but a different organization of the system, an organization that was constructed by the person himself in the course of his life, in the course of his work, as needed in order to meet the tasks that he encountered and that he set himself.
(Howard Gruber, "From Epistemic Subject," 177)

If you're running a footrace against someone and a person gets across the line just ahead of you, you might get jealous. But if they're like 600 yards ahead, you can't get jealous. I was so in awe of what Joss could do that all I could do was marvel. Nobody's jealous of Superman. You just gape.
(Jane Espenson [quoted by Rogers, "With *The Avengers* Joss Whedon Masters the Marvel Universe"])

I am the fan that gets to have the most fun. I get to walk the set every day. I totally get to be there when the story's broken. I get to do all of the fun bits. Every day is fan day for me. That's who I am. I'm the fan that got the closest.
(Joss Whedon, "Pop Culture Q & A")

PROLOGUE

Michael Bay vs. Joss Whedon, Weapons to Be Determined

In which two Wesleyan alumni square off, caveman vs. astronaut, for the future of the imagination.

ooooooooooo

[Bay] has his collar up. The collar on his light-tan jacket. You find yourself wishing he didn't have his collar up ... But soon you are past the collar-up thing. Because now you're wishing he didn't park in the handicapped spot. Oh, you wish he didn't just pull up here to the production office and, without so much as a blip of hesitation, pull his car into the handicapped spot. But he did. And there's nothing you can do. There really is no defense you can give to a healthy thirty-seven-year-old man *parking his $200,000 Ferrari in a handicapped spot*. And why do you wish he wasn't this way? Because you are a generous human being with a regular heart and you like your main character to be sympathetic? Maybe. [my italics]

(Jeanne Marie Laskas, "Bay" [*Esquire* 2001])

In an early scene of "A Hole in the World," the fifteenth episode of the final season of *Angel* – the one in which Fred died, her body commandeered by the ancient god Illyria – we find the ever-contentious Angel (David Boreanaz) and Spike (James Marsters) in mid-argument:

Spike: It's bollocks, Angel! It's your brand of bollocks from the first to last.
Angel: No, you can't ever see the big picture. You can't see any picture!
Spike: I am talking about something primal. Right? Savagery. Brutal animal instinct.
Angel: And that wins out every time with you. (*in Spike's face*) You know, the human race has evolved, Spike! (*walks away from Spike*)

Spike: (*follows Angel making mocking gestures*) Oh, into a bunch of namby-pamby, self-analyzing wankers who could never hope to –

Angel: We're bigger. We're smarter. Plus, there's a thing called teamwork, not to mention the superstitious terror of your pure aggressors!

Spike: You just want it to be the way you want it to be.

Angel: (*yelling*) It's not about what I want![1]

Wesley (Alexis Denisof) interrupts the heated colloquy and asks if the subject at hand is one the entire leadership of Wolfram and Hart should be discussing, and an embarrassed Angel answers in the negative, insisting that the subject was "theoretical." As usual, Spike is more forthcoming:

Spike: (*calmly*) We were just working out a b – (*passionate again*) Look, if cavemen and astronauts got into a fight, who would win?

Wesley: Ah. You've been yelling at each other for 40 minutes about this?

Wesley does have a question, however: "Do the astronauts have weapons?" In unison, Spike and Angel reply: "No."[2]

Figure 1: Whedon Succeeds George Lucas – on a T-Shirt

The subject of this book, and one half of the title of this prologue, is the writer and director of "A Hole," Joss Whedon (1964–), the fan boy, script doctor, librettist, writer, actor, television auteur and movie director who created *Angel* (WB, 1999–2004), spinning it off from his legacy series

Buffy the Vampire Slayer (WB, 1997–2001; UPN, 2001–3). Emblazoned on a T-shirt now for sale on the Internet we find the words, in an imitation of the font used in *Star Wars*, "Joss Whedon Is My Master Now."[3] Among his enthusiastic fans, Whedon, even before the tremendous commercial success of Marvel's *The Avengers*, has acquired unprecedented allegiance, the sort a pre-*Phantom Menace* George Lucas once inspired, or a Darth Vader demanded.

In the period of relative dormancy during which much of this book was written, adherents were so ardent for a crumb of Whedon that even the master's supposed grocery list, an *Onion*esque parody propagated by *Dateline Hollywood* could create a flurry of activity. Later republished in the official *Buffy* magazine as if it were "true," it tells the story of growing fan obsession with the "Master's" leaked-to-the-web personal shopping inventory, said to exhibit "that trademark Whedon wit" in its word choice ("diet moo juice," for example, not "skim milk"). "Devoted fans," we learn, "signed petitions and raised $2.5 million demanding that a network turn 'Joss's Grocery List' into a television series," thus making up for previous sins like the cancellation of *Angel* and *Firefly*. *Dateline Hollywood* reported that the leader of a petition campaign to get Whedon back on the small screen finds it, even after 148 readings, "smarter, funnier, and more compelling than anything currently on TV." We also learn that (1) "sales of the items on Whedon's leaked list have shot up 173% since it began spreading on the Internet" – for obvious reasons, as one fan explains: "I can only hope that by eating what Joss eats, I'll get one-one thousandth of one percent of his genius" and (2) fears of blowback have spread: what if the run on Whedon favourites leads to their absence at his own grocery store – could that not hamper the Master's creativity? *Dateline* also reports news of Whedon's own second-hand response: "Through a publicist, Whedon said he 'appreciates all my fans' support,' but asked that 'Joss's Grocery Shoppers' members 'go bother [cult favourite *Veronica Mars* creator] Rob Thomas for a while and give me a breather.'"[4]

No doubt about it: Joss Whedon has become a "force" to be reckoned with. If critical interest is any indication of merit – no other film and television auteur of comparable age – he just turned 49 – has inspired so much investigation.[5]

Until the Spring of 2012, however, Whedon was thought of almost exclusively as a cult figure, a designation with which he was completely comfortable. In the CHUD interview he told Fred Topel that "the highest compliment I've ever gotten paid was in the first year of *Buffy* when a woman came up to me at Comic-Con in line and said that *Buffy* was her favorite show, in full Klingon makeup."

In perhaps the most oft-quoted response from all of his many interviews, Whedon explains his cultish intentions in the creation of *Buffy*:

> I designed the show to create that strong reaction. I designed Buffy to be an icon, to be an emotional experience, to be loved in a way that other shows can't be loved. Because it's about adolescence, which is the most important thing people go through in their development, becoming an adult. And it mythologizes it in such a way, such a romantic way – it basically says, "Everybody who made it through adolescence is a hero." And I think that's very personal, that people get something from that that's very real. And I don't think I could be more pompous. But I mean every word of it. I wanted her to be a cultural phenomenon. I wanted there to be dolls, Barbie with kung-fu grip. I wanted people to embrace it in a way that exists beyond, "Oh, that was a wonderful show about lawyers, let's have dinner." I wanted people to internalize it, and make up fantasies where they were in the story, to take it home with them, for it to exist beyond the TV show. And we've done exactly that.
>
> *(JWC, 28)*

For personal and professional reasons, Whedon will have none of the widely held belief that obsessive fans should get a life: "I have never had any particular life of my own, so I don't see any particular reason why anyone should run out to get one," he tells *Sci Fi Weekly*.[6] As the maker of shows "designed to foster slavish devotion," Whedon feels it is only natural for him to "entirely respect it in others" (*JWC*, 16) – in that Klingon *Buffy* fan, for example. And in his dialogue with Neil Gaiman, he records his curiosity at Hollywood's "marginalization" of the larger-than-given-credit-for cult market (Grossman): "It's not like *Star Wars* – which came out when I was eleven – was a tiny art house flick," Whedon reminds us.

Which brings us to the other half of our title – the caveman, or is it the astronaut? – Michael Bay (b. 1965), a commercially successful but critically reviled movie director, who, like Whedon, graduated from Wesleyan University, where both studied under legendary film historian Jeanine Basinger. Despite a common alma mater and mentor, Whedon and Bay remain polar opposites, as different as, well, a caveman and an astronaut: each an explorer of one pole of the contemporary media axis, each with his own "weapons" at the ready.

As Table One makes clear, Whedon and Bay have more than just an education in common. Whedon came from a family of television scribes who wrote for a variety of shows in the 1950s, 1960s and 1970s. Bay may have showbiz genes as well; he claims, after all, to be the bastard son of John Frankenheimer (1930–2002), a go-to director of early live American television drama, famous for *The Manchurian Candidate* (1962).

After Wesleyan (about which more later), both Whedon and Bay followed Horace Greely's injunction and went West. Despite a natural desire to avoid becoming ensnared in the family business, Whedon would end up writing for TV (*Roseanne, Parenthood*). Bay quickly became an in-demand director of ads. Not surprisingly his films continue to be full of product placement. One critic observed that sometimes the only images in focus in his "Cuisinart" cinematic style are the products being plugged (Taylor, Review of *Bad Boys 2*). There is no bigger contributor to the creation of what Mark Crispin Miller deemed two decades ago "Hollywood the Ad."

Whedon found work as a sometimes-uncredited but well-paid script-doctor. Bay honed his skills doing music videos, which, like his work in ads, would also influence his "shoot for the edit" style. Whedon's script for *Buffy the Vampire Slayer* would be made into a 1992 movie that failed to get the Whedonesque right but would instil a life-time hatred in the young Whedon for Donald Sutherland and send him back to script-doctoring. Three years after *Buffy* the movie flopped, Bay's *Bad Boys* would gross nearly $149 million worldwide and earn him a Directors Guild award for Commercial Director of the Year. The very next year Bay's *The Rock*, with its big-name stars (including Sean Connery), would gross 330 million worldwide.

Whedon and *Buffy the Vampire Slayer* were reborn together in 1997, this time as a television series. In 1998, *Armageddon* – with its half-a-billion international box office – firmly established Bay as an in-demand director. IMDB Pro lists his current fee as $25,000,000 per picture. Continuing to hint at his desire to escape television and work in film, Whedon remained at work in the family business, spinning off from *Buffy* the new darker, more adult series *Angel*.

In 2001, Buffy the character died, again, and the series moved to UPN, while Bay's *Pearl Harbor* garnered typically harsh reviews and sold only 450 million dollars worth of tickets globally. In 2002, *Firefly* debuted on Fox, which aired it on the graveyard of Friday evening, screwed up its broadcast order, and quickly axed it.

In 2003, after seven seasons and 144 episodes, *Buffy* would come to an end, brought down by Whedon's own burnout and Sarah Michelle Gellar's desire to become a movie star. Also in 2003, Whedon, a comic book geek since his teens, would finish writing *Fray* for Dark Horse Comics, the tale of a future slayer, and Bay did a sequel to his first film, *Bad Boys II*, which, though tremendously more expensive than its predecessor, grossed 50 percent less domestically (slightly more worldwide).

In 2004, *Angel* was cancelled by the WB but, not ready to fade away, ended memorably in a rain-drenched alley after five seasons and 110 episodes. An extraordinary grassroots campaign resulted in *Serenity*, a movie continuation of the *Firefly* saga, but the box office for the 2005 film, Whedon's first as writer/director, was disappointing (though DVD sales were excellent). Bay's *The Island* – the spring release of which, along with George Lucas's *Star Wars: Revenge of the Sith* (2005), forced a delayed premier for Whedon's *Serenity* – became his first outright failure, costing an estimated $126 million to make and earning back only about $36 million in the USA (though it did break even abroad).

During his post-*Serenity* doldrums, Whedon would return to the comic book, including a new, paper-only version of *Buffy* Season 8 as well as his takes on other people's comic franchises, *Astonishing X-Men* and Brian K. Vaughn's *Runaways*, the story of the children of supervillains who band together to become superheroes. Whedon's affection for other television shows led to his directing of two episodes of Greg Daniels's *The Office* – one of which ("Business School") featured Dwight Schrute's encounter with a "vampire" bat. Unable to satisfy his masters (including Joel Silver [*The Matrix*]) with his in-development script, Whedon would officially back out of Wonder Woman in the Fall of 2006.

In 2007, Bay would bounce back from his flop on *The Island* with the franchise-launching *Transformers*, a movie based on a children's toy, which grossed over US$300,000,000 and an astonishing $700,000,000 worldwide, re-establishing him as the king of the blockbuster. In sharp contrast, Whedon headed back to television, reaching agreement with Fox, to which he continued to be obligated in a long-term development deal, to create *Dollhouse*. Starring Eliza Dushku, *Buffy's* Faith, *Dollhouse* debuted in January 2009 and ended, cancelled, a year later after two seasons.

Having found his franchise, Michael Bay went on to direct two more hugely successful *Transformers* films (2009, 2011), while the Whedon Spring of 2012 would see the successful release of the long-on-the-shelf Whedon-authored horror film *The Cabin in the Woods* and then the record-setting blockbuster Marvel's *The Avengers*, which would in short order eclipse all of Bay's films in the box office record book. By August, Whedon would sign a development deal with Marvel Studios to direct an *Avengers* sequel and create properties for television like the much-anticipated Marvel's *Agents of S.H.I.E.L.D* series.

Table 1: Joss Whedon/Michael Bay Timeline

Year(s)	Joss Whedon	Michael Bay
1950–80	Father and grandfather TV writers	
1964	Born	
1965		Born, purportedly the son of film director John Frankenheimer
1980s	Graduates (1985) from Wesleyan University (studies with Jeanine Basinger); goes to Hollywood with aspirations of becoming a filmmaker	Graduates (1986) from Wesleyan University (studies with Jeanine Basinger); goes to Hollywood with aspirations of becoming a filmmaker
Late 80s, early 90s	Writes for television (*Roseanne, Parenthood*)	Directs ads (Nike, Coca-Cola, Got Milk, Reebok)
Early 90s	*Buffy the Vampire Slayer* (1992), first produced film script, bombs	Directs music videos (Donny Osmond, Meat Loaf, Tina Turner, Lionel Richie)
1994	*Speed*, a movie he script-doctored, is released	
1995	*Toy Story* and *Waterworld*, both script-doctored by Whedon, released	*Bad Boys*, first directorial effort, released
1996		*The Rock* released
1997	*Alien Resurrection* (filmed from a script by Whedon) is released; *Buffy the Vampire Slayer* becomes a television series	
1998		*Armageddon* released
1999	*Buffy* spin-off *Angel* premieres	
2001	*Buffy* moves to UPN	*Pearl Harbor* released
2002	*Firefly* debuts on Fox and is cancelled	
2003	*Buffy* comes to an end; *Fray* completed	*Bad Boys II* released
2004	*Angel* cancelled; begins writing *Astonishing X-Men*	
2005	*Serenity* released and does disappointing box office; signs to direct Wonder Woman	*The Island* released
2007	Withdraws from Wonder Woman project; writes comic books; directs "Business School" and "Branch Wars" (*The Office* 3.16 and 4.6)	*Transformers* released
2008	Writes an arc of *Runaways*	
2009	*Dollhouse* debuts on Fox (February 2009)	*Transformers: Revenge of the Fallen* released
2010	*Dollhouse* is cancelled (January 2010); directs "Dream On" (*Glee*, 1.19)	
2011	Filming of Marvel's *The Avengers* and *Much Ado About Nothing* completed	*Transformers: Dark of the Moon* released
2012	*The Cabin in the Woods* and Marvel's *The Avengers* released; Whedon signs to direct *Avengers 2* and develop Marvel properties for television	Producer of an in-development *Ninja Turtles* reboot
2013	Marvel's *Agents of S.H.I.E.L.D.* debuts on ABC in the Fall	Bay's action comedy *Pain and Gain* is a box office hit

Like any good mother, Bay and Whedon's teacher Basinger cannot differentiate her love for all her children – cannot decide whether she prefers a caveman or an astronaut. Her praise for Whedon is well known,[7] and a later chapter (3. Film Studies Major) will examine it carefully. Less well known is her take on Bay.[8] "I often joke that my tombstone will read 'She taught Michael Bay,'" Basinger admits. "But I don't think Michael Bay is the devil. I think he's a good filmmaker. He was an award-winning photographer as a high school student, a fully defined visual artist as a kid, and I don't think he approached the medium with the idea of pleasing other people necessarily" (quoted in Rodriguez, "The Mere Mention"). So Bay has always been an artist and, understood from the right perspective, he is in Basinger's eyes an artist still:

> Ingmar Bergman said, "Every great filmmaker has to define film on his own terms," and in a sense, that's right. [...] For Michael, it's about pace and rapid movement. Michael is actually *an abstract artist* in the way he uses time, space, light and color. He's almost *an experimental filmmaker* in that regard. He uses the medium in the fastest, sharpest way that it can be used, and if you don't like it, tough luck. [my italics]

According to at least one admirer, however, Bay is not bothered by artistic inclinations. Tom Gorai, a producer and collaborator, offers, if you will, the anti-Basinger defence: "Michael's interests line up perfectly with what the American public wants," Gorai observes. "I think a lot of directors would be like that if they could put away their artistic guilt" (quoted in Hochman). As evidence of his connection with his audience, Bay's numbers are, indeed, impressive (as Table 2 demonstrates). His *oeuvre* to date has not given birth to Bay Studies – not a single book on Bay has yet appeared – but his over $4 billion worldwide gross in just over 15 years is indeed impressive in the boardroom if not the classroom.

And Whedon's popularity? Comparing television ratings with movie box office is an apples and oranges affair, but we should note that none of Whedon's four television series, despite their international cult followings, ever made it out of the bottom tier of the Nielsen rankings (three were cancelled), and *Serenity*, his first movie, with an estimated budget of $39,000,000, grossed a disappointing $38,869,464 worldwide. Only this year, over 20 years into his career, has Joss Whedon joined the ranks of blockbuster directors with the $220,000,000 *Avengers*. (See Chapter 13.)

Table 2: Michael Bay Box Office

Bay Movie	US Gross	World Gross
Bad Boys (1995)	$65,807,024	$148,800,000
The Rock (1996)	$134,006,721	$330,500,000
Armageddon (1998)	$201,573,391	$554,600,000
Pearl Harbor (2001)	$198,539,855	$450,400,000
Bad Boys II (2003)	$46,522,560	$261,900,000
The Island (2005)	$35,799,026	$160,299,000
Transformers (2007)	$317,601,309	$701,014,499
Transformers: Revenge of the Fallen (2009)	$402,111,870	$836,303,693
Transformers: Dark of the Moon (2011)	$352,390,543	$1,119,241,043
Totals	**$1,754,352,299**	**$4,563,058,235**

And yet, a quick Google search will reveal that Whedon is a figure of worldwide adoration while Bay is often the target of derision. A quick search on YouTube will uncover some very clever anti-Bay films, both live action and animated, and film critics have been merciless. Described by Rene Rodriguez in *The Miami Herald* as "a stereotypically slick, hotshot director whose movies are all assaultive flash and vacuous thrills – a perfect filmmaker, in other words, for the Xbox generation," Bay has become in one sense a bit of a joke, as Rodriguez notes: "[I]n [...] *Team America: World Police* [2004], *South Park* creators Trey Parker and Matt Stone have one of their marionettes sing the line 'I miss you/ More than Michael Bay missed the mark when he made *Pearl Harbor*' and everyone in the theater got the joke." On NPR's *Wait, Wait, Don't Tell Me!* host Peter Sagal observed that "Michael Bay is to filmmaking what Hurricane Katrina was to urban planning." And the ever-profane *Onion* offers us an imaginary yet accurate exclusive on a future Bay project: "Michael Bay Signs $50M Deal To Fuck Up *ThunderCats*."

Or consider this summary of Bay's critical estimation from David Hochman in *Entertainment Weekly*:

> [M]aking movies by applause meter and then turning them into two-hour commercials for testosterone doesn't exactly improve Hollywood's image as a culture-clotting, intelligence-sapping behemoth. And the critics have not been generous. *Bad Boys*, *The New York Times* said, was

"stitched together, like some cinematic Frankenstein's monster, from the body parts of other movies." And the *Los Angeles Times* said *The Rock* "epitomizes trends in Hollywood filmmaking that have made many people very rich while impoverishing audiences around the world."

Those words appear in an essay (alluded to by Basinger in her defence of her student) entitled "Is Michael Bay the Devil?"

Charles Taylor was thinking about *Bad Boys II* when he made this observation in *Salon* about Bay's crash and burn movie making, but he could have been talking about almost any of his films:

> It's not enough for a bad guy holding onto the side of a speeding Jeep to fly over the edge of a parking garage; his body has to crash into a glass booth below. It's not enough for a villain to go down in a hail of bullets. He has to land in a minefield so we can see the blown-apart bits of his carcass fly up in the air. And when a mortuary van is engaged in a high-speed chase, not only do the back doors fly open so bodies go sprawling all over the highway, we get to see the speeding cars running over them and, in one case, severing a head.

For Taylor, this is not "abstract," "experimental" filmmaking – as Basinger characterizes it; it is not avant-garde but "illiterate": "Michael Bay's career. […] is some sort of reverse triumph, the whomping emergence of illiterate filmmaking. By that I don't mean that the film is made for illiterates, but that his movies are put together seemingly without any grasp of how to construct a story or even a scene." Taylor's damnation is not short on specifics:

> The editing is so manic that during the chases or gun battles you can never tell where the opposing factions are in relation to each other. Whenever something isn't exploding or crashing, whenever Bay has to show two people talking to each other (oh, *those* boring old things), he has no idea how to shoot the scene except in close-ups. Bay's success is proof that sheer incompetence need not deter anyone from becoming a commercially successful director.

Later in these pages, I will have more to say about the distinctive features of Joss Whedon's directorial style, but with Taylor's charge of illiteracy in mind and by way of contrast with his fellow Wesleyanite, let us briefly consider at this point a sequence from the end of "Serenity," written and directed by Whedon – the intended *Firefly* pilot. Having barely escaped from a deal gone bad on Whitefall, Mal and his crew find themselves pursued in atmosphere by the menacing (though not yet seen) Reavers in their oil-smoke-belching spacecraft. Boldly, calmly piloted by the-anything-but-manly-man Wash (Alan Tudyk – earlier we had seen him playing with toy dinosaurs) and engineered by the recovering-from-a-bullet-wound ingenious Kaylee (Jewel Straite), *Serenity* escapes (thanks to a Crazy Ivan) and leaves the cannibals hungry.

The Reaver chase scene is wonderfully clear. We care about the characters throughout, established in all their complexity as only a continuing television series can. We know the terrifying risks and the rewards. Even in the midst of terror, Whedon continues to bring "the funny" (see p. 182) *and* the naughty (after their escape Zoë asks Mal to "take the helm" because "I need this man to tear all my clothes off"). And, despite the paltry budget and the time limitations – American television shows ordinarily have only eight days to get an episode in the can – the sequence looks great, well with the possible exception of that missing steering apparatus Wash is so not hanging onto at the scene's end.

The "Battle of Chicago" in Bay's *Transformers*: *Dark of the Moon* and the final "Battle of New York" in *The Avengers* make the contrast between the two Wesleyanites' directorial style even more apparent. In the former, CGI dominates, and the non-stop action is nearly impossible to follow. In the latter, the characters – Iron Man, The Hulk, Captain America, Thor, Black Widow, Hawkeye, even Loki – are in the forefront, the mêlée is punctuated with character moments, and we know what is going on and who is doing what at every moment.

Caveman vs. Astronaut

Take-it-to-the-bank, "shoot for the edit" summer blockbuster director vs. successful cult television writer and director and showrunner and aspiring filmmaker; Michael Bay playboy and jetsetter and Joss Whedon husband and father; on both the artistic and personal level, a sharp contrast.

Barry Sonnenfeld's caustic response to Bay's work is telling. "I hear he has a very large penis," the *Men in Black* and *Addams Family* director quips (quoted in Hochman), thinking perhaps of Bay's life style – signature Ferrari, companion mastiff,[9] supermodel obsession, up-turned collars or shirts unbuttoned to the waist, a tendency to park in handicapped spaces – as much as his macho film style.

In Bay's *The Rock*, we find the following dialogue between Nicholas Cage's Goodspeed and Mason – you should be hearing the Mason line in a Sean Connery accent (Bay named his mastiff after the character). Bay probably didn't write the line, of course – he has not received writer credit on any of his films,[10] but it is a signature line, informed by swaggering Bay DNA.

Goodspeed: I'll do my best.
Mason: Your best? Losers always whine about their best. Winners go home and fuck the prom queen.

Revealing as well is Bay's Freudian-slip-wearing response to his critics on another occasion: "They castrate me" (quoted in Rodriguez).

Whedon's sensibility is of an entirely different kind. As someone who once described *Buffy* as *My So-Called Life* meets *The X-Files*,[11] Whedon, not surprisingly, contributed an essay ("Reality TV") to a newly released definitive DVD collection of the pioneering 1994–5 series. The end of the truncated teen drama especially captures his attention. In *MSCL*'s final moments, he notes, with characteristic Whedon humour, "[W]e are left with the most crushing cliffhanger in history, with Angela going off on her date with Jordan Catalano having just discovered that it was actually Brian Krakow (*or, as I affectionately call him, 'me'*) who wrote her those love letters" [my italics]. "Or as I affectionately call him 'me.'" Compare, if you will, the photo of a college-age Whedon on the left with that of Brian Krakow (Devon Gummersall) on the right (Figure 2).

In a number of interviews Whedon, who once described *Buffy* as "a show by losers for losers" (crosswinds.net),[12] has hilariously and sadly told of his own loser, aka geeky, youth. Careful to note that he has never been and never will be "this insane recluse with a big beard," Whedon nevertheless admits living "my life feeling alone" (Robinson, *Onion AV Club* 2001; IGN-Film Force Interview). Xander's touching line after a failed attempt in "Prophecy Girl" (*BtVS*S 1.12) to secure Buffy as his date for the Spring Fling – "Look, I'm sorry. I don't handle rejection well. Funny! Considering all the practice I've had, huh?" – had its roots in Whedon's own (often admitted) vast experience.

In a startling, in part tongue-in-cheek (a Whedonesque trademark) reflection, Whedon recalls his childhood:

Well, I had lovely long red hair – less and less of which I have every day – and delicate features. I was quite cute! Something went

Figure 2: Teenage Joss Whedon, Brian Krakow (Devon Gummersall) in *My So-Called Life*

horribly wrong somewhere, but that's OK. But there was a sense of oppression, of not being taken seriously, of physical fear; there were certain things that I had in common – I was very close to my step-sister as well, she was the best friend I had in my family growing up. Plus, I'm super-gay, something my wife has come to accept and even enjoy. It's just something that has always been a part of me. And so I have, I think, a kind of a feminine sensibility. (*JWC* 139; hereafter *JWC*)

Michael Bay or his avatar got the girl when Whedon was in high school. (On the DVD commentary for "Welcome to the Hellmouth" [*BtVS*S 1.1], Whedon reveals that Cordelia's "Don't you have an elsewhere to be?" rejection of Jesse in The Bronze is word for word from his own life.) I suspect that a Michael Bay-type picked on Whedon in the playground as well – perhaps even kicked sand in his face on the beach. For those of you who know *Buffy* well, Bay is Jack Lynch in "The Zeppo"; Xander is of course Joss Whedon.

For the first 20 years of their careers Bay dominated his Wesleyan classmate at the box office. The Wonder Woman film Whedon signed on to write and direct in 2005 was supposed to change all that – putting Whedon on course to compete with Bay. Instead, it led to another humbling rejection. Despite the Marvel Boy Whedon's initial reluctance to take on a DC icon and "a kind of contained, rote superhero franchise" (*JWC* 147) about which he knew little, it was an offer he couldn't refuse. Once, in an interview early in *Buffy's* run, before *The Matrix* trilogy went bust, before *Heroes,* Whedon expressed a-pre-Sylarish desire to eat the Wachowski brothers' brains in order to acquire their powers. Wonder Woman didn't make Wachowski gray matter available, but it did partner Whedon with the powerhouse producer of *The Matrix,* Joel Silver.

"Ultimately you want to move on from [TV]," Whedon had told *The Watchers Guide* in 2000 (Volume 2, 323). Wonder Woman would have given him the chance to move on, giving him a budget in the nine-figure range. It might have altered his "nobody" status. ("I'm still nobody. They're starting to notice me now, so that could change. But nobody in Hollywood seems to be saying, 'Hey, let's go talk to that Sweden guy'" [Havens 162].)

The present book, originally called *Wonder Boy,* was to treat Wonder Woman as the big finish, the dramatic climax, the career equivalent of the defeat of Angelus and Al Franken or the first and second battles of Sunnydale High (*Buffy,* Seasons 2, 3 and 7 respectively), the elimination of the Circle of the Black Thorn (*Angel* Season 5), the vanquishing of The Operative and The Reavers (*Serenity*), the surmounting of the Rossum Corporation in *Dollhouse*: Whedon's conquering of the Big Bad of Hollywood. This didn't happen. Plans change.

The experience left Whedon licking his wounds, extremely wary, but … still Whedonesque: "I'm a moron. I'm a complete dweeb. I don't get it, I never get it. Every time, I think everybody's lovely, and it's all going to work out, and I've never been right. For some reason, I can't get that right, can't figure that out. I think I'm getting better. I think I'm mean now. You're going to see a whole meaner person, now" (*JWC* 148). (For more on Wonder Woman, see Chapter 11 below.)

The Wonder Woman debacle sent Whedon back, for a time, to television, back into the arms of Fox, with which he had a long-term development deal, where he would create *Dollhouse* as an Eliza Dushku vehicle. It would be tempting to view Whedon as the writer/director equivalent of those actors and actresses – from Pernel Roberts (*Bonanza*) to David Caruso (*NYPD Blue*), and Sarah Michelle Gellar – who jumped ship, absolutely certain that the movies were the place to be, only to discover that television was more conducive to their particular talents. After all, it is on the small screen where Whedon's genius had found, pre-*Avengers*, its true home and where (as Table 3 makes clear) he has actually been more productive over the same time period than Michael Bay:

Table 3: Bay/Whedon Productivity

Bay Movie	Running Time (minutes)	TV/Film Directed by Whedon	Running Time (minutes)
Bad Boys	119	*Buffy* (20 episodes)	840
The Rock	136	*Angel* (6 episodes)	252
Armageddon	153	*Firefly* (4 episodes)	168
Pearl Harbor	183	*Serenity*	119
Bad Boys II	147	*The Office* (2 episodes)	44
The Island	136	*Dollhouse* (3 episodes)	129
Transformers	203	*Glee* (1 episode)	43
Transformers: Revenge of the Fallen	150	Marvel's *The Avengers*	143
Transformers: Dark of the Moon	154	*Much Ado About Nothing*	107
Total	**1381 minutes**	**Total**	**1845 minutes**

Two decades out of Wesleyan, the astronaut leads the caveman in narrative production by approximately 7.7 hours – that is almost four two-hour feature films or three Michael Bay films (which average 153 minutes).

But then Marvel's *The Avengers* happened, and Whedon had his shot – the one he hoped for with not only Wonder Woman but, as we shall see, Batman and Iron Man as well – to make not only a summer blockbuster but a superhero movie. The assignment would at last put him on a par with Michael Bay – would make it possible for something more than an apples and oranges comparison.

When, after the flabbergasting numbers were in for Marvel's *The Avengers*' record-breaking opening weekend, Whedon went on Whedonesque, tongue firmly planted in cheek, to thank the fans. He promised "[s]omeday, long from now, [to] […] even have an emotional reaction to it, like a person would. I can't wait!" He was even ready to contemplate the changes it would make in his life and career. His status in the industry could be enhanced: "I may finally be recognized at ComicCon. Imagine!" And the money (see Pomerantz) would certainly come in useful: "I can afford to buy […] a fine meal. But REALLY fine, with truffles and s#!+." Most of all, his new clout, he hoped, might just make it possible to "get a studio to finance [his] dream project, the [long overdue] reboot of *Air Bud*."

Now, thanks to Marvel's *The Avengers*, Whedon need not envy even the box office success of his classmate. Table 4 summarizes the box office performances of all the films Whedon has been involved in – as script doctor (see Chapter 6), writer and director.

Table 4: Box Office for Whedon Doctored/Scripted/Directed Films[13]

Film	Budget	Worldwide Gross
Buffy the Vampire Slayer	$16,000,000	$16,624,456
Speed	$28,000,000	$350,448,145
Toy Story	$30,000,000	$354,300,000
Waterworld	$175,000,000	$255,200,000
Twister	$92,000,000	$494,471,524
Alien Resurrection	$70,000,000	$161,295,658
X-Men	$75,000,000	$295,999,717
Titan AE	$75,000,000	$36,755,000
Serenity	$39,000,000	$38,869,464
The Cabin in the Woods	$30,000,000	$66,486,080
Marvel's *The Avengers*	$22,000,000	$1,511,757,910
Total	**$652,000,000**	**$3,515,721,874**

Whedon's best now stands as the third highest grossing film of all-time, two notches ahead of … of Bay's best (*Transformers: Dark of the Moon*).

There is much more to say about this classic showdown. It is, after all, in part a clash between film and television as narrative media in the twenty-first century (Whedon has worked in both, Bay only in film), a showdown between the inarticulate (have you ever suffered through a Bay DVD commentary?) and the brilliantly articulate (Whedon's hilarious interviews, essays, DVD commentaries and occasional writings are almost always enthralling and illuminating; when Joss uses the phrase "imperialist hegemony" [*Serenity* 14], you cannot help but wonder if Bay would have a clue what his fellow Wesleyanite was talking about); a battle between mainstream and cult media, a coming-to-blows of commerce and art; a confrontation between a prosaic for-pay adapter of other people's ideas and a poetic "maker" of verses[14] – a collision between caveman and astronaut.

INTRODUCTION

From the Mind of Joss Whedon

*An overview of the book's approach, like Whedon's work a hybrid, a fusion of
Howard Gruber's case study method for understanding the nature of the creative
process with a neo-auteurism.*

> Each creative person is unique in a unique way.
>   (Howard Gruber, "From Epistemic Subject," 177)

ooooooooooo

The Genius of Joss Whedon

> You could never hope to grasp the source of our power.
>   (Über Buffy to Adam in "Primeval")

> But Joss just keeps saying, "Don't worry. I have it right here."
>   (Sarah Michelle Gellar on the filming of "Restless" [Udovitch 62])

Describing Joss Whedon as a "genius" has, of course, become commonplace: Candace Havens uses it in the subtitle of her *Joss Whedon*:
The Genius Behind Buffy;[1] cityofangel.com, Kristy Bratton's useful (if
ungrammatical) comprehensive *Angel* website, calls him "a creative force
of unimaginable *genius*"; Buffy herself, Sarah Michelle Gellar, described
her boss as a "mad genius" (Gellar, "An Interview"); key collaborator
David Greenwalt applies the term to his colleague (*Watcher's Guide* I,
244); adherents of the Whedon grocery list use the term; the epilogue
to one of the first academic books on *Buffy* speaks of "The *Genius* of
Joss Whedon."

That last one, of course, is my own, authored just after *Buffy's*
Season 4 finale, written and directed by Whedon, and I am not here
to dispute use of the designation in describing the subject of this book.
Such characterizations, including my own, are in keeping with a long

tradition, going back to the word's Latin origin. In *Speaker's Meaning*, Owen Barfield offers a concise summary of its history: "The Romans [...] would never have said of a man that he is a genius. They would have said that he had, or was accompanied or inspired by, a genius. We prefer to say that he is one" (78). To say Whedon is one is thus to identify him as in possession of (I am quoting the *Oxford English Dictionary*) "that particular kind of intellectual power which has the appearance of proceeding from a supernatural inspiration or possession, and which seems to arrive at its results in an inexplicable and miraculous manner" (*OED* Online, 1989 edition).

The particular example which inspired my use of the term in 2002 was "Restless." When Mim Udovitch visited the set of *Buffy the Vampire Slayer* that year while writing a cover story on the show for *Rolling Stone*, she learned that the final episode of Season 4, then only days away from production,[2] was not yet written. "Like, in a couple of days we start shooting the last episode of the season," Gellar would observe, "and no one has any idea what happens. But Joss just keeps saying, 'Don't worry. I have it right here'" (62). Whedon, we learn later in the article, had an emergency appendectomy earlier in the week, delaying his completion of the script for the season finale.

A few days later Whedon had evidently completed the script for "Restless,"[3] and he would also direct, for the fourth consecutive year, the season's final episode, which would air on 23 May. Confirming his injunction to his star not to worry, "Restless" turned out to be a truly extraordinary hour of television, a kind of TV *8½*,[4] or Eliot's *Wasteland* (Wilcox, *Why*, 162–73), a postmodern, self-referential, diegesis-bending hour that would succeed in summing up *BtVS*'s first four seasons and pointing to its future.

Beyond the sense of high expectation that having the Whedon stamp on it naturally inspired, neither I nor anyone else in *BtVS*'s audience knew what we were in for beyond an Internet rumour, correct as it turned out, that it would be a dream sequence. Whedon had himself disclosed that much (in a Fanforum interview):

> The last episode is all dreams, and it's just about as strange as it needs to be. It was a very fun and beautiful way to sort of sum up everything everyone had gone through, what it meant to them and where they are. It's divided into four acts that are four dreams: Giles, Willow, Xander and Buffy.

We did not know, however, that each of these dreams would in fact be equal in style, strangeness and oneiric suggestiveness to the famous "dancing dwarf" dream of Dale Cooper in the third episode of *Twin Peaks,* a series Whedon has often cited as among his all-time favourites.

Exhausted from their final battle with Adam and from the enjoining spell that made their victory possible, the Gang gathers at Buffy's house to unwind and watch videos. Before they have finished even the coming attractions on the first tape, they are, however, all sound asleep. Their dreams, however, are anything but sweet, as we learn by entering the mindscreen (as Bruce Kawin calls it) of first Willow, then Xander, Giles and Buffy. Each of the four is stalked in turn by the spirit of the First Slayer.

As the Scooby Gang wander through their respective dream worlds – as Willow struggles with her stage fright, fear of opera and doubts about her evolution beyond nerd status during a surreal performance of *Death of a Salesman,* worrying all along that her secret will be discovered; Xander dreams of assignations with not only Willow and Tara but Buffy's mother and worries about his future while finding himself in the midst of an *Apocalypse Now* reddux (Principal Snyder as Kurtz); Giles becomes Buffy's dream dad and frets about the clash between Watcher duties and his "own gig," merging the two as he bursts into song at The Bronze (which has merged with his own living room); and Buffy finds herself perplexed by a purely bureaucratic Riley and a human Adam who accuses her of being a demon (planting questions that would not be answered until Season 7's "Get It Done" [7.15]), before her own final struggle with, and vanquishing of, the First Slayer, the dream diegesis merges with the real set of the Santa Monica studio where *BtVS*S was filmed.

In one captivating tracking shot a fleeing Xander runs from the First Slayer; the camera, in one continuous steadicam take, follows him into Giles's apartment, through a hallway and out into Buffy's dorm, into Buffy and Willow's room, through a closet into his own dank basement apartment, where his stepfather/the First Slayer plucks out his heart. The textual geography of the shot makes perfect dream sense – for in dreams, after all, are not all places and times contiguous? But the dream contiguity of the diegesis of "Restless" is in reality the equally surreal contiguity of the extra-diegetic actual television shooting set. Whedon has simultaneously taken us inside the unconscious minds of the Scooby Gang and behind the scenes of a television show's production.

In Xander's "Restless" dream, Buffy and Giles express their disappointment with *Apocalypse Now,* and Xander finds himself defending it. Then a popcorn-chomping Giles reverses his critical opinion, announcing his sudden realization: "I'm beginning to understand this now. It's all about the journey, isn't it?" Giles's "this," we may say, refers not to Coppola's film but to Whedon's creation. The line is not the only one in "Restless" that takes on self-referential meaning.[5] Even the twice-repeated, first by Tara, then, in the last shot of "Restless," in Buffy's own mind – "You think you know [...] what's to come [...] what you are. You haven't even begun"[6] – seemed to speak not just to the destiny of Buffy the Vampire Slayer but of *Buffy the Vampire Slayer*. Now, over a decade later, the admonition seems even more relevant, with "you" becoming not Buffy or *Buffy* but Joss Whedon himself.

It is not my intent here to dispute Whedon's "genius," but I do want to follow a different tack.

From the Mind ...

Here's how something like this happens. We all sit around scratching our heads. Then Joss says something to the effect of "Can Holland come back all dead and take Angel on an elevator ride to hell but end up right back where he started?" then I just try to work out the details. Bush burning, and its name is Joss.

(Tim Minear, posting to the Bronze after "Reprise" – *Angel* 2.15)

"And the bush was not consumed" (Exodus) is a perfect metaphor of the life of a creative person.

(Howard Gruber, "And the Bush Was not Consumed," 269)

In a Universal Pictures trailer seen in theatres prior to the release of *Serenity* (2005) viewers were greeted by an opening title that reads: "From the Mind of Joss Whedon."[7] The phrasing, intended for both experienced visitors and newcomers to the Whedonverses alike, is telling. *Serenity* – a big screen manifestation of a failed television series – we are being promised, will not be just any work of popular culture; it will not be written by a committee, or rewritten and reshaped according to the findings of focus groups. It will be the product of a particular mind, a unique imagination – the same intelligence, we learn in a subsequent title, that brought *Buffy the Vampire Slayer* and *Angel* into the world.

This book makes a similar assumption. Its subject is not what has come out of that mind – the film scripts (both doctored and original), the television episodes and series, the comic books, song lyrics, the movies. Over 30 scholarly/critical books on that work, well over 200 essays and articles (including over 30 issues of the scholarly journal *Slayage* which I co-edit), and a dozen conferences (in the USA, Canada, Australia, the UK, France, Turkey) have more than satisfactorily examined, and continue to examine, all those.

Nor is this a biography in any traditional sense. As my title suggests, I want to paint a "portrait" of Joss Whedon's creative life. Nicholas Hilliard once proclaimed his desire to paint not just the physical form of his contemporary Sir Francis Bacon (1561–1626), but his extraordinary mind (Eiseley 23). Out of Bacon's mind came the modern scientific world view; out of Whedon have come the 'verses that bear his signature, but I understand Hilliard's desire, though my medium is words and not paint.

In a book called *Waking Dreams*, psychologist Mary Watkins, with the nature of creativity in mind, once observed that the reason we are shocked when magicians pull rabbits out of hats is because we were not around when they inserted them in the first place (137). This book will investigate the creative achievement of Joss Whedon by tracking his rabbits to their source. (A warning to the dearly departed Anya would be necessary here if she were not, well, dearly departed.)

In order to undertake this task I will be adopting an approach every bit as much a hybrid as Whedon's work itself – a critical "combo Buffy,"[8] if you will – which fuses psychologist Howard Gruber's case-study approach to understanding the creative process, applied here for the first time to a pop culture creator, with a grounded-in-television neo-auteurism. Allow me to explain as briefly as possible.

Fast forward through the remainder of this chapter if you like (I have placed Whedon's Gruber's key insights in bold for the speed reader); implement, if you will, the "revolutionary new 'page turning' process" (Whedon, "Introduction," *"Once More with Feeling," Script Book*, ix): it won't hurt my feelings if you move directly to Chapter 1: Television Son. The remainder of this book will not have as much resonance or intellectual depth for readers who zap the next few pages, but it will remain meaningful nonetheless.

Howard Gruber's Approach to the Study of Creative Work

I proceeded like an explorer in a new territory, reading the notebooks [of Darwin] through, over and over again, figuring out what he was focusing on, what his cryptic notes meant, trying to recreate his thought processes from one day to the next. I tried to freeze the current of his thinking at crucial points.

(Howard Gruber)

Simply put, the approach of the late Howard E. Gruber (1922–2005) is "To start with an individual whose creativity is beyond dispute [...] [a]nd then [...] to map, as carefully as I can, what is going on in that person's mind over a period in which creative breakthroughs were occurring" ("Breakaway Minds," 69).[9] What interested Gruber was not the "Aha" experiences so often focused on in the history of creativity. Such moments, he was convinced, are always "part of a longer creative process, which in its turn is part of a creative life." "How are such lives lived?" – that was what Howard Gruber wanted to know.[10]

"There is no need," Gruber was convinced, *"to think of the individual as solving problems in a mysterious way called 'genius'"* ("The Emergence of a Sense of Purpose," 6). Creativity, in fact, is not "a set of properties that a person has in a certain moment and carries around with him. [...] The question is really not the 'ivity' of it – the property list – but how people go about doing it when they do it" ("From Epistemic Subject," 175).

Historically speaking, *creative individuals often "leave better traces."* Indeed, "the making and leaving of tracks [...] is part and parcel of the process itself [...] a kind of activity characteristic of people doing creative work." "Wittingly or not," he notes, *they "create the conditions under which we can study their development"* ("Which Way Is Up?" 119). What sort of traces are to be discovered?

[N]otions that seemed too absurd to be written down, transient thoughts still too fleeting or awkward for written expression, taboo ideas that can be expressed only when muted or transformed. And there is another sort of thinking that leaves very little trace, although it is not rejected or suppressed: the personal imagery one uses to carry a thought along, the personal knowledge one gains of a situation only by actually being in it – seeing, hearing, feeling, tasting, smelling it. Doing, enjoying, remembering, imagining it. This is the fine-structure of experience, well nigh invisible except to the person himself.

(*Darwin on Man*, 253)

For creative people "a long and well-worked through apprenticeship is vital to the development of a creative life." The particular circumstances vary: "Teachers and mentors may be imposed upon the young person, or sought out, or discovered in a lucky accident. They may be physically present or far away, living or dead models." But the end result is the same: "models and mentors there must be, as well as the disciplined work necessary to profit from them" ("Foreword to *Notebooks of the Mind*," x).

Early in their life's work, *creative individuals make "good moves"* – strategies, "first stroke[s] of the brush [which] transform the canvas" – that "set the stage for the protracted creative work of which it is only a part" ("From Epistemic Subject," 172). (These moves are often recorded in an "initial sketch": a "rough draft or early notebook to which the worker can repair from time to time – that serves as a sort of gyroscope for the oeuvre" ["Inching," 265–6].) Though "delays, tangents, and false starts" are equally common and "almost inevitable," creative individuals find ways of managing their work "so that these inconclusive moves become fruitful and enriching, and at the same time so that a sense of direction is maintained." "Without such a sense of direction," in fact, as Gruber shows, "the would-be creator may produce a number of fine strokes, but they will not accumulate toward a great work" ("Inching," 265).

Creative people, Gruber found, are not as isolated as once believed: they are, in fact, extremely good at collaborating, at interacting with peers. They often devote their skills and a surprising amount of time to establish environments and peer groups ("personal allegiances") capable of nurturing their work ("Breakaway Minds," 72; "And the Bush," 294–5).

Creative people are willing to work hard for a very long time, even if such work does not produce immediate results or rewards, and this work remains enjoyable for them. "Perhaps the single most reliable finding in our studies," Gruber observes, "is that *creative work takes a long time. With all due apologies to thunderbolts, creative work is not a matter of milliseconds, minutes, or even hours – but of months, years, and decades*" ("Inching," 265). Creative individuals should not be thought of as obsessed or fanatic: "the creative person cannot simply be driven," Gruber writes. "He must be drawn to his work by visions, hopes, joy of discovery, love of truth, and sensuous pleasure in the creative activity itself" ("And the Bush," 294).

Creative individuals, Gruber discovers, "need to know a lot and cultivate special skills" ("Breakaway Minds," 71): Darwin, for example, knew a tremendous amount about such esoteric subjects as barnacles and animal breeding, knowledge which shaped his discoveries about evolution; Leonardo's precise knowledge of anatomy informed his art; Newton's hands-on experience as the maker of scientific instruments was "instrumental" to his theory-making ("Foreword to *Notebooks of the Mind*," x). Creative individuals sometimes acquire this knowledge through a "special kind of narcissism" ("And the Bush," 280) such as that exhibited by Darwin when he used himself as his subject in order to study man's higher faculties.

Creative individuals possess a "network of enterprises." "In the course of a single day or week," Gruber notes, "the activities of the person may appear, from the outside, as a bewildering miscellany. But the person is not disoriented or dazzled. He or she can readily map each activity onto one or another enterprise" ("The Evolving Systems Approach," 13). That creative work is often "spread out over months and years has consequences for the organization of purpose." For "in order to make grand goals attainable, the creator must invent and pursue subgoals." Individuals must find ways of managing their tasks through a network of enterprises ("Inching," 265).

"The creative person must develop a sense of identity as a creative person, a sense of his or her own specialness" ("And the Bush," 294–5). *Creative people possess, and seek to possess, unique points of view, special perspectives on the world.* Such points of view, in fact, are likely to distinguish the creative person more than any particular problem solving ability.

The ongoing work of creation is often guided by what Gruber calls "images of wide scope." "There is probably a place," Gruber writes, "for a special term such as 'image of wide scope,' distinct from metaphor, to refer to the potential vehicle of a metaphor that has not yet been formulated or to refer to supple schematization [...] that might enter into a number of metaphors" ("Inching," 256). Darwin's notebook sketches of the tree of evolution, Einstein's "thought experiment" of a voyage on a beam of light in order to understand reality from its perspective – these are classic examples of images of wide scope, Freud's numerous drawings, his rendering of neurons in the brain, which recently inspired an entire art exhibition at the SUNY Binghamton.

Creative individuals [...] "have at [their] disposal a number of modalities of representation. Systems of laws, taxonomic systems, and thematic repertoires [the term is Gerald Holton's] [...] – are all pertinent" ("Cognitive Psychology," 315). Various thinkers develop direct, special ways of thinking: Wordsworth in iambic pentameter, von Neumann in mathematical equations, Dr Johnson in prose ("Aha Experiences," 48). These "private languages and modes of thought" must be translated, however, into "public discourse."

Ordinarily, an "overriding project [emerges] that unites all the enterprises," though this is not always the case ("History and Creative Work," 9). Each enterprise is governed by plans and intentions, but, due to the nature of the coupling, the frustration of one plan does not bring the whole system to a halt. Rather the individual overcomes obstacles through new procedures: he or she may, for example, turn to a related enterprise which had been placed on the "back burner." "How the individual decides whether to struggle with [...] difficulties or to shift to some other activity," Gruber notes, "is regulated by the organization of purposes as a whole" ("Cognitive Psychology," 315).

The pages ahead will plot the conformity of Whedon's life and work through application of Gruber's scheme. Think of the epigraphs highlighting key Gruber ideas that serve to presage each of the book's two parts and every chapter as roadmarkers intended to "place" the stages of Whedon's creative development across his career.

My subject, however, is not a great figure in the history of science or a canonical writer. Joss Whedon's creative achievements have been in popular culture, most significantly in television and film, so it is my intent to enhance Gruber's method by melding it with a medium-specific approach.

Neo-Auteurism

It may well be that the early development of art forms and/or new media of communication exhibits a natural tendency to anonymity. Poetry, for example, is authored by "anonymous" before Homer or Chaucer or Dante appear on the scene; *Gilgamesh* and *Beowulf* precede *The Iliad* or *The Canterbury Tales*. In architecture, the Gothic cathedral, the anonymous work of thousands, comes before the acknowledged creations of a Christopher Wren or Frank Lloyd Wright.

In the first four decades of the movies, authorship was seldom at issue. Though directors like D.W. Griffith, Erich von Stroheim, Sergei Eisenstein and Charlie Chaplin were recognized as artists of the medium, in the normal course of things it was more customary to credit a producer or even a studio as the true origin of a work of movie art. It was only after World War II, when French "cinéastes" associated with the journal *Cahiers du Cinéma* – chief among them François Truffaut, a future important director of the New Wave, in his essay on the "politiques des auteurs" (1954), began to speak of movie auteurs: the French word for "author."[11]

Only now, half a century into the medium's existence, have we come to recognize that television as well might have authors.[12] Anti-television scholars like Todd Gitlin have insisted (in 1994) that "There is still virtually no place in American television, commercial or public, for a serious writer or director to make a career" (xiii) in a medium in which all artistic purposes are "subordinated to the larger design of keeping a sufficient number of people tuned in" (56). "In headlong pursuit of the logic of safety," Gitlin writes, "the networks ordinarily intervene at every step of the development process. It is as if there were not only too many cooks planning the broth, but the landlord kept interfering as well" (85).

But in this century, in an era in which Jason Mittell detects a growing interest in television's "operational aesthetic," a foregrounding of "the constructed nature of the narration," and new audience interest in how favourite shows get made (Mittell 35), such figures as Aaron Sorkin (*West Wing*, NBC, 1999–2003), David Chase (*The Sopranos*, HBO, 1999–2007), Alan Ball (*Six Feet Under*, HBO, 2001–5), Amy Sherman-Paladino (*Gilmore Girls*, WB, 2000–6; CW, 2006–7); J.J. Abrams (*Alias*, ABC, 2001-6), Damon Lindelof and Carlton Cuse (*Lost*, ABC, 2004–10), and Joss Whedon have emerged as television auteurs.[13] The original auteur theory's appeal, the critic Peter Wollen has noted, was obvious: it "implie[d] an operation of decipherment [...] reveal[ing] authors where none had been seen before" (77). Television scholars, myself included, were struck anew by that appeal.

In the 1970s and 1980s, however, not only auteurism, but literary authorship as well, faced dire challenges from new theoretical trends:

> After hundreds of years of outstanding health, and as fetishised intellectual superhero and focal point for art and literature, under the Tel Quel theorists, the author had suddenly withered and perished. As is the case with quick passings, though, many who were close to the author – namely, large numbers of art history and literature academics – have had great problems dealing with the death, and some still refuse to let go, their work a continuing eulogy. By contrast, and almost Oedipally, many of academia's next generation were only too happy to witness the death and have whole-heartedly welcomed the text and the reader's inheritance of the author's ‚powers, estate, and superhero [...] status. And, of course, political economists who do not particularly believe in texts, readers, *or* authors, instead regarding the world as populated by products and producers, were keen to see discussion of the author come to an end.

In "Resurrecting the Author: Joss Whedon's Place in *Buffy's* Textual Universe," the work from which I have been quoting, a brilliant, knowledgeable and suggestive talk given at the first scholarly conference on *Buffy* in 2002, Jonathan Gray not only supplies a multi-media history of authorship but issues a call for bringing the auteur back from his current "undead" status.[14] These pages intend to answer Gray's call, but in synchrony with Gruber's understanding of creative work.

PART I:
Apprentice

It is safe to say that no case of creative achievement
occurs without a long apprenticeship.

(Howard Gruber,
"The Evolving System Approach to Creative Work," 15)

1 TELEVISION SON

In which the offspring of two generations of television writers, John Whedon and Tom Whedon, enters this dimension.

Being creative means striking out in new directions and not accepting ready-made relationships, which take stamina and a willingness to be alone for a while.

(Howard Gruber, "Breakaway Minds," 72)

oooooooooo

I think my father's best work was probably done at our dinner table. [...] It was great to live around a writer, and my mother also wrote in her spare time, so the sound of typewriters was probably the most comforting sound in the world to me. I loved that. And while I really enjoyed all of the funny things my dad was working on, it was really just being *around* someone who was that funny. And all of his friends were comedy writers. So the house was constantly filled with these very sweet, erudite, intelligent guys just trying to crack jokes – my father's friends, my mother's friends, teachers, drama people. It just had a great air to it, and what you wanted to do is to go into that room and make those guys laugh.

(Joss Whedon, *JWC* 43)

You know, I literally had left college going, "I'm not going to be a television writer." And my friend would go, "Three-G TV!" Third generation. He'd taunt me all the time. "It's not going to happen!"

(Joss Whedon, IGN-Film Force)

The year is 1978. At a birthday party for younger brother Jed (1969–), a teenage Joss Whedon screens a film entitled *Stupidman* starring the birthday boy, a work inspired by the release of Richard Donner's *Superman* that year. It would not be the only film Joss and his brothers would make. He and his brothers recall a parody of *Gone with the Wind*, a Western, a *noir*, the heavily-indebted to *Alien Creature from the Planet*

Hell, and *Back to 'Nam,* "a documentary about war movies," a musical based on the Iran-Contra hearings (*Dr. Horrible's Sing-Along Blog: The Book* 8). Tom Whedon, a veteran television writer (he was then on the staff of *Alice* [CBS, 1976–85]), recalls that his son's 15-minute film was a huge hit with its audience, which demanded repeated screenings, and that the occasion was the "[b]est birthday party I've ever been to." The director, however, remembers it somewhat differently. "The embarrassing thing about that," he told Lisa Rosen ("Family Tradition"), "is that it was a group of eight-year-olds, and I did stand in the next room pacing back and forth going 'They're not laughing, they're not laughing,' like it was a Broadway opening" (35).

That would be at least two years before Whedon's pivotal "existential epiphany" (examined in detail in the next chapter), an important chapter in his "History of Me" eloquently described in the DVD commentary for "Objects in Space" (*Firefly* 1.14). Teenage Joss may not yet have been contemplating the nature of existence, but he was evidently already worrying about his future, contemplating the pros and cons of being "Three-G TV."[1]

As already noted, both Whedon's grandfather and father had been writers, and both had worked in television. John Ogden Whedon (1904–91) had already contributed to *Harper's Magazine* when his short story "Fighting Blood" appeared in 1929 in the *New Yorker.* For the latter periodical, under famous editor Harold Ross and alongside legends like James Thurber (1894–1961) and E.B. White (1889–1985), Whedon wrote on a regular basis for over a decade, during an era of Prohibition and Depression, first poems – "Chinatown" (1928), "Theme Song for a Movie" (1928), "Chantey for a Ferryboat" (1928), "Soda-Counter Lunch" (1928), "Speakeasy" (1928), "To a Worm" (1929), "Plans for a Horrid Old Age" (1929), "The Merry Round" (1929); then occasional short fiction – "A Crash in Tin Pan Alley" (1929) and essays – "Recognition" (1933); and regular contributions to the magazine's famous "Talk of the Town" section – "Steam" (1932), "Merry Christmas" (1933), "Framed" (1933), "James" (1934), "Miracle in 23rd Street" (1935), "More Inscriptions" (1937), "Uprising" (1938), "Little Business" (1938).

In 1950, the ancestor of the author of "Once More with Feeling," the famous musical episode of *Buffy the Vampire Slayer,* would see his musical *Texas, Lil' Darlin* – co-written with Sam Moore and scored by the legendary Johnny Mercer (1909–76) – have a good run (283 performances) on Broadway. In the same decade John Whedon would begin writing for the new medium of television, first for the one-hour drama showcases so common in television's early years: *Lux Video Theatre* (1951–5), *Kraft*

Television Theatre (1956), *The Alcoa Hour* (1957); later for many popular sitcoms: *Leave It to Beaver* (1958–9), *The Donna Reed Show* (1961), *The Dick Van Dyke Show* (1962–4), *The Andy Griffith Show* (1963–4). Late in his career he would work for *Disneyland*.

In a fine piece on multi-generation Hollywood writer families, Lisa Rosen quotes John Whedon's son's memory of his writing practice: "When I was a child, my father wrote at home. [...] He locked himself in the study, and no one was allowed in there. He worked a real nine-to-five day, and he'd break out for lunch for a half-hour. I kept hearing the typewriter going all the time" (35). Tom caught the habit and wrote for his entire career on a manual typewriter.

Joss's father's career would be not quite as successful, long, or varied, but Tom Whedon would write for *Captain Kangaroo* (1962–5), *The Dick Cavett Show* (1971), *The Electric Company* (1972–7), *Alice* (1977–80), *United States* (1980), *Benson* (1980–1), *It's a Living* and *The Golden Girls* (1989–91). Like both his father *and* his son, Whedon's dad exhibited musical inclinations. While a student at Harvard, Tom had written and performed with the university's Hasty Pudding Theatricals (Davis 157); later, in the 1960s, he would write, with frequent collaborator Jon Stone, a musical called *Money* that was performed at New York's Upstairs at the Downstairs;[2] and later he would also author at least 50 songs for *The Electric Company*. "Some fathers can't really talk to their sons," Joss Whedon told Lisa Rosen, "but they can throw a baseball. [...] We'd throw on all the Sondheim albums" (Rosen 35).

Tom's collaboration with Bob Keeshan (Captain Kangaroo) on the iconic 1960s children's show was anything but positive. Michael Davis recounts how Whedon and the other writers lived in constant fear of the Captain's "mean streak," his tendency to fire people on the spot for giving him "crap" to work with, and his stinginess – writers were required to accompany Keeshan on his public appearances and create material for a spin-off without additional compensation. The writers, who "loved the Captain but hated Keeshan," drowned their sorrows, as Whedon recalled: "There was a bar across the street from the studio that sold a triple martini for a dollar fifty and it got a lot of us in deep trouble. [...] It was the hardest drinking crowd I ever worked with." Eventually, when Joss was not even a year old, Tom Whedon and Stone would walk away from the show (51, 52, 56, 57, 59).

Tom Whedon's time on *The Electric Company* resulted in another unexpected legacy to his son. Trying to heighten its coolness for its demographic, the show began to air segments featuring Spider-Man (1974–7),[3] Tom brought home a bunch of Marvel comic books as research, dropping them in his son's lap. "I'm like, 'What's all this?'" Joss would recall in a March 2008 piece on National Public Radio's *Morning Edition*. "What's all this that will now obsess me for the rest of my life?'" (Ridley). The path from that Marvelous moment to the making of Marvel's *The Avengers* over three decades later is the subject of this book.

The picture Joss offered James Longworth (see the epigraph to this chapter) of a day in the life of a television son as an inspiration – the reassuring sound of typewriters, the high value placed on intelligence and wit – is revealing and helpful to our understanding of the formation of his imagination. We get a somewhat less nostalgic, but equally revealing glimpse of the life of a television son in Tom's memory of his influence on Joss's brother Sam.

> When I was first writing *Captain Kangaroo*, my oldest son Sam was three years old, and we were living in a Westside [New York City] apartment with a long hall. I would go down this long hall to my office and write. I came out one day, and my son was marching up and down the hall, saying "Shit, fuck, shit, fuck," – he had been listening to his father write. (Rosen 35)

Is this why John Whedon cloistered himself away when he wrote?

Joss would offer IGN-Film Force an illuminating account of his sense of his father's place in television:

> I loved when my father was working on *The Electric Company* when I was younger [...] I liked the shows he did, but I never thought they were as funny as he was. In my mind, I thought that he was running them, because he'd run *The Electric Company*. I don't think he was, but it felt like *Alice*, *Benson*, and even *Golden Girls* – which I think was hilarious and was a classic[4] – this is the wittiest man I'd ever met, and all of his friends were extraordinary, and the sitcoms were never quite the same as my father.

Whedon's inherited creativity was not solely on his father's side. "My entire family was very creative, theatrical, and artistic," he would tell Priggé. His mother "directed and starred in a lot of theater" and wrote but never published several novels. Whedon "also knew many poets and musicians. As children, we all knew that we could never be able to hold real jobs"[5] (Priggé 51; *JWC* 65).

Still, Joss himself remained "a bit of a TV snob, as a child"[6] (IGN-Film Force Interview). In an interview with noted television critic David

Bianculli on NPR's *Fresh Air*, Whedon admits that in his (potentially) "Three-G TV" household there was a "a bit of 'Oh, maybe he'll do something better than we did,'" but more significantly his own attitude was "'I shall never write for television.' [...] I never watched American TV, I only watched, like, *Masterpiece Theatre*" [PBS, 1971–] (*JWC* 5) – that quintessentially British import that would provide the imaginary setting for Andrew's-on-the-toilet introduction to *Buffy, Slayer of the Vampyres* in "Storyteller" (*BtVS* 7.16). How he overcame this condescension is the subject of a later chapter (4. "Television Writer"), but where the attitude came from in a family of television writers needs consideration here.

One cause was a basic lack of familiarity with television. Joss Whedon has customarily responded to frequent questions about his own adult television tastes with the same basic refrain: those who make television do not have time to watch it.[7] Such, too, was the case with Tom Whedon: "my father wasn't an avid TV watcher either. He would enjoy himself, there were things we watched, but it wasn't like we all sat down" (*JWC* 48). The other cause was the influence of his decidedly Anglophile mother, with whom young Joss would live after her relatively amicable divorce from Tom Whedon in 1973.

"She really was more into the *Masterpiece Theatre* of it [television]," Whedon would recall, "and I kind of just followed in her footsteps – except for the part where she watched the news, which I didn't. It was depressing. It was really my mother's influence [...] a lot of stuff I do traces back to her" (IGN-Film Force). Other major British "telly" influences via his mother included *Monty Python* (BBC, 1969–74), *Upstairs Downstairs* (ITV, 1971–5), *Love for Lydia* (ITV, 1979), *Jenny*, and the BBC Shakespeares (*JWC* 51; Priggé 47–8).

Whedon's mother influenced much more than his television tastes. In Whedon's 2006 speech before Equality Now, an organization Lee Stearns helped to found, he would speak movingly about her sway (as well as his wife's):

> I think it's because of my mother. She really was an extraordinary, inspirational, tough, cool, sexy, funny woman. And that's the kind of woman I've always surrounded myself with, particularly my wife, who is not only smarter and stronger than I am, but occasionally actually taller too. But only sometimes taller. And, uh, I think it all goes back to my mother.

Lee Stearns was very demanding but always supportive: "You had to prove yourself – not that she wouldn't come through if you didn't, but she expected you to hold your own," Whedon would tell Felicity Nussbaum. Prior to her death in 1992, "they had talked about his *Buffy* screenplay, and [...] knew he was on his way" (*JWC* 65–6).

As a child, Whedon's future may have been indeterminate, but one thing was absolutely clear. He knew "from day one" (IGN-Film Force) he "wanted to do something that wasn't a real job": "I wanted to be an artist. I loved drawing, I loved singing, I loved acting, I love every kind of art that there is. So I had never really narrowed it down, and it wasn't like I was slaving away" (*JWC* 51).

2 FAN BOY

In which the young Joss Whedon grows up, here and in the UK, under a variety of high and popular cultural influences.

In his explorations of the world, the individual finds out what needs doing. In his attempts to do some of it, he finds out what he can and what he cannot. He also comes to see what he need not do. From the intersection of these possibilities there emerges a new imperative, his sense of what he must do. How "it needs" and "I can" give birth to "I must" remain enigmatic.

(Howard Gruber, *Darwin on Man*, 257)

ooooooooo

He's not the normal adult in any way that I can see. [...] He's the mischievous kid and the wise-adult kid in one package.

(J.J. Abrams on Joss Whedon [quoted in Nussbaum, *JWC* 67])

Joss Whedon has always liked to create imaginary worlds. When he was eleven or twelve, for example, he had one featuring hero Harry Egg, itinerant space traveler, and his androgynous demigod sidekick, Mouseflesh.

(Mimi Udovitch 62)

I think everybody always feels they're different. I did feel different from the people around me. I've always felt that I was the outsider in every group I've ever been in, except my staff.

(Joss Whedon, IGN-Film Force)

Asked in an interview if he had a nickname in school, Joss Whedon revealed, perhaps tongue-in-cheek, that it was "Who are you again?" (*JWC* 37). He tells Longworth that the Season 1 *Buffy* episode "Out of Sight, Out of Mind," in which a constantly overlooked female Sunnydale student finds herself becoming more than metaphorically invisible, had its origin in his own "invisibility" as an "extraordinarily alienated" child: he even recorded his experience in a cartoon (*JWC* 50).

"I lived my life feeling alone," Whedon would tell IGN-Film Force, "That's just the way of it. I always did. As soon as I was old enough to have a feeling about it, I felt like I was alone. No matter how much I loved my family – and I actually got along better with my family than I think most people do – but I just always felt separate from everybody, and was terribly lonely all the time."

On another occasion, as we saw in the Prologue, Whedon spoke of his childhood as more than merely lonely, recalling "a sense of oppression, of not being taken seriously, of physical fear" (*JWC* 139). In the same interview he speaks of his "merciless – charming, but merciless" older brothers and being "very afraid of my father [...] an incredibly dear man [...] not necessarily great with kids" (*JWC* 39).

Escape was nevertheless at hand. Writing was something Whedon did "[s]ort of always, and never": "Stories, poems, songs, plays, comic books. Whatever came to mind. And I always sort of vaguely associated writing with my life, in that I thought I could make movies. I always assumed making them meant writing them, but I never really thought about that." The writing included longer efforts: he would try his hand at novels, none of which got past page 12 (*JWC* 51). "I was always trying to communicate something," he has acknowledged, "even if I was just, 'Pay attention to me!'" (IGN-Film Force).[1] Whedon, alas, was ahead of his time, as he recognizes: thanks to the Internet, today "much teenage writing is for the consumption of everybody in the universe. Had there been the Internet, I probably would have been on it like a bandit" (IGN-Film Force).

If juvenile writing was a diversion for Whedon, so too were musicals. We already saw that in the Whedon household, where both his grandfather and father could claim credits as songwriters, listening to Sondheim served as a substitute for parent–child interaction. For young Joss himself "Musicals were my absolute bread and butter. [...] That has never changed. I'm absolutely a musicals boy" (*JWC* 159). But by far the greatest imaginative release came in the form of the comic book.

Marvel Boy

We saw in "Television Son" how Joss Whedon's father literally dropped his obsession-to-be for Marvel comics into his lap sometime in the mid-1970s. For those of us who grew up with comic books, as I did in the 1950s, an avid fan of superhero comics (all purchased at a "mom and pop" neighbourhood grocery run by holocaust-survivor European Jews in Oil City, Pennsylvania), completely obsessed with Challengers of the Unknown, Green Lantern, Batman, The Flash and Justice League of America (somewhat less with Superman and Wonder Woman), the DC universe was all I knew.

Marvel's decade would be the next one. (By the 1960s, my own boyish comic book passion had somewhat waned, and I was no more willing to switch allegiances between comic book universes than I was ready to surrender to the Beatles and the British Invasion – I was still loyal to the King.) In the years just prior to the birth of Joss Whedon in 1964, DC's upstart rival gave birth, in an astonishing burst of pop culture creativity, to The Fantastic Four (1961), The Incredible Hulk (1962), Spider-Man (1962), Iron Man (1963), The X-Men (1963), and the new Daredevil (1964), all franchises in which Stan Lee (often working with Jack Kirby) had a hand. Comic book historian Peter Sanderson has observed that "DC was the equivalent of the big Hollywood studios." It had reinvented superheroes just in time for the pre-teen me but then succumbed to a "creative drought" just as the superhero demographic had changed. "There was a new audience for comics now, and it wasn't just the little kids [aka David Lavery at 10] that traditionally had read the books." The Marvel that emerged contemporaneously with Joss Whedon was, according to Sanderson "in its own way the counterpart of the French New Wave [...]":

Marvel was pioneering new methods of comics storytelling and characterization, addressing more serious themes, and in the process keeping and attracting readers in their teens and beyond. Moreover, among this new generation of readers were people who wanted to write or draw comics themselves, within the new style that Marvel had pioneered, and push the creative envelope still further.

A decade later, Marvel Boy Joss Whedon was, of course, one of those.

Marvel's appeal for Whedon was not just to his inner television writer/director-filmmaker-comic book author; the Marvelverse presented an inviting imaginative home for Whedon's own childhood psyche. In Comic Book Nation, Bradford W. Wright observes that Stan Lee had succeeded in creating "a clear alternative to the competition" by recognizing "the particular themes of the genre that seemed to fascinate contemporary young people the most."[2] In contradistinction to DC's tendency toward "moral platitudes," All-American heroes (Batman being the major exception), and a "triumphalist" mind-set, the "cautionary tales" presented by Marvel, Wright argues, featured instead "alienated antiheroes":

> On the surface these characters were not sympathetic, they were hopelessly selfish individuals who planted the seeds of their own destruction. Yet in these pathetic characters, readers recognized familiar human failings and glimpsed their own anxieties. The Marvel sci-fi formula essentially amounted to a less sophisticated variation on television's *Twilight Zone*, which had recently won a large and loyal youth audience for its twisted tales about the moral and emotional fragility of human beings. (203)

Characteristically, when fan boy Joss Whedon tried to explain his sense of loneliness in his youth, his answer was Marvelous: "Well, you know, it wasn't what I wanted. I wanted to be a part of a group. But I felt like Luke Cage in the Fantastic Four. [...][3] That's just always been the way. You know, very often you'll be in a group and you'll discover that every single person in it feels like they're the one on the perimeter. It's like everybody has their own moment that's going on, some more than others" (IGN-Film Force). Joss Whedon's fan boy mind was inseminated with Marvel memes.

Riverdale to Winchester

> Buffy: You! I mean I can't believe you got into Oxford!
> Willow: It's pretty exciting.
> Oz: That's some deep academia there.
> Buffy: That's where they make Gileses.
>
> ("Choices," *BtVS* 3.19)

After his parents divorced when Whedon was nine, he would live with his mother and stepfather in New York in a "matriarchal household" (*JWC* 139), continuing to attend, as he had since first grade, Riverdale School, a "progressive" private institution where his mother taught.

When Lee Stearns secured a sabbatical year in the UK,[4] Whedon would accompany her to England, "where they make Gileses." His first trip abroad, his matriculation in an English school induced more than a little culture shock: at the over-six-centuries-old, all-male school, he found himself listening to a "lecture on why co-education will never work" and was immediately pegged as "the token lazy American."

Figure 3: The Chapel at Winchester College, where Whedon studied from 1979 to 1981

Two aspects of both his educations were the same: at both Riverdale and Winchester, Whedon "had no money and was surrounded by very rich people"; at neither school did he have any success with women: "I wish that I could have made some moves on a girl at some point in my high school career," Whedon would lament, "but that probably wasn't going to happen at Riverdale, either." Contact with women was, of course, on purpose a remote possibility at Winchester, but as Whedon recognized, the loneliness he felt was not unique: "I was just as lonely when I was around girls as when I wasn't." And there were mitigating circumstances: good friends, for example, and "very good pot." Still, "Socially, every boy that comes out of Winchester was completely pathetic" (IGN-Film Force). Every Winchester male, whether "head boy" or not, in other words, was potentially a Wesley Wyndham-Pryce.

Whedon evidently excelled in English class, where he recalls being "relentless and unstoppable," and he came away certain that while his American education had been at "a good school," his British Alma Mater, often ranked as the top private school in England, was on a different plane: "a great school. An incredible school." "Intellectually, it was a staggering gift to be able to be around that much intelligence," Whedon recalled

41

(IGN-Film Force).[5] It is no wonder, then, that he accepted the school's invitation to stay on after his mother returned to the United States, finally graduating in 1981.

One of Winchester's lasting legacies was Whedon's love of Shakespeare. His infatuation with the greatest of English writers predates his time in The Bard's homeland. "As far back as I can remember. I used to read plays when I was a kid" (the first play he read was *Henry IV*[6]), and he watched the BBC Shakespeares with his mother. The in-depth examination of plays from *Othello* to *Hamlet* at Winchester took his understanding and appreciation of Shakespeare to another level.[7]

Consider, for example, the scene from "Earshot" (*BtVS* 3.18) – a scene written by Whedon (as the episode's author Jane Espenson reveals on the DVD commentary) – in which a newly telepathic Buffy shines as the result of reading the mind of her English teacher in a discussion of *Othello*, much to the chagrin of know-it-all classmate Nancy and the puzzlement of Willow and Xander:

> Teacher: Jealousy clearly is the tool that Iago uses to undo Othello. But what's his motivation? What reason does Iago give for destroying his superior officer?
>
> Nancy (Voice over): Cassio has my place. Twix my sheets, he's done my office.
>
> Buffy: Well, he was passed over for promotion. Cassio was picked instead and people were saying that Othello slept with his wife.
>
> Willow (VO): Buffy did the reading? Buffy understood the reading?
>
> Xander (VO): When did she study? Was I supposed to study? Ms. Murray's kinda hot.
>
> Nancy (VO): I was gonna say Cassio. Uh, I hate her.
>
> Teacher: Any other reason?
>
> Nancy (blurting out): Race!
>
> Teacher: Uh … good Nancy. Can't overlook that … There's something else at work here.
>
> Buffy: Well, he, um, he sort of admits himself that his motives are … spurious! He, um, he does things because he, he enjoys them. It's like he's not, he's not really a person. He's a, the dark half of Othello himself.
>
> Teacher: Buffy. Really. Very astute. I said something quite like that in my dissertation.
>
> Buffy: I know. Uh, I mean … I agree. With that.
>
> Teacher: Yes, and doesn't that also explain Othello's readiness to believe Iago. Within seconds he turns on Desdomona … He believes that

she's been unfaithful. And we're all like that. We all have our little internal Iagos, that tell us our husbands or our girlfriends or whatever, don't really love us. But you never really see what's in someone's heart.

It's a hilarious scene (and not just to English professors), but it's actually Whedon showing off his Winchester education.

The Bard's influence on Whedon's creative life would lead to the regular Shakespeare readings of writers and cast held at his house – the seed crystal for the *Buffy* musical "Once More with Feeling," to naming the planet that spawned the Reavers (in *Serenity*) after Prospero's daughter in *The Tempest* (Miranda), and most significantly to his 2011 radically independent filming – on location at his house in the wake of the big budget *Avengers* – of *Much Ado About Nothing* (see Chapter 12).

Winchester was not known for fostering creativity or even acknow-ledging that the movies and popular culture even existed. Whedon recalls wondering why he was being asked to write about the Crusades instead of going to see *Manhattan* (Woody Allen, 1979) at the local theatre. Still, Whedon remembers it as being an inspiration nonetheless:

> At Winchester, they tried to squash a lot of things. Certainly everything I wore or said bothered them, but at the same time I studied classic literature and drama with some of the greatest teachers out there. You couldn't help but become more creative.[8]

Frequent trips to see movies and plays in London – only a little over an hour away by train – fed his creative energies as well. On one of them he experienced a major epiphany that would be a turning point in his life.

Epiphany

On one of those trips to London, a Fall 1980 screening of the Special Edition of Spielberg's *Close Encounters of the Third Kind* (*CE3K*), occasioned an "existential epiphany" for the sixteen-year-old Whedon (the "very pretentious" designation is his own). We know this because he talks about this important chapter in the "History of Me" in some detail in the DVD commentary that accompanies "Objects in Space," a River-centric episode of *Firefly* in which a sadistic bounty hunter enters *Serenity* and is defeated by his prey, River Tam.[9]

Figure 4: Angel reads one of Joss Whedon's most influential books in "Lovers Walk" (*Buffy the Vampire Slayer* 3.8)

It was a time in Whedon's life when all the basic questions about the nature of time, life, reality and death had come to seem unanswerable. Thinking in adult fashion for the first time, Whedon found himself "presented with the totality of things but no coherent pattern to put them in." "I just suddenly understood that real life was happening," Whedon recalls, and that it did not need him in order to happen. Back at Winchester, a friend loaned him the novel *Nausea* (1938) by the French father of existentialism Jean-Paul Sartre,[10] which became the most important book he had ever read. He would also dip into *The Myth of Sisyphus* (1942) by Albert Camus (1913–60).

While insisting he is not knowledgeable about matters philosophical, Whedon goes on to describe how the heady brew of *CE3K*, Sartre and Camus had made him hyper-conscious of the "pain of being aware of things" – of "objects in space." "Nothing can exist only slightly," passages like the following from *Nausea*, the narrator Roquentin's meditation on the "in-the-wayness" of the natural world, had taught him:

> I sank down on the bench, stupefied, stunned by the profusion of beings without origin: everywhere blossomings, hatchings out, my ears buzzed with existence, my very flesh throbbed and opened, abandoned itself to the universal burgeoning. It was repugnant. But why, I thought, why so many existences, since they all look alike? What good are so many duplicates of trees. (133)

Because they epitomize what Sartre calls "being-in-itself," Roquentin finds their existence inconvenient – in the way. He wants them to exist, he says, "more abstractly," more, that is, like him.

A bit abstract himself, Whedon would return from his UK sojourn ready to take his education to the next level.

3 FILM STUDIES MAJOR

In which a creator-in-the-making goes to college and falls under the influence of the movies and mentors like Jeanine Basinger and Richard Slotkin.

A long and well-worked through apprenticeship is vital to the development of a creative life. Teachers and mentors may be imposed upon the young person, or sought out, or discovered in a lucky accident. They may be physically present or far away, living or dead models. But models and mentors there must be, as well as the disciplined work necessary to profit from them.

> (Howard Gruber, "Foreword" to *Notebooks of the Mind*, x)

When we say that great insights come only to the prepared mind, we do not mean that the mind is prepared merely by steeping it in pre-digested knowledge. The way is made ready by active search and inquiry. The welcoming mind belongs to one who has prepared it by his own efforts, as a field in which new ideas can flower.

> (Howard Gruber, *Darwin on Man*, 246, 248)

ooooooooooo

[T]he teachers [at Wesleyan] understand that they are not there to tell you what to think. They are there to tell you how to think. To show you how to see. They do not make clones at Wesleyan. [...] The study of film ultimately is the study of yourself.

> (Joss Whedon's Ad for the Wesleyan University Film Studies Program)

Asked by Tasha Robinson whether his degree in film studies at Wesleyan University had been useful or had merely instilled "a lot of useless abstract knowledge," Whedon's response was unequivocal:

I walked out with unbelievably essential knowledge. I happened to study under the people that I believe are the best film teachers ever. Film hasn't existed that long, so I say that with a certain amount of confidence. The teachers at Wesleyan were brilliant, the most brilliant people I've been around, and there is not a story that I tell that does not reflect something I either learned, or learned but already knew, from my professors. In terms of production, the place was useless. In terms of connections, I suppose you could go there, but it wasn't the fast track to becoming a hotshot producer. But my. It was just an undergraduate degree, but I'm talking about an education, the most valuable thing I ever learned. Oddly enough, I never studied writing. I studied almost everything except writing.

(Robinson, *Onion AV Club*, 2007)

Since the beginning of film history, the path to becoming a filmmaker has been anything but predetermined. In Peter Bogdanovich's otherwise forgettable *Nickelodeon* (1976), a lawyer is transformed into a director in the second decade of film's first century by a variety of misunderstandings. The Pantheon director Howard Hawks (1896–1977) parlayed a college degree in mechanical engineering into 40 years of filmmaking. Federico Fellini (1920–91) came to Rome as a cartoonist after World War II and became one of the medium's greatest auteurs.

By the 1970s, the rite of passage had become clearer – and cred-entialled. Francis Ford Coppola (b. 1939; MFA, UCLA); Martin Scorsese (b. 1942; MFA, NYU) George Lucas (b. 1944; BFA, USC), Robert Zemeckis (b. 1952; BFA, USC), Spike Lee (b. 1957; MFA, NYU) – all were Film School Auteurs who had studied moviemaking in all its aspects in a university setting. By century's end, however, different paradigms had presented themselves. David Fincher (b. 1962), Michel Gondry (b. 1963), Spike Jonze (b. 1969), Michael Bay – all came to feature film directing via an apprenticeship in shooting commercials and/or music videos; and the success of high-school dropout Quentin Tarantino (b. 1963) even suggested that his highly informal training – as a video store employee and movie junkie – might be a path to auteurhood. "Actors wait tables, directors work at video stores," Whedon himself would quip, no doubt with his contemporary Tarantino in mind (Robinson, *Onion AV Club*, 2001). Others, Michael Bay's supposed real father John Frankenheimer (in the 1950s) and no less than cinema titan Steven Spielberg (b. 1946) (in the late 1960s and early 1970s), would, like Whedon, hone their skills as directors in television before becoming film directors.

That Whedon would find himself at Wesleyan was, in a sense, pre-ordained: since his parents had old college friends on the faculty there, he had been to Middletown often as a child (their daughter would later give

Whedon his very candid insider college tour), and a friend from Riverdale was already matriculating there when Whedon was choosing a school. Although he would visit several schools, he applied only to Wesleyan and, despite not being exactly a stellar applicant (he refers to himself as a "n'er-do-well"),[1] he was admitted, leaning toward a major in theatre (IGN-Film Force).[2]

Although Whedon would write and make "little movies" during his years at Wesleyan, the school did not offer courses in either screenwriting or film production. What Whedon did study was film theory and film history: "Watching films over and over again and dissecting them, really understanding what they were trying to do, and all that good stuff. The best film theory study available. But, really, sort of crap production – as my movies evident" (IGN-Film Force).[3] Still, he remembers Wesleyan as a time when "I was exposed to every damn thing and my brain was exploding with creative thoughts" (Priggé, 61). A time, in other words, that was the direct opposite of his years at Winchester.

Acknowledging that learning the essentials of film production is, of course, essential for any would-be filmmaker,[4] Whedon insists on the significance as well of the kind of foundational film studies education he received: "[I]t's more important at that age to be studying the meaning thing, to be studying what builds up the great movies. Where the simplicity is, where the complexity is. [...] You get so many people out here with incredible technical expertise who have nothing to say, or no idea of the importance of having something to say, or the importance of understanding what they're saying" (IGN-Film Force).

What he learned at Wesleyan would shape the way Whedon would make television. A case in point: asked by Edward Gross if he envisioned ever having Angel battle Angelus, Whedon would reply: "It's not a priority, because it's not something you want to do right away. You want to save a show like that *for your Baroque period*, which *Buffy* entered during episode two. But, sure, why not? Angel vs. Angelus? How much fun would David have?" (my italics). Whedon's choice of words here, especially the reference to "Baroque period," may seem obscure, but it seems certain he is referring to a passage from Thomas Schatz's *Hollywood Genres: Formulas, Filmmaking, and the Studio System*, a 1981 book which he no doubt read at Wesleyan, in which the author identifies a four-phase evolutionary pattern for the historical development of a genre:

> an experimental stage, during which its conventions are isolated and established, a classic stage, in which the conventions reach their "equilibrium" and are mutually understood by artist and audience, an

age of refinement, during which certain formal and stylistic details embellish the form, and finally *a baroque (or "mannerist," or "self-reflexive") stage,* when the form and its establishments are accented to the point where they "themselves become the "substance" or "content" of the work. (37–8; my italics)

Over a decade after college, "A+" film major still,[5] Whedon's use of the term "baroque" to describe the postmodern-out-of-the-gate *Buffy* is precisely accurate, and sure enough, Angel would battle Angelus, but not until Season 4's "Orpheus" (4.15) when Whedon's second child had become more self-aware and self-referential.

"[R]aised by teachers," Whedon grew up with "a very different idea of school than most of the kids around me" (*JWC* 59). His admiration for his Wesleyan professors was profound, his description of their influence eloquent and moving (at least to a teacher like myself):

Again, people who understand theory in terms of filmmaking and film storytelling, and film mythos and film genre, better than anybody else does. Lectures that were so complete, so complex, so dense and so simple that I almost had trouble following them, and by the end would realize they were dealing with things that were already in me. They were already incorporated in the way I thought about story, because they are the American mythos. Just having that dissected and presented by people who understood the very basics from the brain of the film, to the Greek myth aspect of the story, to every single thing you could learn without actually making film yourself – when I say making the film, I mean coming to Hollywood and doing it – was there. I don't have a thought about story that is not influenced by those teachers.

(IGN-Film Force)

Although Wesleyan graduates would later help to set up a career path into the film and television industry,[6] Wesleyan was, in the 1980s at least, more about art than commerce, more about aspiring cinéastes "watching *Johnny Guitar* [Nicholas Ray, 1954] at 4:00 in the morning, [...] [and] seeing *Day of the Outlaw* [1959] – a bizarre, black and white, Andre de Toth Western" (IGN-Film Force).[7] The 4:00 am screening would bear fruit later, in the last words – "I'm a stranger here myself" – of *Alien Resurrection,* Whedon's second produced film script (Ripley [Sigourney Weaver] is quoting Ray's eponymous male hero [played by Sterling Hayden]). In Whedon's time a film major was "prepared [...] for the thinking process more than the technical filmmaking process" (Basinger, quoted in Havens, 15).

Waiting for him in Middletown were two "extraordinarily brilliant professors" (Priggé, 61) who would have a powerful effect on his mind and art.

Jeanine Basinger

Born in Arkansas in 1936, Jeanine Basinger earned BS and MS degrees at South Dakota State University in the late 1950s. After working in publishing during the 1960s, she began teaching at Wesleyan College in 1971, and she has been there ever since, a professor without her doctorate who settled into a long career in the last decade in which a "terminal degree" was not a rite of passage. Forty-one years later, Basinger, now 77, continues to teach at Wesleyan, and the university's $10,000,000 film complex, named for her, was dedicated in the summer of 2008.

A legion of Basinger's students now working in film and television has talked of her teaching and her influence.[8] Dana Delaney recalls that she "dignified" her subject, proving that film studies "could be as rigorous and intellectually demanding as any other discipline." Deemed a "force of nature," "Hollywood's secret weapon," and "an unlikely superhero,"[9] her enthusiasm for her subject has been described as "infectious," but the word "intimidating" is often used as well. Domenica Cameron-Scorsese recalls that Basinger's pedagogical style was a successful amalgam of "positive reinforcement" and "putting the fear of God into you." According to *Variety*, Basinger's "policies are legendary, draconian – and inarguably effective: No missed classes. No extensions. No exceptions. (She even holds her senior seminar on Sunday!)" According to Garcia, the only excuse she would accept for being tardy was death. Does this sound familiar? Basinger's tough love must have reminded Whedon a bit of his mother, and she might have been the basic model for one of his characters. Buffy and Willow's psychology professor comes into the lecture hall on the first day of class and introduces herself:

> Professor Walsh: I'm Professor Walsh. Those of you who fall under my good graces will come to know me as Maggie. Those of you who don't will come to know me by the name my TAs use, and think I don't know about, "The Evil Bitch Monster of Death." Make no mistake, I run a hard class, I assign a lot of work, I talk fast and I expect you to keep up.
>
> ("The Freshman," *BtVS*S 4.1 – written by Joss Whedon)

Figure 5: Joss
Whedon and
Jeanine Basinger

Basinger, however, was not running a secret government "initiative" below the Wesleyan campus or propagating a "bio-mechanical demonoid" in her spare time. With ingenious assignments – she once required students to translate/reconceptualize a work by Ernst Lubitsch into a Frank Capra or Howard Hawks film (Loewenstein) – and a great deal of loving concern (*Variety* tells stories about her taking in homeless students, ferrying the sick to the hospital, and counselling the troubled, perhaps even helping the helpless), Basinger has become a legend.

The "wholly unpretentious" (Turteltaub) Basinger requires no books in her classes, insisting instead that her students concentrate on the films under discussion in a given course, and her classes, in a time when film studies has developed a formidable, often incomprehensible, parlance, are refreshingly free of jargon. "Nobody is smarter than Jeanine," Jeffrey Lane observes, "but she doesn't feel the need to be above the subject."

Her own books, always a testimony to her encyclopedic lover's knowledge of the movies, are likewise devoid of affectation. A review in *Bright Lights Film Journal* of *A Woman's View* characterizes her as a "critic with a legitimate passion for movies who has seen practically everything and can make the kind of connections that are possible only through immersion in the subject" (Morris and Thesiger). When a *New York Times* critic, Manohla Dargis, reviewing *The Star Machine*, her latest work, finds Basinger guilty of "sentimentalism," "anti-intellectualism" and "moony appreciation"; accuses her of making an argument "Kindly, somewhat ludicrously" and of a failure to document sources properly; laments her dismissal of Mulvey's theory of the gaze; and finds her "attempt to restore agency" to those enfolded into the Hollywood machine "touching," we are witnessing, in part, a generational argument.[10] Basinger's cinephilia is simply not theoretical enough for film studies' Next Gen. "To go four years studying film without hearing the word 'semiotics' – amazing!" another Basinger student would recall – that student being Joss Whedon.[11]

Whedon was Basinger's Riley, serving as her teaching assistant. She remembers him as a "joyous student" and the "crème de la crème." "He's incredibly smart," she told Havens, and "deeply, widely read. He's not one of those who falls into show business because he taps the popular culture and nothing else. He has read the classics. He knows history. His mother was a great schoolteacher. He was raised by a wonderful teacher, and he reflects that." (Havens 14) She reports that Whedon "continues to study and grow and learn" (when he returns to Wesleyan for visits, Basinger sometimes arranges for mutual screenings of esoteric film offerings at the Museum of Modern Art). "Most people have an idea that a genius is someone who never studies, or works hard," she hastens to remind, but "it's quite the opposite" – as the example of Whedon demonstrates (Havens 15). Asked if his "fame" has changed him, her answer is adamant: not at all. "He has matured even more and deepened as a person. He's more thoughtful and caring. He's the same guy. The work is everything to him. Not the fame. It's all about the work" (Havens 15).

Richard Slotkin

Whedon also counts the now retired Wesleyan University scholar Richard Slotkin as a major influence.[12] Born in Brooklyn, educated at CCNY and Brown University, where he would earn his Ph.D. in 1967, "Richie" Slotkin joined the faculty at Wesleyan in 1966, becoming Olin Professor of English in 1982. He is the author of a trilogy of books investigating American mythology, *Regeneration Through Violence: The Mythology of the American Frontier, 1600–1860* (1973), *Fatal Environment: The Myth of the Frontier in the Age of Industrialization, 1800–1890* (1985), *Gunfighter Nation: The Myth of the Frontier in Twentieth-Century America* (1992),[13] as well as novels like *The Return of Henry Starr* (1988) and *Abe* (2000). His most recent critical work is *Lost Battalions: The Great War and the Crisis of American Nationality* (2005).

Figure 6: Richard
Slotkin

Slotkin's life's work has been to examine the deep cultural roots of
American "mythogenesis," "the creation, 'in both maker and audience, [of
tales that are] mystical and religious, drawing heavily on the unconscious
and the deepest levels of the psyche, defining relationships between human
and divine things, between temporalities and ultimates" (Slotkin, quoted
by Tucker).

Whedon had been Slotkin's student in "Introduction to Myth and
Popular Culture," a course required of all American Studies students at
the junior year.[14] Slotkin recalls that the course was founded on his "own
work on the role of myth-making in the creation of national culture"
and included "some theory (including [Joseph] Campbell – though
with warnings about his a-historical bent and religious bias)." Whedon
examined the development of genres such as Westerns, detective novels,
and science fiction "in any popular commercial form – first Colonial
'captivity' narratives, then the Frontier romances of [James Fenimore]
Cooper,[15] then a sampling of other popular genres and series." Whedon
would also enroll in a senior seminar with Slotkin: "a film course which
(if memory serves) might have been 'Mexico Westerns' – the subject of my
book, *Gunfighter Nation*, which traces the interaction of Westerns with
politics in the Vietnam War era."

Asked if he detected any sign of his influence in Whedon's work,
Slotkin's response was wonderfully articulate and revealing:

The most basic is his understanding that when you work in certain genres, you are playing with symbols and themes that are fundamental and seriously important to American culture. So you can augment the power of your work by subtly reminding your audience of what they already know about your story – suggesting they recall the resonances and meanings similar imagery had for them in the past.

This is most obvious in *Firefly/Serenity*, which invoked the Western to give the science fiction a kind of historical resonance – alerting the audience, without being heavy-handed, that like the Western, this kind of film can also be a mythic reflection of and on American culture. I think something similar happens in Buffy, but the range of myths and genres is broader – high school films, horror movies, Westerns, etc. Joss understands that movie genres are a kind of lexicon or repertoire of ideological tropes (he wouldn't put it that way), each expressing some essential aspect of the culture. The power and appeal of Buffy comes, in part, from the breadth of its generic reach.

"Beyond that," Slotkin concludes, "I think he picked up on and shared my engagement with the Western as an American master-narrative."

Whedon's introduction to the work of Joseph Campbell might well be cited as another Slotkin legacy. Rhonda Wilcox's *Why* Buffy *Matters*, Greg Stevenson's *Televised Morality*, Zoe-Jane Playdon's "The Outsiders' Society": Religious Imagery in Buffy the Vampire Slayer," David Fritts's "Warrior Heroes: *Buffy the Vampire Slayer* and *Beowulf*," Mary Alice Money's "*Firefly* 'Out of Gas': Genre Echoes and the Hero's Journey," Dale Koontz's *Faith and Choice in the Works of Joss Whedon* – all find Campbell a useful source in interpreting Whedon's work, but their discovery of *The Hero with a Thousand Faces*' "monomyth" in Whedon's work is not quite the same as plotting its undeniable presence in the work of, say, the Nigerian novelist Amos Tutuola (*The Palm-Wine Drinkard, My Life in the Bush of Ghosts*), where the author would seem to be unconsciously tapping narrative archetypes. If Campbell helps us make sense of Whedon, it is because the film studies auteur learned the topography of the monomyth in class.[16]

What Whedon Learned

What precisely did Whedon take away from Wesleyan? After making an obscure reference in an interview to *Deep Rising* (Stephen Sommers, 1998), Whedon acknowledges, "Yes, I'm quoting a Stephen Sommers movie – my knowledge of film is that deep" (IGN-Film Force). With the help of the film studies auteur's DVD commentaries and interviews we get a sense of just how deep. Not all the cinematic intertexts detailed below date back to Whedon's film education, but his signature importation of theme and technique from film history into his (mainly) television art had its beginnings in Wesleyan classrooms.

- At the outset of his commentary on "Innocence" (2.14), Whedon acknowledges that every aspiring television director thinks of his work, however minor it may be, as equal in weight and importance to *Citizen Kane* (Orson Welles, 1941) – which, should we have forgotten, he describes as a "black and white film about a bald guy."
- The clash in the *Buffy* opening theme music, in which the drone of an organ, a staple of horror movie music, is replaced by rock and roll, was intended to signal that *Buffy* would not play by the rules of the traditional horror film. This collision is echoed, as Whedon also points out, in the frequent altercations between Giles, whose generic roots are in the Van Helsings of British horror, and Buffy.
- The backward head-butt Buffy uses in the showdown with Luke in The Bronze (in "The Harvest," *BtVS* S 1.2) was inspired by Abel Ferrara's *China Girl* (1987).
- Describing the final showdown with The Judge in the shopping mall in "Innocence," Whedon acknowledges that the slow-motion violence of the scene is his "incredibly low budget attempt" to "do Peckinpah."
- As Drusilla and Angelus flee from the oncoming rocket Buffy uses to destroy The Judge, Whedon admits his indebtedness to a similarly choreographed scene in Luc Besson's *The Professional* (aka *Leon*, 1994) ("Innocence").
- With images from *Blue Velvet* in mind, Whedon describes the sex scene between Buffy and Angel in "Innocence" as Lynchian.
- Discussing his love of long takes ("one-ers"), he cites the influence of French New Wave director [Max] Ophüls and American auteur Woody Allen. And he seeks to distinguish his intention in using them from the style of "Brian DePalma-see-how-far-I-can-take-my-steadicam-before-I-run-out-of-film" ("Innocence").
- In Whedon's eyes, the three-way standoff in "Innocence" between Xander and Jenny Callendar, Angelus (holding Willow captive), and Buffy (the scene in which Angelus first reveals himself without a soul to the Scoobies) evokes the style of a gunfight in a Western

(the films of Spaghetti-Western master Sergio Leone are alluded to). In the same scene, the shot of Angelus in vamp face standing in shadow, not quite visible, in the school doorway recalls for Whedon the Joker's first appearance before Boss Grissom in Tim Burton's *Batman* (1989).

- Emphasizing his view that a horror narrative should abide by its own rules and exhibit internal consistency, Whedon speaks sarcastically of the scene in *Blade* (Steven Norrington, 1998) in which vampire Deacon Frost is able to walk in sunlight thanks to his use of a special sunscreen ("The Harvest").[17]

- "Restless" (*BtVS* 4.22) has several shots that are *The Limey*-ish (Steven Soderberg, 1999), and Buffy's mom in the wall was suggested by Orson Welles's *The Trial* (1962).

- The one-er that follows the doctor from the morgue to his meeting with the Scoobies in "The Body" (5.16), Whedon acknowledges, was "borrowed" from Paul Thomas Anderson's *Magnolia* (1999): "What can I say?" Whedon confesses on the DVD. "I'm a hack." Moments later, a wide-angle shot, "where everything is a bit too big, wide, and harsh," evokes Stanley Kubrick.[18]

- Buffy's in-a-cemetery rendition of "Going Through the Motions" in "Once More with Feeling" was a homage to the "I Want" songs in Disney/Howard Ashman-Alan Menken musicals (*Little Mermaid* [Ron Clements and John Musker, 1989], *Beauty and the Beast* [Gary Trousdale and Kirk Wise, 1991]).[19] Spike's number, "Rest in Peace," on the other hand, was inspired by both *Brigadoon* (Vincente Minnelli, 1954) and *West Side Story* (Robert Wise, 1961).

- The tone of "Doublemeat Palace" (*BtVS* 6.12) was suggested by *Parents* (Bob Balaban, 1989), which Whedon made screenwriter Jane Espenson watch (Kaveney, "Writing the Vampire Slayer," 114).

- That early slow-mo of Angel walking toward the camera in "City of" (*Angel* 1.1) – John Woo indebted.

- Whedon had asked Russ Berryman, DP on *Angel*, to light the confrontation between Gunn and Wesley in "Spin the Bottle" (*Angel* 4.6) to make Angel Investigations' "muscle" look like Michael Corleone in *Godfather III* (Francis Ford Coppola, 1990).

- The "*Moulin Rougeiness*" and "almost mannered" stylization of "Waiting in the Wings" is an amalgam of Vincent Minnelli, Baz Luhrman and Douglas Sirk (*Angel* 3.13).

- The second fight outside "The Well" in "A Hole in the World" (*Angel* 5.15) would use a "45 shutter thing" indebted to both *Gladiator*

(Ridley Scott, 2000) and *Saving Private Ryan* (Steven Spielberg, 1998). (He also acknowledges a possible dept in the name of "The Well" to the "Well of Souls" in *Raiders of the Lost Ark* (Spielberg, 1981). Oh, and a shot of Wesley and Fred at the beginning of the fourth act elicits an unexplained "Ingmar Bergman" from Whedon.

- John Ford's *Stagecoach* (1939) was a major template for *Firefly*, though at the urging of Fox to amp-up the action and the gunplay it became more like *The Wild Bunch* (Sam Peckinpah, 1969) (*Firefly: The Official Companion* 6).

- The cgi zoom-in on *Serenity* at the end of the Reaver chase (*Firefly*, "Serenity" 1.2) would have been perhaps the first use of the technique – if *Star Wars: Attack of the Clones* (George Lucas, 2002) hadn't been screened first, a fact that, Whedon admits, "pissed" him off.

- *McCabe and Mrs. Miller* (Robert Altman, 1971) and *Die Hard* (John McTiernan, 1988) influenced the look of the ship in "Serenity," Part I.

- The character of the bounty hunter Jubal Early in "Objects in Space" (*Firefly* 1.10) was in part inspired by Vann Siegert (Owen Wilson) in *Minus Man* (Hampton Fancher, 1999).

- The Operative in *Serenity* was strongly influenced by Bill the Butcher (Daniel Day Lewis) in *The Gangs of New York* (Martin Scorsese, 2002), while Mal was indebted to John Wayne in *The Searchers* (John Ford, 1956). (On another occasion Whedon would praise Nathan Fillion's ability to go "from Harrison Ford to Franklin Prangborn on a very thin dime"[20] [*Serenity* 16].)

- To help think through his concern in *Serenity* that "Mal's in a Western and River's in a noir," Whedon consulted "noir westerns" recommended by Jeanine Basinger: *Pursued* (Raoul Walsh, 1947), *The Furies* (Anthony Mann, 1950), *Johnny Guitar*.

- River's triggered explosion in The Maidenhead in *Serenity* Whedon thought of as "Robert Altman's *The Matrix*" (*Serenity* 32).

- We know, thanks to a series of rapid questions to Whedon ("Joss Answers 100 Questions," the CHUD interview), Whedon's favourite Western: *Once Upon a Time in the West* (Leone, 1968); his favourite science fiction film: *The Matrix* (The Wachowski Brothers, 1999); number one musical: *The Band Wagon* (Vincente Minnelli, 1953); all-time favourite movie: also *The Matrix* – "Despite everything that's happened after"[21] (Topel, CHUD Interview); and last movie seen in a theatre (at the time of the interview): *Punch Drunk Love* (Paul Thomas Anderson, 2002). We know that "The

Coen Brothers [Joel and Ethan Coen] still continue to amaze [Whedon] on a regular basis" and that he will "watch anything David Fincher shoots" – "he's one of the few nonwriting directors who really excites me" (*JWC* 34–41).

- We know the *Cabin in the Woods*-influencing horror films he watched before and after his college years. (See the section on *Cabin* in Chapter 12.)
- As Ensley Guffey demonstrates in his essay on *The Avengers* in the *Joss Whedon Reader*, the director's blockbuster is at heart a war movie greatly indebted to Professor Basinger's *The World War II Combat Film: Anatomy of a Genre.*
- And we know the filmmaker whose "respect" he would welcome the most:

Actually, the person that has plagued me has been Spielberg because I keep like seeing bits of *Minority Report* [2002], *Catch Me if You Can* [2002], whatever he's doing and I'll come in the next day and be a wreck. It's like I'll watch five minutes of it and like every shot was sexy, every shot was useful. I'm a hack. I'm nothing. Somebody kill me. Wait, I've rethought this whole scene and it's going to be totally wrong now. I don't look at his stuff anymore. He's just bugging me. He's someone I think everything he's done is totally fascinating.

(Topel, CHUD Interview)

Whedon and Michael Bay are not the only film and television makers to have come out of Wesleyan. An estimated 400 Wesleyan alumni now work in Hollywood: heads of studios – Toby Emmerich at New Line, Nick Meyer at Paramount, and Marc Shmuger at Universal; producers – Paul Schiff (*Rushmore*, *Mona Lisa Smiles*), Laurence Mark (*As Good as It Gets*, *Deep Rising*, *Glitter*), Brad Fuller (*Texas Chainsaw Massacre*), Toni Ross (*Gravesend*), Liz Garcia (*Cold Case*); agents – Rick Nicita; actors and actresses – Bradley Whitford (*West Wing*, *Studio 60 on the Sunset Strip*),[22] Dana Delany (*China Beach*, *Desperate Housewives*), Domenica Cameron-Scorsese[23] (*The Age of Innocence*, *Absence* [a director and writer as well]), Willie Garson (*Sex and the City*, *NYPD Blue*); writers – David Kohan (co-creator of *Will and Grace*), Matthew Weiner (a writer for *The Sopranos* and creator/showrunner of *Mad Men*), Jennifer Crittenden (*The Simpsons*, *Seinfeld*, *Everybody Loves Raymond*, *New Adventures of Old Christine*), Akiva Goldman (*A Beautiful Mind*), Jeffrey Lane (*Mad About You*), Stephen Schiff (*Lolita*), Alex Kurtzman (*Alias*, *Transformers*, *Star Trek*), Bruce Eric Kaplan (*Seinfeld*, *Six Feet Under*); and directors

– Rodger Grossman (*What We Do in Secret*), Jon Turteltaub (*National Treasure, National Treasure: Book of Secrets*), Marc Longenecker (*Beach Demons*), Paul Weitz (*American Pie, About a Boy*), and Miguel Arteta (*Six Feet Under, The Office, Ugly Betty*).

In 1988, Whedon would head to California hoping to become a founding member of the Wesleyan mafia.

4 TELEVISION WRITER

In which the college grad goes West in hope of realizing his dreams of becoming a filmmaker and discovers television.

> The creative person must develop a sense of identity as a creative person, a sense of his or her own specialness. But this cannot be founded on empty fantasies. Tasks must be self-set. A personal point of view must emerge that gives meaning to the choice of tasks. A group of personal allegiances must be formed to provide the mutual support (and sometimes collaboration) that creative work requires. As the individual senses this entire system beginning to function, a new excitement must rise in him and he must be willing and able to assimilate this state of heightened emotionality without retreating into ordinariness.
>
> (Howard Gruber, "And the Bush Was not Consumed," 294–5)

oooooooooo

> [W]hat most showrunners really want is a writer who has a fresh and distinctive voice; but at the same time, they want a writer who can suppress his or her fresh and distinctive voice and conform to the voice of the show.
>
> (Jeffrey Stepakoff, *Billion-Dollar Kiss*)

When Whedon headed west after Wesleyan, "[a]n eccentric wannabe auteur with bright red hair down to his waist" (*JWC* 66), the plan was still to become a filmmaker. Averse, as we have already seen, to the "Three-G TV!" label, as luck would have it he would find himself living with "Two-G TV" and his new stepmother. In LA he would work briefly for the American Film Institute (doing research for Gregory Peck's lifetime achievement award)[1] and (almost) at a video store, while becoming, by his own admission, closer to his father than he had ever been before. Gradually, he found his creative mantra morphing: "Television is lame-o, I am a film student, I shall never write for. They pay *how* much?" (Robinson, *Onion AV Club* 2001).[2]

Whedon had begun to watch more television than he had as a boy: *Hill Street Blues* (NBC, 1981–7) and *Wiseguy* (CBS, 1987–90), for example, and, later *Twin Peaks* (ABC, 1990–1) and *My So-Called Life* (ABC, 1993–4) – series, he acknowledged, that "hit me right where I live, creatively" (Priggé 47–8). Plunging into television – urged on by his father, as he would later joke, because he was trying to get him to move out (Gross, "Life in the Whedonverse," 5) – he wrote no fewer than five uncompensated spec scripts:[3] an *It's a Living* – a show for which his dad was writing (ABC, 1980–2), a *Just in Time* (ABC, 1988), an *It's Garry Shandling's Show* (Showtime, 1986–90), a *Wonder Years* (ABC, 1988–93), a *Roseanne*. His father's praise and career advice[4] and insider connections to the television industry contributed to a sea change. Most of all, another epiphany – the second key one of his life, equal in importance to the *Close Encounters/Nausea* revelation in the UK – resulted in a rethinking of his life plan: "I sat down and really tried to write a script and found the great happiness of my life" (Robinson, *Onion AV Club* 2001) – "discovered [...] that I love writing more than anything on this earth [...]" (IGN-Film Force). As we have seen, he had always assumed he would be a filmmaker, but "never thought about writing" (Gross, "Life in the Whedonverse," 5). Now being a writer dominated Whedon's sense of himself and his future, and in the Fall of 1989, a paid television writer, he would accept the mantle of "Three-G TV!"

Roseanne

I always say, I will never do anything that's not genre. People go, well, what about *Roseanne*? I'm like, yeah, okay, but [...] That to me was genre because it was a sitcom with real people in it which, to me, was at that point a fantasy. I always tend to think just left of center, to remove myself from the world by one step. It is very freeing, and it's a particular way of coming at stories and looking at them that I find the most beautiful stuff that I know comes from, ultimately.

(Grossman)

Whedon's frenzy of spec-ulating resulted in a job offer from *Roseanne*, which would soon begin its second season on ABC. The hiring came as a bit of a shock since when he had watched the first season of his future employer, he found himself "completely blown away" and recognized immediately that his own "writing was not as good as the show I was watching, which was very daunting" (Priggé 73).

The fullest account of Whedon's time on *Roseanne* is to be found in the IGN-Film Force interview. We learn there why he was originally attracted to the show – because "it had a feminist agenda, because it was real, and decent, and incredibly funny"; the advantage of being part of the *Roseanne* writers' room – in the "studied chaos" of the show he had a unique opportunity to do a great deal of writing (to the astonishment of his father and his colleagues[5]); and his impressions of Roseanne herself – "grouchy as hell." ("I don't think I'm breaking a big news story by explaining [the difficulty of working with Roseanne]," he would tell Bianculli (*JWC* 5).[6]) But he found himself becoming frustrated as his fledgling efforts were overwritten by producers before Roseanne ever saw them. Eventually finding an advocate in Tom Arnold, he did have one memorable, positive lunch meeting with the "good Roseanne."[7] The next time they met, however, Whedon recalls:

> I saw her walk by the office, look at me – and not only not recognize me, but not recognize that there was someone standing in front of her. I had never seen somebody like that before. I was like, "This is like the lady from *Misery*! Oh boy." (IGN-Film Force)

Whedon's tales of his conflicts with the boss must have found a sympathetic ear in his father, who over two decades before had suffered under the autocracy of Bob Keeshan.

Whedon was credited with writing four episodes in *Roseanne*'s 2nd Season (1989–90).[8] "Little Sister" (2.2) concerned Roseanne's strong reservations about her sister Jackie (Laurie Metcalf) becoming a cop. In "House of Grown-Ups" (2.5) Jackie leaves for the police academy, and Becky takes Darlene on to a high school party (where kissing is involved). Darlene must read (against her will) an award-winning poem at Culture Night at her school in "Brain-Dead Poet's Society" (2.10). In "Chicken Hearts" Roseanne battles her 17-year-old manager at the fast-food restaurant. In each one we catch glimpses of the future Whedon, only 24 at the time and qualified for "puppy status" (Bianculli).[9]

"Little Sister" shows Whedon already adept at writing about women. The "A" story of the episode has Roseanne trying to convince her younger sister not to pursue her latest plan to join the police force, culminating in a famous wrestling match between them. In the parallel "B" plot Becky (Lecy Goranson) and Darlene (Sara Gilbert) also exhibit sibling rivalry (when the youngest sister claims she is blamed for everything in the Conner household, her mother corrects her: "Only the stuff since you were born"). The episode is full of funny set-pieces: Dan making chili so good that it will one day be "hanging from the ceiling in the Smithsonian" and doing a spot-on imitation of Julia Child; Darlene's slumber party with her hilarious drunken aunt; the Roseanne versus Jackie showdown. Memorable lines, exhibiting *Roseanne's* characteristic dark humour and presaging Whedon's own future signature funny, abound: when Jackie exits the Conner house yelling an angry "Go to hell" at her sister, Roseanne replies "This is hell!"; when Dan asks at breakfast, "Are we missing an offspring?" Roseanne replies, "Where do you think I got the bacon?"; Darlene's claim (in response to her mother's query about how they spent their night together) that she and Jackie "went into Chicago and picked up a couple of sailors." In a "C" storyline, we learn about Becky's discovery of her father's adult magazines, which results in a seemingly text-book feminist mother-daughter discussion of objectification, somewhat subverted by Roseanne's sly, subversive smile when she claims to agree with Becky's insistence that she feels sorry for the centrefolds.

Though much in the style of its younger contemporary sitcom *Seinfeld* (NBC, 1990–8), a show "about nothing" (nothing in particular, that is), "House of Grown-Ups" is a better, funnier episode than Whedon's first outing. With Jackie about to leave for police training, the Conner house inherits her VCR (so they can tape her favourite soap), resulting in a slew of Whedonian pop culture references (to *Davy Crockett King of the Wild Frontier* [Norman Foster, 1955], *Dirty Harry* [Don Siegel, 1971], *Star Wars* [George Lucas, 1977], *Nightmare on Elm Street 4: The Dream Master* [Renny Harlin, 1989]). Again, we are given hilariously anti-PC lines and situations. When six-year-old DJ, trying unsuccessfully to play *Davy Crockett*, proclaims "I can't work this damn thing," his mother immediately "scolds" him: "Where did you get that language? *It's called a VCR.*" In the aftermath of "Little Sister's" concern over porn, we find Roseanne asking Dan, just back from the video store, if he has rented something just for them later; when he shows her an evidently adult film (they both grin slyly). While urinating (out of frame), Dan asks Roseanne, meddling in her sister's life, why she doesn't fix South Africa while she's at it, and she replies, in a kind of henpecking-housewife-ad-absurdum, "I would of, if you fixed those nuclear weapons like I told you to."

But the best moments are in the Conner girls' bedroom, as Becky prepares for a party and tutors her younger sister how to dress, how to toss her hair (an echo of a Jackie and Roseanne scene in "Guilt by Disassociation" 2.3), how to breathe while making out, and, to Darlene's revulsion, how to French kiss (a conversation interrupted by their mother, who continues the tutelage). A *Buffy* fan will be reminded of the Slayer's before-a-mirror – "Hi! I'm an enormous slut! Hello! Would you like a copy of *The Watchtower*?" – wardrobe debate in "Welcome to the Hellmouth" (1.1). "I don't mean he's girly or anything. He's definitely a manly man. But there's this sensitivity to him where women are concerned. He gets girls. He understands how we think," Alyson Hannigan (Willow) would say a decade and a half later about her *Buffy* boss (quoted in Havens 9), but the signs were there, as this episode makes clear, when he was 25.

"Brain-Dead Poets Society" (2.10), its title a reference to the 1989 Peter Weir-directed Robin Williams vehicle released only months before, would demonstrate his ability to "get girls" even better. In an episode that begins with Darlene playing and talking basketball with her dad, an English class assignment to write a poem results in parent–child discussions of her mother's own poetry (salvaged from a notebook in the garage), Sylvia Plath, and songwriters as poetic models (Edie Brickell, Chrissie Hynde, Rickie Lee Jones are mentioned). She writes the poem and is chosen to read it at an evening gathering at her school. Not surprisingly, she refuses to participate, leading to a marvellous exchange – I can think of no more representative anti-*Cosby Show Roseanne* moment – between Dan and Roseanne over whether they should force her to appear:

> Dan: That's funny, because I thought Darlene had two parents. And this is a decision both of us should be involved in.
> Roseanne: We obviously have to come to a decision, and one of us is going to be wrong. You just give me the chance to be wrong this time. Look, no matter what we do we're going to screw our kids up. You let me mess up Darlene and you can have Becky.
> Dan: What about DJ?
> Roseanne: We'll flip for it.

The episode gives Whedon a chance to pen some truly horrible poems – by her mother, Crystal's child, the boy who takes the podium just before Darlene reads hers. Darlene's poem, however, is quite wonderful, funny and touching, in its combination of humour *and* pathos distinctly Whedonian:

> To Whom It Concerns
> To whom it concerns, Darlene's work will be late.
> It fell on her pancakes and stuck to her plate.
> To whom it concerns, my mom made me write this,
> And I'm just a kid so how could I fight this?
> To whom it concerns, I lost my assignment.
> Maybe I'll get lucky – solitary confinement.

Figure 7: Darlene
(Sara Gilbert) and
Roseanne (Roseanne
Barr) in *Roseanne*

To whom it concerns, Darlene's great with a ball,
But guys don't watch tomboys when they're cruising the hall.
To whom it concerns, I just turned 13,
Too short to be quarterback, too plain to be queen.
To whom it concerns, I am not made of steel.
When I get blindsided my pain is quite real.
I don't mean to squawk, but it really burns.
I just thought I'd mention it, to whom it concerns.

If Darlene had been in Sunnydale during Sweet's visit ("Once More with Feeling," *BtVS*S 6.7), these heartfelt, honest lines might have been sung.

"Chicken Hearts" would also presage *Buffy*, though admittedly not Whedon's masterpiece series at its most memorable. Anyone watching the episode today cannot help but think of the "Doublemeat Palace" episode of *BtVS*S (6.12), written by the ordinarily brilliant Jane Espenson and directed by Nick Marck), named by TVSquad.com as the single worst episode of the series (McDuffee). Because the Conners need the income, Roseanne is forced to work in fast food (Margaret Thatcher, Vanna White and Delta Burke already have all the good jobs for women she quips), where she suffers under Brian, a pompous 17-year-old manager.

Roseanne, of course, counters her unhappiness with her usual wit. When Brian chastises his crew's slow response time by telling them "we can't exactly call it fast," Roseanne's reply is "Why not? We call it food." When told that her "negative attitude will get [her] nowhere," she answers "This *is* nowhere." When a ludicrously dithering customer cannot decide what to order from the tempting menu, he finally asks, "What you recommend?" Roseanne quickly replies, "Psychotherapy." The timing and structure of the joke may remind veteran Whedonians of a justifiably famous exchange between Cordelia and Xander in "Graduation Day," Part 2 (*BtVS*S 3.22) – written by Joss Whedon:

> Xander: Cordy! What's up?
> Cordelia: I demand an explanation.
> Xander: For what?
> Cordelia: Wesley.
> Xander: Uh – inbreeding?

When he demands that she work weekends, however, Roseanne resorts to placating him, asking him over for dinner so that Dan can fix his carburettor. When Brian fires her anyway, the Conners send him packing, his carburettor returned to its constituent parts: "Do you want fries with that?" Roseanne triumphantly asks while giving him the boot. Contemplating a career in diplomacy at episode's end, she laments that she's just been fired by Opie – the sheriff's young son (played by future Oscar-winning director Ron Howard) on *The Andy Griffith Show* (CBS, 1960–8), a series Whedon's grandfather had written for 25 years before.

We should note in passing that "Chicken Hearts" may have been just a tad autobiographical. In the *Master at Play* conversation Whedon recalls that the Friday before he was offered a position on *Roseanne* he had begun work at a video store, which tried to convince him to stay, telling him he had "managerial potential" (*The Master at Play*).

On *Fresh Air*, Whedon explained to Bianculli the circumstances of his exit from the show:

> [F]or a while, the chaos worked for me because I got to write a lot of scripts and I really got to work; I got in there. And then I sort of got shut out of the process by the producers. As it got more insane there, they got more insular and they just sort of locked themselves in a room and I found myself with nothing to do, so I'd come in, work on *Buffy*, the movie script, and go home. And I realized that was not what I wanted to do, so I quit. (*JWC* 5)

Or, as he put it in another interview, "I couldn't work for them anymore, because I don't like getting paid to do nothing" (IGN-Film Force). He remembers his time with *Roseanne* as "a good stepping-stone, not a good experience" (IGN-Film Force).

Like his fellow WB showrunner Amy Sherman-Palladino (*Gilmore Girls*, 2000–8), who would praise her time on *Roseanne* as instrumental to her own development,[10] Whedon would come away from his year with the Conners having learned a great deal. From *Roseanne* writer and producer Danny Jacobsen (who would later create *Mad About You* (NBC, 1992–9), Whedon would take away a new understanding of how to discover "the emotional truth of a moment and what's funny about it. That's the real basis of all writing [...] the ability to find the important moment" (Priggé 84).

Parenthood

Whedon would end up writing for one other show: the short-lived *Parenthood* (NBC, 1990–1), a sitcom that brought the Steve Martin comedy (Ron [Opie] Howard, 1989) to the small screen. Whedon would author at least three episodes of the series – the one in which all the children get chicken pox ("The Plague" 1.2); the one in which Helen (Maryedith Burrell) catches her son Garry (a young Leonardo DiCaprio) making out in his bedroom ("Small Surprises" 1.7); and the one in which the stripper mother of Tod (David Arquette) pays a visit ("Fun for Kids" 1.11).[11] Given the failed show's mission statement,[12] inherited from the Lowell Ganz and Babaloo Mandel movie screenplay, to provide a realistic, unsentimental, character-driven look at family life, Whedon's attraction to the show seemed obvious. When *Parenthood* would return to the air in 2010, this time showrun by *Friday Night Lights* mastermind Jason Katims, it would finally become the sort of series Whedon had hoped it might be last century.

Meanwhile, the movies were calling: the script downtime on *Roseanne* had enabled was about to be made.

5 *BUFFY* GOES TO THE MOVIES

In which his first film script (and greatest creation) is ruined by others and disillusionment sets in.

[Gregor Mendel and Alfred Wegener[1]] made fundamental discoveries, attempted to disseminate their ideas, and ran into the stone wall of intellectual inertia (either through being ignored or ridiculed), only to be "rehabilitated" years later.

It is not so obvious that the long "moment" necessary for the construction of a new idea is the same as that necessary for its acceptance.

(Howard Gruber, "History and Creative Work," 6)

○○○○○○○○○○

It didn't turn out to be the movie that I had written. They never do, but that was my first lesson in that. Not that the movie is without merit, but I just watched a lot of stupid wannabestar behavior and a director with a different vision than mine – which was her right, it was her movie – but it was still frustrating. Eventually, I was like, "I need to be away from here."

(Joss Whedon on *Buffy the Vampire Slayer* the Movie [*JWC* 24])

The idea that became *Buffy the Vampire Slayer* (1992) was born in Whedon's mind soon after graduation from Wesleyan, but it stayed there for at least two years before he wrote it down (Ervin-Gore). The *Buffy* seed crystal is well known – Whedon has told the story hundreds of times): Whedon's long-time love of horror movies had led him to wonder what the result might be if the (usually) blonde-girl killed/terrorized by the monster in the alley were to kick its butt instead. (The particular blonde Whedon had in mind, as he would tell James Longworth [*JWC* 53], was the character played by P.J. Soles [Lynda vander Klok] in the original *Halloween*.)

If a movie were ever to be made of his script, Whedon imagined it could likely become, like *"Revenge of the Killer Bimbos"*[2]: essentially one of those "'T&A' fests" "picked off the video shelf because it had a funny title." His movie, of course, would be different – would do something new and unusual with a preposterous premise: "titles like that leap out at me because I *want* them to have their revenge because everybody's been calling them bimbos. So I wanted to make a movie that would grab you in that same way. That juxtaposition of something very frivolous versus something very serious." In Whedon's mind's eye, *Buffy* on the big screen would become "a good, responsible, feminist, exciting, enjoyable movie, and not just a titty bash" (*JWC* 53).

Like any piece of culture, *Buffy the Vampire Slayer* the movie (hereafter *BtVStM*) was the product of its place and time. Gabrielle Moss's "From the Valley to the Hellmouth: *Buffy's* Transition from Film to Television" (2001) reconstructs the context. For Moss, *BtVStM* was "a campy send-up of the era's reigning teen film genres, supernatural horror as exemplified by the *Nightmare on Elm Street* series [1984–9] and *The Lost Boys* [Joel Schumacher, 1987] (a film Paul Reubens's glam vampire henchman is clearly meant to lampoon) and teen comedy such as *Fast Times at Ridgemont High* [Amy Heckerling, 1982] and *Valley Girl* [Martha Coolidge, 1983]." In Moss's estimation a "paper-thin parody," its main target being its "Valley Girl caricature heroine," the *BtVStM* that made it to the screens was anything but feminist. Its Buffy constantly finds herself in peril because of her "vapidity and stereotypical femininity"; she controls neither her mind nor her body nor her sexuality (Lothos easily places her in a trance, which results in the death of her watcher Merrick, and also seeks to seduce her in her dreams; her "menstrual cramps act as a danger-detection system"). *BtVStM*, according to Moss,

> sticks to an obvious and physical gender logic, displaying her triumph over feminine weakness by wearing pants. Buffy's struggle as a woman and slayer is one to feel comfortable in both her womanly body and powerful role, and in the end, she is neither; at the film's close, dancing with her boyfriend Pike [Luke Perry], Buffy tells him she does not want to lead, and he says the same. Not comfortable leading or being led, "Buffy" exists in a limbo, not ready to be a powerful warrior nor content being her former beautiful airhead self.

Like almost all of its contemporary critics, Moss finds *BtVStM* too inclined towards the comic depiction of a "gum-cracking Valley teen being accorded power and responsibility."

Hal Hinson, writing in *The Washington Post*, would describe *BtVStM* as "a mess from start to finish," though he does acknowledge its "goofy charm." He singles out the director for most of the blame – for "[beginning] scenes that dribble off to no real purpose or are broken off abruptly without resolution. [...]" *BtVStM* "doesn't attempt to disguise the fact that the picture is a junk food item; instead, [it] simply lets the jokes fly in a spirit of disheveled camp." For the same paper's Desson Howe, *BtVStM* "lacks the insidious import of its *Heathers* [Michael Lehmann, 1988] model. Even in its knowing twitting of the teen-blasé society, it's not satirically thorough about the task. Its comic creativity is patchy. [...]" Peter Travers (*Rolling Stone*), struck by the "resigned look of an actor who's landed a role he'll never live down" on the face of Donald Sutherland, comments on the director's "deadly" pacing, and uses Buffy's own words as his final verdict: "It's *so* five minutes ago."

Whedon, of course, was not making the film on his own. A viewer of *Buffy* and *Angel* who had never seen the original *Buffy* movie would still know the name of the woman who secured financing for filming Whedon's script and assigned herself as director, for Fran Rubel Kuzui and Kaz Kuzui appear as Executive Producers in the credits of (and receive checks for) every single episode of both series. Writer and director came to the film with very different agendas.

Fran Kuzui was best known at the time for *Tokyo Pop* (1988), a film about a New Jersey punk singer, Wendy Reed (Carrie Hamilton), who moves to Japan in hopes of making it as a singer; falls for a guy named Hiro (Diamond Yukai) – not the one from *Heroes*; has her 15 minutes of fame; and then returns to the USA. After earning an MA at NYU, Kubui and her Japanese husband had slowly, painstakingly developed a successful business distributing American (and later European) films in Japan (*Stop Making Sense* [Jonathan Demme, 1984] was one of their first successes) and Japanese films in the USA. *Tokyo Pop* was born out of encouragement from Japanese interests in having the Kuzuis turn to filmmaking, and she wrote it herself when she could find no other takers (late in the process, however, she would partner with Lynn Grossman).

In an interview with *Wide Angle* (done while *Buffy* was still in production), Kuzui would admit that "*Tokyo Pop* I really didn't do for myself. I tried to do it to show what I could do. And after I made it, I knew I *could* make movies, so I wanted to make a movie for myself, and I wanted to make a movie as much inside the system as I could, to see whether I could do that, too." *Buffy* was, of course, that movie.

But Kuzui came to *Buffy* on the rebound after being badly burned in another development deal – "I got fucked every way you can possibly fuck a director," she would tell *Wide Angle*. (In *The Watcher's Guide* I [247] she identifies the project as *Cool Runnings* [1993 – directed by fellow Wesleyan alum Jon Turteltaub].) Not surprisingly, unlike *Buffy's* author, she would have mostly positive things to say about her next project. Her producers at Fox, Joe Roth and Roger Birnbaum, had

> seen my other film, and I was working with responsible producers, and they looked at dailies every day, and so the irony for me is that when I was working outside the studio system [on *Tokyo Pop*], I didn't feel I had enough direction, and found I had to work more for myself than I wanted to. And when I wound up making *Buffy* I was told to work for myself! And they never ever interfered while I was filming, never once. In the case of *Buffy*, I had five really high-profile actors, and they gave me all the freedom to work with them, and them the freedom they wanted, which was pretty amazing.
>
> (*Wide Angle*)

Kuzui had nothing but praise for her veteran actors, who taught her a great deal about her craft. Needless to say, Whedon's memories of making *Buffy* were a tad darker.

A decade after the grave disappointment of *BtVStM*, Whedon would still characterize himself as "a very gentle man, not unlike Gandhi,"[3] but "kind of a company man" as well and reiterate his goal "to maintain a good relationship with the people I work with" (Longworth 219), so it should not surprise us that he has been relatively diplomatic in characterizing the director's part in destroying the film. He recalls a conversation during filming with Kristy Swanson (Buffy), who came to the writer seeking advice on how to play her character:

> I literally said, "I can't." Because I have always treated film and television like the army, and I'm very strict about it. It was not my place. It was the director's movie. At that point I was there to try and help the director realize her vision, and that's all.

His debt to Kuzui, who "came in when nobody else wanted the film, said, 'We're going to put this together'" and worked, like the experienced film distributor she was, to put together financing (in co-operation with Howard Rosenman and Sandollar), also made the careful-to-be-realistic Whedon reluctant to be critical. "Without them," he would tell IGN-Film Force, "there would be no film – and possibly not this phone conversation." In other words, if Kuzui hadn't made *Buffy*, no matter how badly, the chain of life events that would follow, including

Buffy's eventual transformation into one of the greatest series in television history, might well never have happened and there would have been no reason for the interview (or this book).

Unhappy with what he saw transpiring on the set of *Buffy* the movie, Whedon held his tongue: "You do that. You respect the person above you, and you make suggestions and you do your best. [...] you don't ever disrupt the chain of command. You have to have faith in the person who's running it or things will fall apart" (Robinson, *Onion AV Club*, 2001). Kuzui, he acknowledged, had "a thing she wanted to do. She was into the comedy of it – she didn't want to make a B horror movie, that's not her style" (IGN-Film Force). Was Kuzui's clear inability to succeed at the narrative challenge of doing all the genres at once caused by her genre inflexibility or foreordained by the supreme difficulty of the task Whedon had set? It was, after all, an achievement Whedon himself would not be able to claim until later in the decade and in another narrative medium. What bothered Whedon the most was not Kuzui's direction but that nobody was protecting the script – his script (IGN-Film Force).

Whedon reported being there during shooting through much of the production, absenting himself only after he could not stand to be around Donald Sutherland any more (*JWC* 24). Sutherland, whom Whedon came to despise (and still despises), was *Buffy's* big problem, not Kuzui. The Canadian-born Sutherland (b. 1935) has been an incredibly busy actor in film and television both in the USA and abroad since 1962 (the IMDB lists over 150 roles in a 50-year career), and when he took the role of Merrick, he had already worked with many well-known directors: Alan Pakula (*Klute*, 1971), Nicholas Roeg (*Don't Look Now*, 1973), Federico Fellini (*Casanova*, 1976), Bernardo Bertolucci (*1900*, 1976), Philip Kaufmann (*Invasion of the Body Snatchers*, 1978), Robert Redford (*Ordinary People*, 1980), Richard Marquand (*Eye of the Needle*, 1981), and Oliver Stone (*JFK*, 1991). The relative novice Kuzui simply could not control him.

Whedon was fine with Rutger Hauer, who played Lothar, an ancient vampire and the movie's Big Bad. Admittedly "big and silly and [...] kind of goofy in the movie," he was at least "into it" (*JWC* 24) and Whedon gave him points for that. And he loved the turn of Paul Reubens – whose cult children's show *Pee-wee's Playhouse* (1985–91) had then just come to an end – as Amilyn. With what is described as a "weepy, awed voice," he spoke of Rubens to Robinson as "a god that walks among us [...] one of the sweetest, most professional and delightful people I've ever worked with."[4]

Sutherland, however, "was just a prick" and a "real pain," who, with the director's acquiescence, rewrote Whedon's dialogue and exhibited a constantly nasty attitude, full-of-himself, "incredibly rude" to Kuzui and "everyone around him" (*JWC* 24). Anyone who thinks Whedon's antipathy for Sutherland is merely subjective or that Donald's behaviour on the set of *Buffy* was the result of a veteran's perhaps understandable impatience with a novice director, would do well to watch Damian Pettigrew's documentary about Federico Fellini, *I Am a Born Liar*, in which Sutherland unashamedly exhibits every attribute Whedon accuses him of and speaks of the late pantheon director Fellini as "childish," "hysterical," "a tartar," a "demon," a "martinet" and insists working with him was a "torment" and "hell on earth."[5]

A younger, more candid Whedon would have his say on the *BtVS*tM experience in a 1997 interview with Edward Gross. The movie he had imagined was to have been "a horror action comedy" with "fright [...] camera movement [...] acting – all kinds of interesting things that weren't in the final film." All of his best jokes were cut; the Kuzui version was neither edgy nor "visceral" but rather "a glorified sitcom where everyone pretty much stands in front of the camera, says their joke and exited" ("Life in the Whedonverse," 6).

"It didn't turn out to be the movie that I had written" (Ervin-Gore). That "[t]hey never do," Whedon acknowledges, "was my first lesson." A decade later, he would damn it with faint praise as "not [...] without merit" but a frustrating experience (*JWC* 24) that basically soured him on filmmaking – and *Buffy* – for quite some time. In 1997, he would confess prematurely to Edward Gross that he looked forward to the day when his name was *not* immediately associated with *Buffy the Vampire Slayer*.

Popular culture has long been defined by, and relegated to oblivion because of, its own tendency towards the ephemeral. *BtVS*tM might well stand as Exhibit A of the tendency. As Moss notes, the movies "lampoon[ed]" by it "fell out of fashion soon after *Buffy the Vampire Slayer* was made, leading popular cinema into several years of dominance by action films and the occasional 'chick flick' emotional drama." But other cultural forces were at work, as Moss observes: "in other forms of media, the roots of the Girl Power movement which would one day allow *Buffy* to exist as a serious girl power feminist heroine were beginning to grow." Meanwhile, Whedon would turn to other projects.

6 SCRIPT DOCTOR/SCREENWRITER

In which Whedon tries his hand, with some success, at saving the work of others and writing for the movies.

It is useful to think of the creative individual's thought as forming a set of evolving structures. During a given period of activity, the person works with one such structure, finds its inadequacies – internal faults, disharmonies with other structures, etc. – and revises. Thought evolves from structure to structure. These structures are not static entities but regulatory systems that govern the intellectual activity of the person.

(Howard Gruber, "And the Bush Was not Consumed," 289)

ooooooooo

I find that when you read a script, or rewrite something, or look at something that's been gone over, you can tell, like rings on a tree, by how bad it is, how long it's been in development.

(Grossman)

In the "Innocence" DVD commentary (*BtVS* 2.14), Joss Whedon speaks of his proudest moment-to-date as a writer. With all the memorable lines and events in an episode he would later rank as his own personal *Buffy* favourite,[1] Whedon singles out "the boring Gypsy scene where the guy talks rather pompously about vengeance and what not." How to make sense of Jenny Calendar's role and of the curse and its escape clause (that it would be lifted if Angel were ever to experience a single moment of pure happiness)?[2] Whedon's solution was the following exchange:

Enyos: You know what it is, this thing vengeance?
Jenny: Uncle, I have served you. I have been faithful. I need to know
   [...]
Enyos: (interrupts) To the modern man vengeance is a verb, an
   idea. Payback. One thing for another. Like commerce. Not with

us. Vengeance is a living thing. It passes through generations. It commands. It kills.

Jenny: You told me to watch Angel. You told me to keep him from the Slayer. I tried. But there are other factors. There are terrible things happening here that we cannot control.

Enyos: We control nothing. We are not wizards, Janna. We merely play our part.

The kind of obstacle the scene presented, its disparate elements, each of which was valuable and worthy of retention in itself but that didn't really connect, was not new to Whedon. As a script doctor he had faced even larger, more intimidating challenges, more substantial plot holes, character inconsistencies, narrative conundrums. He tells how, walking along Santa Monica Pier, the phrase "vengeance is a living thing" came to him, and he knew he had found the cure.

The unofficial history of script doctoring probably stretches back to the beginning of the movies. Is it not possible even a Griffith or a Chaplin needed an uncredited helping hand with a script? And Ben Hecht (1894–1964) was well known in his day for having operated on many in-need-of-medical-attention screenplays. Its contemporary emergence from the closet, however, begins with Francis Ford Coppola's public acknowledgement (at the 1973 Oscars) of Robert Towne's contribution to *The Godfather* (1972) or "creative consultant" Tom Mankiewicz's redrafting of Mario Puzo's *Superman* (1978).[3] In recent decades scripts and their physicians (see Table 5) have included some significant figures.

Table 5: Contemporary Script Doctors

Movie	Director	Year	Script Doctor
Hook	Steven Spielberg	1991	Carrie Fisher – Princess Leia in *Star Wars*
Last Action Hero	John McTiernan	1993	William Goldman – Oscar-winning screenwriter of *All the President's Men* and *Butch Cassidy and the Sundance Kid*
Crimson Tide	Tony Scott	1995	Quentin Tarantino – writer–director of *Pulp Fiction* and *Kill Bill*
Bulworth	Warren Beatty	1998	Aaron Sorkin – creator of *The West Wing*
Ronin	John Frankenheimer	1998	David Mamet – Pulitzer Prize-winning playwright, Oscar-nominated screenwriter, and director
Charlie's Angels	McG	2000	Akiva Goldman – Oscar-nominated screenwriter of *A Beautiful Mind* and Wesleyanite
Minority Report	Steven Spielberg	2002	Frank Darabont – writer and director of *The Shawshank Redemption* [1994]

Whedon himself provides a cogent sense of the script doctor's job description in an interview with Edward Gross. Acknowledging that the assignments vary considerably, he explains that the call usually comes "when they are making a movie already and they should not be. [...]" Once onboard, the doctor may face any number of challenges, from "Gosh, this one scene doesn't work," to "Wow, this script sucks," but the basic charge remains the same: "connecting whatever dots they already have; it's taking whatever they're wed to and then trying to work something good in between the cracks of it" (Gross, "Life in the Whedonverse," 7).

Whedon found himself practising this shadow craft primarily in the years between the release of *BtVStM* and *Buffy's* rebirth on television. He had a patron – "a huge benefactor and collaborator of sorts" – Jorge Saralegui,[4] a Fox executive who encouraged Whedon to write "the spec that sort of made my bones" – *Suspension* (see below) – and helped to get him consequential assignments for both *Speed* and *Alien Resurrection*.

The money was good and the opportunities varied. He loved the plot of *Speed* and "was very anxious to come in and rewrite the characters." *Toy Story*, on the other hand, "was the greatest opportunity in the world, because it was a great idea, with a script I didn't like at all." His response to some potential assignments, however, was "You don't need me. You need to [*shouting*] *not make this*" (Robinson, *Onion AV Club*, 2001). His rule of thumb was always that "a good idea with a terrible script" still held promise, while the opposite was not necessarily true.[5] As he would put it in discussing the challenge he faced with *Toy Story:*

> the dream job for a script doctor: a great structure with a script that doesn't work. A script that's pretty good? Where you can't really figure out what's wrong, because there's something structural that's hard to put your finger on? Death. But a good structure that just needs a new body on it is the best. (*JWC* 91)

Scripts Doctored

Speed (Jan De Bont, 1994)
By any measure, *Speed* was a huge success. Made on a budget of approximately $28 million, it would gross over $350 worldwide. But a week before filming was to start, concern about the film's script would result in Whedon being brought in to punch it up.[6] (His patron, Fox's Saralegui, was behind the assignment.) The movie was already cast, though Whedon would make some modifications: for example, he felt

the character played by Alan Ruck (Stephens), a boilerplate "asshole" lawyer in the original script, was wasted and offered a quickly accepted alternative: "Why don't we just make him a tourist? A guy, just a nice, totally out-of-his-depth guy?" Ortiz (Carlos Carrasco) was already "on board," but fan boy Whedon would have Jack deem him "Gigantor" (and explain the reference to a giant Manga robot to Reeves). In Whedon's hands, Jack became less of a "maverick hotshot" and more of a "polite guy trying not to get anybody killed" who is still able to think in unorthodox ways. Whedon gives Keanu Reeves himself a great deal of the credit for the character.

Told that he was not permitted to change any of the stunts but that he had a blank check to alter every word, Whedon authored most of the dialogue in the final film (*JWC* 95). When Jack, inspecting the bomb beneath the in-motion bus, passes his profane realization of their precarious situation up to Stephens (on the radio with the police) – "Fuck me!" – we might not recognize it as Whedonesque, but when we hear Stephens's not quite faithful translation – "Oh darn!" – we are certain of the author. He had a hand, too, in minor reconstruction of the plot: in the death of Jack's partner, Harry Temple (Jeff Daniels); in the search for the bomber, Howard Payne (Dennis Hopper). His task, as he understood it, was to find "the emotional reality of the characters and [get] them from A to B in a realistic fashion" (*JWC* 96). Because of Writers Guild of America rules, however, his name did not appear on the finished film, and Graham Yost (who would later create the excellent FX TV series *Justified*) was given sole credit as *Speed's* author.

Toy Story (John Lasseter, 1995)

Like *Speed, Toy Story* would also prove to be a tremendous success, earning over $354 million worldwide on a budget of $30 million, but like *Speed* the film had a somewhat troubled production that resulted in a call for a doctor.[7]

In a roundtable discussion ("Filmmakers Reflect") on the DVD of *Toy Story*, four individual prime movers in the making of the film – John Lasseter (director), Andrew Stanton (screenwriter), Pete Docter (supervising animator), and Joe Ranft (story supervisor) – mull over, ten years after, its genesis. They recall coming up with the idea of a buddy film, their establishment of a "don't list" (no villain, no singing, no "I want"); their give and take hammering out of the story and characters into the wee small hours. Joss Whedon's name is never mentioned.[8]

The four also reminisce about how, "just before Christmas" in 1994,[9] just after a horrible screening for the Disney bosses and just before

Figure 8: Whedon's Creation: The T-Rex with an inferiority complex in *Toy Story*

animation was to begin, the production was shut down. Lasseter and company begged for another two weeks to make things right. Again Whedon is not mentioned, although if this were a play, it would be time to cue his entrance: "They had shut the movie down," Whedon tells Kozak (*JWC* 92). "I went up to Pixar, and they actually said, 'Listen, we're having to shut down for a while because we're having story problems. Many of you are going to be laid off, and Joss is here to fix the script.' And then I was just like, 'Why are you pointing at me? What's going on? This is horrible!' I think this was 'Black Monday.' I don't know if it was a Monday. I think it was a Monday. But it was definitely referred to as 'Black.'"[10]

Conveniently, Whedon was already under contract with Disney at the time. He had come to work for the Mouse because of his long-standing love of musicals and his desire to follow in the footsteps of *Little Mermaid* (1989) and *Beauty and the Beast* (1992) but quickly found that the "animated musical died with Howard Ashman [1950–91]" (*JWC* 97).[11]

Whedon was involved in several animated projects. He would write not only a script but the lyrics for three songs for *Marco Polo*, a film they wanted to turn into "My Fair Lady" (Broadway composer Robert

Lindsey Nassif wrote the music), but which would never appear. For the film that would eventually become, in the next century, *Atlantis: The Lost Empire* (Gary Trousdale and Kirk Wise, 2001), a project conceived, in recombinant style, as "Journey to the Center of the Earth" meets "The Man Who Would Be King," Whedon would earn a screen credit, but only because he was the first writer assigned to it. In fact, he contributed "not a shred" to the film.[12]

When Whedon got the call from Pixar, he quickly discovered that he loved Lasseter's idea – toys having a life of their own – but the script was "a shambles," and "Woody was a thundering asshole. So it was my job to make him somewhat likable" (Tracey 23). "Thrilled" by the project, he moved to Northern California, where Pixar's animation studio was located, and would remain there for months working on the film, leaving only when the film was finally greenlit. He would return a month later for another session (a total of six months' work in all). In the parlance of the script doctor, the job was "not a polish; it was a rewrite. [...]"

He would add only one new character, Rex (see Figure 7), the terribly insecure but adorable Tyrannosaurus voiced by Wallace Shawn (contrary to popular opinion, the little three-eyed aliens were *not* his invention), but he would make some difficult decisions about what might be cut, excising "a lot of extraneous stuff, including the neighbor giving [Andy] a bad haircut before he leaves," and he would be involved, too, in "finding the voices." In the wake of Disney's decision not to use Jim Carrey as Buzz Lightyear (not a big enough star!), he was instrumental in identifying how Tom Hanks should voice Woody. Whedon told Michael Sragow that "John [Lasseter] suggested I watch a scene near the beginning of *Nothing in Common* [Garry Marshall, 1986] where he jokes with everybody as he walks through his office." The suggestion proved useful.

It will surprise no one that "The whole thing with the mutant toys, as we referred to them, forming the skateboard thing to bring [Buzz and Woody] out" was Whedon's idea, but it was actually a substitute for what he refers to as "my Barbie-as-Sarah-Connor rescue scene," nixed after Mattel would not grant the requisite permission to transplant their franchise toy into a Terminator scenario.

In retrospect, Whedon's greatest pride in his contribution to *Toy Story* was "the voice and the sensibility of the characters, keeping them from being that sort of old-school Disney – what my wife would refer to as 'old-man humor.' Getting a little more voice and a little more edge into the jokes and into the bits, and just helping the structure, seeing it through."

Whedon enjoyed working with Lasseter and company, fellow fan boys:

We were raised on the same cartoons and toys. [...] It was a great, great process because you're sitting around with a bunch of animators who are basically drawing caricatures of each other, getting Sharpie headaches and making a lot of jokes, and they're the sweetest bunch of guys.

Although they were breaking new ground in digital animation, it was the dedication of the *Toy Story* team to the narrative that most impressed Whedon:

John Lasseter was like, "We're telling a story. We're making a cell-animation film. We'll never think of it as anything else. We'll never place CGI just to show what it can do, just to play tricks. This isn't a 3D movie. This is a story." Everything was very old-school in that sense. That's what made it stand out and that's what spawned the generation of movies that came after it. It was simply, "Oh! We already know how to do this; we've just got a slightly new medium to do it in."

Toy Story would receive an Academy Award nomination for best screenplay, earning Whedon the right to forever call himself an Oscar-nominee.

Waterworld (Kevin Reynolds, 1995)

Already infamous before its release for its troubled production (long-time friends Kevin Reynolds, its director, and Kevin Costner, its star, had a major falling out) and its soaring budget (at the time of its release it was the most expensive movie ever made at approximately $175,000,000), *Waterworld* bombed in the United States and only barely eeked out a profit abroad (earning $255 million worldwide).

Whedon had been brought in to work on the post-apocalyptic tale of a mutant hero trying to survive in a flooded, landless world (the ice-caps have melted) which the media had already begun routinely referring to it as *Fishtar* and *Kevingate*.[13] Whedon came on very late in the process, worked on location in Hawaii for seven weeks in 1994, and was quickly reduced to "the world's highest-paid stenographer" (*JWC* 26) as he recorded the ideas of Costner, et al., only to see them all jettisoned (Jacobs). Although he told Legel that "there's a draft of *Waterworld*" – apparently one he wrote – "that's pretty cool," Whedon had no choice but to concede that, as a script doctor, he had "lost the patient."

Twister (Jan De Bont, 1996)

Whedon has had almost nothing to say about his work on *Twister*, where, working again with *Speed* director De Bont, he would so some doctoring of a script credited to no less than Michael Crichton (and Anne-Marie Martin). "In *Twister*, there are things that worked and things that weren't the way I'd intended them," he would tell Tasha Robinson (*Onion AV Club*, 2001). On the DVD commentary, De Bont makes mention of the "very edgy, very fresh, very young" dialogue provided by his fellow *Speed* collaborator in the film's first major sequence (following the flashback in which Helen Hunt's character's father, in a career-inspiring tragedy, is snatched away by a tornado).

The following dialogue – between Rabbit (Alan Ruck, who had also been in *Speed*), Laurence (Jeremy Davies), Dusty (Philip Seymour Hoffman), and Bill Harding (Bill Paxton) – sounds like it could well be Whedon's:

> Rabbit: All I'm saying is don't fold the maps!
> Laurence: I didn't fold the map!
> Rabbit: Yeah, well Kansas is a mess, there's a big crease right through Wichita. Roll the maps.
> Bill: What do you know, the storm chasers.
> Rabbit: Hey, I don't believe it! Who is that handsome devil!
> Bill: Gentleman.
> Dusty: The Extreme! IT'S THE EXTREME!!
> Bill: Oh man, don't start that shit!
> Dusty: Oh manly hand shakin' Zeus. How you doin', man?
> Bill: Doin' great, doin' great.
> Dusty: Oh bad!

It seems entirely possible that *Twister's* iconic comic tornado debris moments – "Cow!" "Another cow!" "I gotta go, Julie, we got cows" – were Whedon contributions as well.

Titan A.E. (Don Bluth and Gary Goldman, 2000)

Another project he would sooner forget – he tells Tasha Robinson that he is "happier having my name on [*Atlantis*]," a movie to which he contributed not a thing (*Onion AV Club* 2001) – *Titan A.E.*, for which he shares a credit with future *Angel* and *Firefly* collaborator Ben Edlund, is not without interest to followers of Whedon's development, containing as it does a few elements of the *Firefly/Serenity*verse in germ. Both, for example, are set in an after-earth (AE) future – *Titan* at the dawn of the thirty-first century. This time earth has been destroyed, not abandoned as overpopulated, obliterated by a race of energy beings called the Drej, who fear what the human race, about to develop radical new "Titan" technology, may become. Unlike *Firefly*, *Titan A.E.* is overflowing with aliens of many varieties – in this 'verse humans are the abnormality since few survived destruction of the home world. We also have a hovercraft – an absolute necessity according to Whedon (*Serenity* DVD commentary), and a Jayne prototype – two of them in a sense: for both Korso (voiced by Bill Pullman) and Preed, Corso's right-hand-lizard (Nathan Lane), are willing to sell out to the highest bidder (though Corso does prove finally heroic). Neither, however, has Jayne's stupid charm, nor a big gun named Vera, nor a cool hat with earflaps. When Cale, the story's tousle-haired, blonde hero, succeeds in the end in fulfilling his father's plan for him and creating a new earth, he decides to name the planet "Bob" – a disconcerting choice for Whedon and Edlund who surely were aware that the name evoked the supernatural, parasitic serial killer in *Twin Peaks* (or perhaps they were just referencing Microsoft's disastrous, user-friendly Windows system from the mid-1990s). It is really not a bad film and is rather beautiful to look at. Whedon's distaste for it must be, like his dismissal of *Alien Resurrection*, an insider's aversion.

X-Men (Bryan Singer, 2000)

In a 1999 interview with *Science Fiction Weekly*, conducted just after he had finished taking another pass at the script of Bryan Singer's initial *X-Men* outing, Whedon made this prediction about his success: "I'm not too hopeful my version will show up," he responded presciently. "[T]here may be some stuff left when the dust settles, but no, it looks like they went a different way" (*JWC* 17).

Indeed, as Whedon would later report, only one line survived. In a late scene of the film, Cyclops demands, after a battle in which the shape-shifting Mystique has mimicked both Wolverine and Storm, how he is to be certain the being he faces is indeed his-anything-but-friend, fellow X-man, and rival for the affections of Jean Grey, to which Wolverine replies: "You're a dick." It would be Whedon's sole contribution to *X-Men*, a film he became involved in because of his fascination with the incredibly complex X-man universe and his love for the characters.

The opportunity to have his own way with the 'verse and its inhabitants would not come until the next century when, working in a different medium, he would succeed Grant Morrison as the author of *Astonishing X-Men*. In 2006, the Great Mentioner, with some justification, would have him succeeding Bryan Singer as the master of the X-Men movie franchise, but the GM was wrong, and Whedon would sign on to do (or not) Wonder Woman instead. It would not be until the second decade of the new century that he would again have the chance to work in the Marvelverse – this time as the director of Marvel's *The Avengers* (see Chapter 13).

Scripts

Suspension

Inspired in part by the tremendous box office success of *Die Hard* (John McTiernan, 1988), Whedon's "*Die Hard* on a bridge" script for *Suspension* was sold to Largo Entertainment for a reported $750,000. Whedon would tell Edward Gross that the attraction of the story, as with *Speed*, was in "creating a situation that is immediate, in your face, exciting and then playing every variation that you can." With the relentlessness of *The Terminator* (James Cameron, 1984) likewise in mind, Whedon set out to write one of those "great premise movies that cannot be stopped." The challenge was to discover "How many unbelievable things can happen on a bridge."

In Whedon's film terrorists take over the George Washington Bridge in New York in what is essentially a kidnapping of a wealthy oil executive. His hero is a former cop, Harry Monk, who has just been released from jail and finds himself the only one with a chance to stop the scheme. "It's a redemption through violence story, actually, which I like a lot," Whedon explained.

A writer for screenwritersutopia who managed somehow to gain access to Whedon's script, reports (in an ungrammatical review) that it is full of "early John Woo shenanigans" and "[l]ike a theme-park ride [...] keeps your screams shaded with laughter." "[W]ith his kid-high-on-sugar take on the action genre," Mayflower reports, Whedon "wows us without an ounce of self-seriousness or allusion [*sic*] of anything more momentous than a man bungee-jumping down the side of a bridge."

Afterlife

Reportedly sold to Columbia for $1.5 million, Whedon's script for *Afterlife* now appears to be dead in the water. Whedon has rarely mentioned it in interviews, and virtually all that is known of it is from Mayflower's review of the purported text.[14] *Afterlife's* hero, Daniel Hofstetter, a scientist, dies and finds his consciousness reborn, thanks to the intervention of a government agency, into the body of a younger man, the serial killer Jamie

Snows; goes in search of his beloved wife Laura; is, of course, presumed to be the monster he now looks like; and is hunted by the cop who had sent Snows to the chair.

Mayflower reports that "what makes this script special, beyond its action-and-intrigue trappings" is the reunion of the dead husband and wife: "They are rediscovering one another and able to do what each couple wishes they could: bring it back to that indescribable electric charge of their first touch. Joss is also smart enough to know that Laura and Daniel would indulge in his newfound strength. Which translates to heating up the sheets like hog-wild teenagers." Such scenes presage the writer Whedon will become. As Mayflower writes with some apostrophe-less eloquence:

> this is why I think Joss Whedon is such a good writer. He simply knows people. Hes [*sic*] always right on and with it when it comes to human interaction and when his characters are faced with extraordinary situations. Add that to his knowledge of the little things – the small asides and quirks that make up life – and Joss is able to draw true human portraits of the true human condition even in action scripts and a show about a young vampire-slayer.

Alien Resurrection (Jean-Pierre Jeunet, 1997)

> Trish Burkle: I mean, Rog's always had a thing for those disgusting *Alien* movies with all the slime and teeth. He just can't get enough of 'em. Except for that last one they made – I think he dozed off.
> ("Fredless," *Angel* 3.5)

The chance to write the fourth instalment in the *Alien* franchise[15] was of an entirely different kind from Whedon's work on *Speed*, *Toy Story*, *Waterworld* and *Twister*. As an admitted ardent lover of "sequels [...] franchises, and [...] big epic stories that go on and on" and a jilted devotee of "summer movies, before every single one of them was crap," the attraction was obvious, and Fox had enough faith in Whedon's earlier doctoring achievements to commission a script. His first draft was sans-Ripley – Weaver was not interested in another sequel. After she was persuaded to at least be open to another outing, however, Whedon's next Ripleyed draft won her over. (In the next century, it should be noted, Whedon would succeed again in securing Weaver's services, this time to play The Director in the final moments of *The Cabin in the Woods*.) Once Jeunet, the barely conversant-in-English French director of such "art" films as *Delicatessen* (1990) and *City of Lost Children* (1995), signed on to direct (after Danny Boyle [*Trainspotting*, 1995] and Peter Jackson [*The Lord of the Rings*, 2001–3], among others, took a pass), *Alien Resurrection* was greenlit.

Although the film that would be made from his original screenplay would bring tears to his eyes (actually a "single manly tear"[16]); although he would insist sardonically to Tasha Robinson that the episode of *Boy Meets World* (ABC, 1993–2000) he never wrote (despite an erroneous IMDB listing) gives him more pride than *Alien Resurrection* (*Onion AV Club* 2001), it was, in retrospect, a learning experience. In bringing his heroine back from the dead – Ripley (Sigourney Weaver) is cloned, with an alien inside her, 200 years after she has died – he recalls beginning to master in the process the art of narrative metaphor which would become his trademark when he created the *Buffy*verse. As he would tell shebytches.com:

> When I was writing *Alien: Resurrection*, I began to understand, on a level that I hadn't before, what I was trying to do. Before it was even metaphor, it was simply, "What experience are these people going through that people can relate to? What is the thing that's going to make people say, 'I am Ripley,' not just, 'There's Ripley'?" And I was particularly dealing with this because she was coming back from the dead, and people had to accept that. So I realized, "I have to make it difficult for Ripley to have come back from the dead, because it's going to be difficult for the audience to accept it – but if it's difficult for her to accept it too, they will identify with her, that will be the in.
>
> (*JWC* 141)

On *Buffy* he would, of course, bring the same kind of character thinking to Buffy's harsh return to the living in Season 6.

Whedon provides a fairly precise phenomenology of what went wrong with *Alien Resurrection* in a conversation with Will Harris, admitting, finally, that "it wasn't a question of doing everything differently, although they changed the ending." The source of his pain was "mostly a matter of doing everything *wrong*":

> They said the lines […] *mostly* […] but they said them all wrong. And they cast it wrong. And they designed it wrong. And they scored it wrong. They did everything wrong that they could possibly do. There's actually a fascinating lesson in filmmaking, because everything that

they did reflects back to the script or looks like something from the
script, and people assume that, if I hated it, then they'd changed the
script.

Jeunet and company "just executed it in such a ghastly fashion as to render
it almost unwatchable" (Harris). The experience inspired Whedon to vow
with characteristic humour that "the next person who ruins one of my
scripts is going to be me" (*JWC* 81, 131).

Nevertheless, in a movie he "loathes," he can still "see the germ of
everything I've tried to do in my career. It's the moment when Winona
Ryder, who is such a porcelain beauty, looks at herself and says, 'Look at
me, I'm disgusting.' And that's when I said, 'OK, now I understand what
I'm doing with my writing'" (*JWC* 141). And he would learn too that he
should perhaps prefer "work[ing] on something that 19 people don't own
and control," that "isn't just somebody else's" (Robinson, *Onion AV Club*,
2001).

In (non-Whedon) retrospect, *Alien Resurrection* wasn't quite a disaster.
With a budget of approximately $70,000,000, it did manage to earn
$161,295,658 worldwide, and the reviews, though hardly laudatory,
sometimes had kind things to say. While Roger Ebert would deem it
"a nine days' wonder, a geek show designed to win a weekend or two at
the box office and then fade from memory," and Stephen Hunter (in *The
Washington Post*) reduced it to "an art film with bugs that explode out of
people's chests," Laura Miller (in *Salon*) would praise "the cranky banter
of the smugglers" which "hearkens back to one of the most likable aspects
of the first *Alien*, its depiction of the boredom of everyday space travel."
Nearly every review would extol Sigourney Weaver's performance as an
über Ripley.

Revealingly, the biggest complaint of the reviewer for AIN'T IT
COOL NEWS, who had read the screenplay in advance, was the film's
unfaithfulness to it: "It's like they always took the path less cool. For
example there was a chance to do the Cameron dream of having a kickass
smaller person whup up on the bigger things, with Winona [Call], but
instead they were biased by her petite frame."[17] And Hunter would
register his surprise at its humour: "The movie never scales the heights of
pure skull-in-the-vise horror that Ridley Scott's original managed. And
it never develops the cool marines-vs.-bugs carnage of James Cameron's
second installment. But it brings a mordant, crackerjack wit to the world
of chest-busting, head-ripping creepazoids from beyond." The source of
the dark comedy? Hunter's answer – "The French, they have a knack,
no?" – would credit, wrongly, Jean-Pierre Jeunet. Whedon had brought

the funny – mostly in the mouth of Ripley. It was Whedon who wrote this exchange between Call and Ripley:

> Call: You're a thing. A construct. They grew you in a fucking lab.
> Ripley: But only God can make a tree.

This was perhaps the first ever SF reference to Joyce Kilmer. It was Whedon who had Ripley later ask Call, "Are you programmed to be such an asshole? Are you the new asshole model they're putting out?" It was Whedon who gave Ripley the very Buffy-like response to a soldier's question:

> Distephano: Man, I thought you were dead.
> Ripley: I get that a lot.

Although Whedon tells Tasha Robinson that he always enjoyed the challenges of script doctoring, noting that the process is not unlike "being an executive producer, finding out what's wrong with a story and fixing it. [...] That's fun" (*JWC* 148), he retains from his experience in the Nineties a strong aversion to "factory bullshit. When you get notes on a script that are good but then that same studio puts out something redonkulous [...]. you just wonder 'How did that happen?' If you start using that perspective you'll make yourself insane. And nobody has the code, do they?" (Legel, Comic-Con Interview). Writers-at-heart Whedon and Neil Gaiman are in agreement on the source of the "odour" they detect in the film industry:

> Gaiman: Yes. It really is this thing of executives loving the smell of their
>   own urine and urinating on things. And then more execs come in,
>   and they urinate. And then the next round. By the end, they have
>   this thing which just smells like pee, and nobody likes it.
> Whedon: There's really no better way to put it.
>
>   (Grossman)

Given the opportunity to return to the more writer-friendly medium of television, as he soon would be, Whedon would take down his script doctor shingle and put his at-that-point-disappointing movie career on hold.

PART II:
Creator

The question of novelty [...] is central. How is it that certain individuals have devoted their lives or large portions of their lives to the construction of novelty?

(Howard Gruber, "From Epistemic Subject," 171)

We are not talking about species typical behavior. Rather, we are talking about the maximum of which members of the species are capable.

(Howard Gruber, "From Epistemic Subject," 175)

Creative works are constructed over long periods of time.

(Howard Gruber, "From Epistemic Subject," 171–2)

The creator may or may not be obsessed with [the] idea of uniqueness, but it is my conviction that people who lead creative lives generally intend to do so, and define themselves accordingly.

(Howard Gruber, "The Evolving System at Work," 13)

[T]he main function of ordinary work is reliable production, whereas innovation is always potentially disruptive.

(Howard Gruber, "The Evolving System at Work," 11–12)

7 *BUFFY* DOES TELEVISION

In which a botched movie becomes a TV masterpiece.

A creative moment is part of a longer creative process, which in its turn is part of a creative life. How are such lives lived? How can I express the peculiar idea that such an individual must be a self-regenerating system? Not a system that comes to rest when it has done good work, but one that urges itself onward. And yet, not a runaway system that accelerates its activity to the point where it burns itself out in one great flash. The system regenerates the activity and the creativity regenerates the system. The creative life happens in a being who can continue to work.

(Howard Gruber, "And the Bush Was not Consumed," 269)

ooooooooooo

And Buffy was very much an attempt to create an icon – to do it subtly, I didn't expect people to catch wind of what I was doing, I expected her to become an underground icon – but in fact she lived above ground, and could eat roots and berries.

(Joss Whedon, *JWC* 140)

I didn't want to say "Look, we're better than a TV show." I wanted to say "You can do all of this in an episode of television. It just depends on how much you care." [...] I love TV. I love what you can do with it [...]. It's not better, it's just TV in all its glory. The way I celebrate musicals I celebrate this medium.

(Joss Whedon, "Once More with Feeling" – DVD Commentary)

I could hear Joss's voice. I could feel his heartbeat.

(Jeanine Basinger on watching *Buffy the Vampire Slayer* on television for the first time – "Joss Whedon, A+ Film Major")

"As far as I'm concerned, the first episode of *Buffy* was the beginning of my career," Joss Whedon would tell *Entertainment Weekly*. "It was the first time I told a story from start to finish the way I wanted."

In an article about a later Whedon show, *Firefly*, Felicity Nussbaum reports being eyewitness to a moment when "a dewy young woman leaned forward and gripped [Whedon's] hand between hers, pulling him in for enforced eye contact: 'I just want you to know – we trust you. We know you know what you're doing. We know it will be great'" (*JWC* 70). This kind of allegiance – the avowal that "Joss Whedon is My Master Now" – the ever-modest Whedon, as we have already seen, tends to make light of and depersonalize: the devotion of *his* fans, he insists, is not, after all, anything like that experienced by an actor: "it's not, 'I love your face' – only my wife loves that – but it's about the work." The atheist's refusal to be worshipped is not just a matter of temperament, however. Taking it seriously, he fears, would be a creative disaster: "You have to reality check. When somebody calls you a 'god' the first thing you have to ask yourself is, 'How sh[it]ty am I?' because if you start believing it, guess how badly you're about to start writing?" (Spiegel). No one called Whedon a god before *Buffy the Vampire Slayer* was reborn on TV.

Begin at the end. In 2005, two years after *Buffy the Vampire Slayer* had gone off the air after seven seasons, Whedon would tell Priggé:

> I was not very upset ending Buffy: I'm not a guy who cries and looks back at things. In my high school, we didn't even have a graduation ceremony. We just left. At the end of *Buffy*, I was totally exhausted and we had to shut down filming one night because I was too tired to go on. That has never happened before. I was exhausted from seven years of telling stories – 144 stories to be exact. I knew it was time to stop. I knew it in every fiber of my being. You can love pasta like nothing else, but when you're full, you're full. (160)[1]

Sated, Whedon did not push away from the table; Sarah Michelle Gellar did, deciding not to renew her contract so she could pursue her movie career. "Buffy Quits!" a 7 March 2003 cover story in *Entertainment Weekly* proclaimed.

The idea of reincarnating *Buffy the Vampire Slayer* on television in the first place was not Whedon's either. As he would tell Tasha Robinson, "After the première of the movie, my wife said, 'You know, honey, maybe a few years from now, you'll get to make it again, the way you want to make it! [Robinson describes Whedon's voice here as "broad, condescending."] Ha ha ha, you little naïve fool. It doesn't work that way. That'll never happen" (*JWC* 25). Recall, too, as we saw earlier, that Whedon had been anxious to shed the "man who created *Buffy*" label. Depending on which version you believe, credit goes either solely to Gail Berman, the head of Sandollar Productions (later to be President of Fox Broadcasting),[2] or to *BtVStM* director Fran Rubel Kuzui, working in conjunction with Berman.[3] This time, all agreed, Joss Whedon would be put in charge. "I was pretty much out of TV completely at that point," Whedon recalls, "and my agent asked me, 'Now, come on, really what do you want to do?' I said, 'I'm already writing scenes for this in my head,' and he said, 'Fine, I'll make the deal.' I did not expect it to take over my life like this. I did not expect it to move me as much as it did" (*Watcher's Guide* I, 241). Many of us who fell for *Buffy* could say exactly the same.

The original idea was for a children's programme, a 30-minute show that would be a kind of *Power Rangers* [Fox, 1993–2001] clone – a show that was then making a fortune as a "merchandising cornucopia" (*TV Guide Guide to TV* 448) for the new network. But when he began to seriously ponder *Buffy* the series, that notion morphed, with help from Whedon's agent Chris Harbert,[4] into something "a little more tongue in cheek, [an] hour-long drama – a real show with lots of schtik and spoof" (Ervin-Gore).

Network after network would pass on the show, however (in the *A&E Biography* episode on *Buffy* Berman speaks of "lots of sets of rolling eyes"), before the WB, then a relatively new netlet, would buy it. The "B movie that had something more going on" (IGN-Film Force interview) name of the in-development series became a problem, of course. The suits pleaded that it be altered, but there was a clear method in Whedon's titular madness:

> I believe that anyone who isn't open to a show with this title isn't invited to the party. I made the title very specifically to say, "This is what it is." It wears itself on its sleeve. It's sophomoric, it's silly, it's comedy-horror-action; it's all there in the title. Having the metaphor to work with makes the show better, and having the silly title makes the show cooler. At least to me. ("Joss Whedon on Sex, Death")[5]

He knew, too, that a slight tweek might produce a different result. Asked if "the series would stand more chance at the Emmys with a different name?" his answer was clear: "Buffy the Vampire Slayer, MD" (*JWC* 39). He refused to change the title and has never looked back: "To this day, everyone says, 'Oh, the title kept it from being taken seriously.' I'm like, 'Well, f[uck] them. It's a B movie, and if you don't love B movies, then I won't let you play in my clubhouse.' Now, I'm not an exclusionary person, I don't like to drive people away, but honestly, if people have trouble with that title" (IGN-Film Force).

In the earlier chapter on *BtVS*tM, I have already touched on the Buffyverse origin myth. *Buffy's* migration to the small screen would lead him to reveal more about its genesis. "The vampire angle," he now acknowledges, "was kind of irrelevant in a way. The story was more about a girl who no one takes seriously, but has incredible responsibility and power" (Priggé 96–7). In fact, the original working title, Whedon has claimed, was "Rhonda the Immortal Waitress" (AE Biography).[6]

It has been known for some time that Whedon had imagined *Buffy the Vampire Slayer* the Series (hereafter *BtVS*S) as a kind of cross between *The X-Files* and the iconic, but short-lived, teen drama *My So-Called Life* (ABC, 1994–5; see my own article "*My So-Called Life* Meets *The X-Files*" in *Dear Angela*: *Remembering* My So-Called Life). But until Whedon wrote an essay on the series for the new, definitive DVD release of *MSCL*, we did not have the story quite right. In "Reality TV," Whedon not only heaps praise on Winnie Holzman's creation –

> no show on TV has ever come close to capturing as truly the lovely pain of teendom as well as *My So-Called Life*. And yes, I'm including my own. We all stole fr- I mean *learned* from it, but we never matched it. I doubt anyone will. (After all, it doesn't pay.)

– he also explains its part in selling *Buffy*:

> When I pitched *Buffy the Vampire Slayer*, I told executives it was a cross between *The X-Files* and [...] and then I always took a moment to judge how smart they were. If they seemed like empty suits, I'd go with *90210*. It was a big hit. But if they seemed like they knew their business, I'd use another example. The example that every writer I know still references. The show that – forget what it did for my writing and my career – I'll love the way you can only love as a youth: with fierce bewilderment and unembarrassed passion.

He does not say whether the WB was a (*Beverly Hills*), *90210* (Fox, 1990–2000) or *MSCL* pitch; we do know that the WB allowed him to have his own way with his new show.

*BtVS*S had additional agendas to simply giving the world a kickass cult woman hero; Whedon hoped to create as well (his own words) "a world in which adolescent boys would see a girl who takes charge as the sexiest goddamn thing they ever saw" (*JWC* 66), or as he put it in his Equality Now speech:

I wanted to create a female icon but I also wanted to be very careful to surround her with men who not only had no problem with the idea of a female leader, but were in fact, engaged and even attracted to the idea. That came from my father and step-father, the men who created this man, who created those men, if you can follow that [...]

Whedon's master plan was nevertheless without pretension. *Buffy* would be a television entertainment and not a treatise. "It's better to be a spy in the house of love, you know? [...]," he would explain to Nussbaum. "If I made 'Buffy the Lesbian Separatist,' a series of lectures on PBS on why there should be feminism, no one would be coming to the party, and it would be boring. The idea of changing culture is important to me, and it can only be done in a popular medium" (*JWC* 65).

Another strong factor in *Buffy's* genesis was Whedon's childhood love of comics and his disappointment with the absence of strong female characters. As he explains in his foreword to *Fray*: "The idea for *Buffy the Vampire Slayer* came from that same lack I had felt as a child. Where are the girls? Girls who can fight, who can stand up for themselves, who have opinions and fears and cute outfits? Buffy was designed to fill that void in movies – and then, ultimately, in TV." Whedon also wanted to explore in depth a metaphor implicit in *MSCL*: the idea that high school is hell. *BtVS*S and *Angel* collaborator (and *Grimm* co-creator) David Greenwalt would famously remark that "If Joss Whedon had had even one happy day in high school, none of us would be here" (*Watchers Guide* I, 240) – we would never have had *Buffy*.

Anyone who has seen the original pilot (still available on YouTube), with the very goth Riff Regan impersonating Willow, knows that the *Buffy* which would eventually be named (by both *TV Guide* and *Entertainment Weekly* – #3 and #1 respectively) one of the greatest cult shows of all time and inspire more scholarly and critical interest than any series in the history of the medium was still a long way off.[7]

It would not be unfair to say that, like many a television series, *Buffy* was still finding its feet throughout its first, partial season (*BtVS*S was a midseason replacement show, which began airing on 10 March 1997). Whedon himself has said as much: "The WB let me create a really weird show. If you think about the first season of *Buffy*, it is not a show in full maturity, but it is definitely a show that is bizarre, often dark, and strange. The WB Network never once really questioned me, and I was lucky enough to have them go along with me" (Priggé 190). As Whedon would quip to James Longworth, clearly the still-wet-behind-the-ears netlet had no idea what they were doing (*JWC* 46).

*BtVS*S differed a great deal from *BtVS*tM. The series would relocate Buffy from Los Angeles to Sunnydale, California, a town conveniently located on a "Hellmouth" – a centre of demonic energy. In the show's Lovecraftian mythology,[8] demons were the original inhabitants of the earth, and vampires are demon/human hybrids. As the series begins, Buffy, a "Gidget for the fin de siècle" (Siemann), has already discovered (in the movie) her chosen role as the "one girl in all the world with the strength and skill to fight the vampires." Having moved to Sunnydale to escape her past, she would prefer to be a normal teenager, but her new hometown, plagued by vampires, demons and other evils, will not permit her to ignore her calling. With the ongoing help of her "Scooby Gang" friends like Xander Harris (Nicholas Brendon) and Willow Rosenberg (Alyson Hanigan), and Rupert Giles, her Watcher (Anthony Stewart Head), a tremendous upgrade on Donald Sutherland's Merrick, Buffy continues to battle not only the forces of darkness but also her own inner demons. Beginning with Season 4, Buffy and the Scoobies head off to college (at the University of California, Sunnydale) but with no let-up in the enemies they must confront.[9]

*BtVS*S, more than the movie, had an autobiographical element. Whedon readily admits the basic "idea of somebody that nobody would take account of, who just had more power than was imaginable" was in reality "a pathetically obvious metaphor for what I wanted my life to be. Like, 'I'm the guy that nobody paid attention to. What they didn't know was that I'm really important. I can save the world. So, you know, that's pretty cool, too'" (IGN-Film Force).

And *BtVS*S had at least two Whedon avatars in the narrative itself: Xander and Giles. As he would tell David Bianculli, Xander "was obviously based on me, the sort of guy that all the girls want to be best friends with in high school, and who's, you know, kind of a loser, but is more or less articulate and someone you can trust. That part wasn't like me, but the rest was." Giles, too, was Whedonish in that they were both "English boarding school" products (at Winchester, Whedon had known "a lot of Gilesy people") and also because Giles manifested his adult showrunner and director self – "when I'm working and I just – I feel like I'm supposed to be the grown-up in an insane group of children who are not paying attention to me when we have this mission which, in my case, is to create this show" (*JWC* 6).

During *BtVS*S's first season Whedon himself would write the two-part official pilot, "Welcome to the Hellmouth" and "The Harvest" (1.1 and 1.2), a greatly enhanced version of the Alyson Hannigan-less pilot, but he would not direct an episode until the season finale, "Prophecy Girl" (1.12).

Whedon was now running his own television series in his own way. "I have control over all the shows," he explained in 2000:

> That means that I break the stories. I often come up with the ideas and I certainly break the stories with the writers so that we all know what's going to happen. Then once the writers are done, I rewrite every script [...]. Then I oversee production and edit every show, work with the composers and sound mixers. Inevitably every single show has my name on it somewhere and it is my responsibility to make it good [...]. Every week that show is on, I'm standing in the back row, biting my nails, hoping people like it, so I feel a great responsibility. The good thing is that I'm surrounded by people who are much smarter than I am. So gradually I have been able to let certain things take care of themselves, because my crew, my writers, my post-production crew, everybody is so competent, that I don't have to run around quite as much as I used to.
>
> (Lavery, "A Religion in Narrative")

He still had many lessons to learn.

The "dog and pony show" of series television production provided a rapid education for Whedon, and thanks to his DVD commentaries we can recapitulate that learning. In reality, the strict parameters imposed on creative inclinations by budget and time constraints force novice and veteran alike to find less expensive and more expeditious paths to quality. Whedon's commentaries have much to say about this process.[10]

- The skateboard on which Xander makes his first appearance on the show (crashing into a railing on his first sight of Buffy) was quickly jettisoned because lighting such a moving figure was too complicated and expensive ("Hellmouth").
- The dream sequence which follows the opening credits in "Welcome" was supposed to be elaborate and original. To save time and money it was in the end constructed out of imagery from future episodes of Season 1 ("Hellmouth").
- In "The Harvest" Xander asks if vampires can fly. The possibility of flying vampires had to be rejected because of the special effects cost, as did other vampire motifs (e.g. vampires turning into bats).[11]
- When Whedon first envisioned the Sunnydale High School Library, Rupert Giles proprietor, he had in mind something dark and labyrinthine (the paintings of Piranesi are evoked), but at the

time he had not given any thought to how such a design might be lit. The idea was jettisoned, and the library became more modern and bright ("Hellmouth").

- Whedon had toyed with the idea of placing Eric Balfour (Jesse in the first two episodes) in the opening credit sequence, thereby leading viewers to conclude that he would be a regular, only to kill him off in "The Harvest" ("Hellmouth") but learned that re-editing the sequence was cost-prohibitive.

As is often the case with innovators in all fields, Whedon's ignorance of the rules, as he admits in the *A&E Biography*, would actually prove to be a powerful spur to originality.

When *Buffy* became a series, Whedon still had no training as a director, not at Wesleyan, not in his career-to-date as a television writer or script doctor, but he did have a hidden agenda. Five years into *BtVS*S, he would own up to his evil Steven Spielbergish plan: "I'll create a television show, and I'll use it as a film school, and I'll teach myself to direct on TV."[12] "I'm sure a lot of writers want to direct because they're bitter," Whedon would acknowledge – and certainly he had experienced some disillusionment in his experiences with *BtVS*tM and *Alien Resurrection*, but he knew very well that "is not a reason to direct." Instead, Whedon turned to directing because he "want[ed] to speak visually, and writing is just a way of communicating visually" (Robinson, *Onion AV Club* 2001).

No one would place his rookie outing, "Prophecy Girl," in the same league with such later efforts as "Innocence," "Hush," "Restless," "The Body," "Waiting in the Wings," and "Objects in Space," but there are moments in it where we catch a glimpse of what Whedon would become as a television auteur. In the scene in the library in which Buffy first learns of the prophecy that she will die in her showdown with The Master, the shocking emotional power of Whedon's creation first manifests itself in Buffy's protest, brilliantly acted by Gellar, against her mortality. Later, after Xander brings Buffy back from the dead, she marches in Spring Fling formal wear with joyous determination, in lock step to Nerf Herder's theme, towards the final battle and rebuffs her friend's concern:

Xander: You're still weak.
Buffy: (stops) No. No, I feel strong. I feel different.

She feels different because Whedon is in control. This is precisely the sort of postmodern sublime that Fran Rubel Kuzui (or Kristy Swanson) did not have a clue how to deliver but at which Joss Whedon excelled. When, face-to-face with her nemesis moments later, she sends him to hell (after telling him he has "fruit punch mouth"), we know we have seen the death of the series' first Big Bad and the birth, the real imaginative birth, of both *Buffy the Vampire Slayer* and Joss Whedon the director.

Whedon both wrote and directed many of the truly memorable and innovative individual milestones of *Buffy*, including "Innocence" (2.14), the episode that sees Angelus emerge after "one perfect moment of happiness" with Buffy; "Hush" (4.10), in which The Gentlemen, fairy-tale monsters, steal the voices of the residents of Sunnydale and fully half the show transpires without a word of dialogue; "Restless" (4.22), comprised of four astonishing dream sequences in which the spirit of the First Slayer tries to kill the Scoobies after they have defeated Adam; "The Body" (5.16), minutely detailing the emotional aftermath of the sudden death of Buffy's mother; and "Once More with Feeling" (6.7), a long anticipated musical episode in which a visiting demon causes the Scoobies and all of Sunnydale to behave as if trapped in a Broadway musical.

As "long haul" shows (the term is Sarah Vowell's) became more and more the order of the day in American television in the 1990s, different approaches had evolved in order to face "the peaks and valleys of serial creativity," as Marc Dolan called the intimidating challenges facing the makers of multi-year television series. *Twin Peaks*, the subject of Dolan's essay, had failed to solve the problem, burning itself out early with no way of replenishing or indefinitely extending its narrative; in its wake, *The X-Files* would prove somewhat more successful with its "flexi-narrative" (the term is Robin Nelson's), combining individual, non-serial "monster of the week" episodes with a multi-season "mythology" arc concerning an alien invasion of earth, but it, too, lost steam, and its final seasons proved forgettable.

Though new to the demands of television storytelling, Whedon would succeed where others had failed, following a model that owed much to *The X-Files* but with a twist, For the most part *BtVS*S would wrap up its multi-episode arcs in a single season. Every year, Buffy and the Scooby Gang would do battle with a unique "Big Bad" – The Master, Angelus, The Mayor, Adam, Glory, the Nerd Troika and Dark Willow, The First; every year they would defeat their foe and save the world before or in the season finale. This new model had its beginning in Season 1. Unsure whether there would even be a Season 2, and anxious not to repeat *MSCL's* cancellation-engendered "most crushing cliffhanger in history," Whedon decided to make "Prophecy Girl" simultaneously a season and a series ender. Henceforth, each season would be largely self-contained.

Rather than having a mythology develop over many seasons, *Buffy's* characters – every one of them, major and minor – would develop and evolve. "[T]he shows that I've always loved the best," Whedon would tell David Bianculli, "have accumulative knowledge. One of the reasons why *The X-Files* started to leave me cold was that after five years, I just started yelling at Scully, 'You're an idiot. It's a monster,' and I couldn't take it anymore. I need people to grow, I need them to change, I need them to learn and explore, you know, and die and do all of the things that people do in real life" (*JWC* 4). The application of that need in *BtVS*S was a story that ran for 144 episodes, almost 100 hours of narrative, the equivalent of 50 feature films – in less than seven years.

As *Buffy* begat *Angel* in 1999 – simultaneously with Season 4 of *BtVS*S; as Whedon expanded the Whedonverses in space and time with *Firefly* in 2002 – concurrently with the inception of what would be the final season of *Buffy*, Whedon's commitment to his first-born diminished. In *BtVS*S Seasons 4 and 5, he would direct both the first and last episodes, just as he had done in Seasons 2 and 3. Season 5, however, would begin with an episode, "Buffy vs. Dracula," that Whedon neither wrote nor directed, an unprecedented development, though as the season progressed he did write and direct three episodes, "Family" (5.6), "The Body" and "The Gift" (5.22) – the latter being not only the season finale, the series' landmark 100th episode, the final episode on the WB, and the episode in which Buffy dies (for the second time). The only episode of Season 6 he would write and direct was the extraordinary (in every sense of the word) "Once More with Feeling," and his credited involvement in Season 7 was likewise light: writing, but not directing (the first time this had happened since the pilot), the season premiere ("Lessons") and writing and directing "Chosen" (7.22), the epic series finale.

If in 1997 Whedon dreamed of never again being associated with *Buffy the Vampire Slayer*, *BtVS*S guaranteed that that would never again be a possibility. Whedon would be no one-hit wonder, of course, but *Buffy* will forever remain his greatest achievement.

8 CREATOR OF *ANGEL* AND *FIREFLY*

In which the Whedonverses expand and the pains of cancellation are known.

Creative people have a network of enterprises. They become the sort of people who can easily handle seemingly different but intimately related activities. They become highly skilled jugglers.

(Howard Gruber, "Breakaway Minds," 71)

ooooooooooo

Angel

"I have this series and I have this son and between the two of them, one of them is always crying," Joss Whedon started our discussion, referring to his only show currently on the air, *Angel*, and his nearly one-year-old child. "That's not true," he clarified. "My son hardly ever cries, but the series. That's another story."

(Joss Whedon – Sullivan, *Underground*)

We thought [*Angel*] was going to be, as we liked to call it, "Touched by an Equalizer," but we realized we can't write that show. We can only write shows where terrible things happen to the people we love, and we come back every week to find out how they deal with it.

(Joss Whedon, in *Geek Monthly*)

Less than three years into an unanticipated television career, during *Buffy's* 1998–9 season, Joss Whedon had begun plans to expand the Whedonverse. By September 2002, he would have three shows on the air: *Buffy* in its seventh (and last) season, *Angel* in its fourth, and *Firefly* in its first (and only). The Whedonverse had become the Whedonverses. Felicity Nussbaum observed Whedon editing *Buffy* and *Angel* scripts on the set of *Firefly* in Fall 2002 (*JWC* 64). By Fall 2004, for the first time since March 1997, not a single Whedon show was on television.

Joyce Millman has noted that "Angel seemed like an odd character around which to build a spin-off. What could you do with a tongue-tied slab of beefcake who avoids sex (lest he lose his soul again), hides from daylight, and morphs an ugly prehensile forehead and fangs?" ("Angel," *Essential Cult Television Reader* 29). As Millman shows, Whedon knew better. The creation of *Angel*, deemed with brilliant playfulness "The Spin-Off with a Soul" in Stacey Abbott's pioneering collection of essays on the show, was a multi-stage process, as Whedon explained to Stephen Priggé (96–7).

Stage One came with the realization that the character of Angel on *Buffy* was "really popping" and would soon outgrow the narrative that had given him birth. Buffy and Angel's unrequitedness, Whedon had become certain, did not have a narrative future. "I also knew that the romance between Buffy and Angel could go so far before it became incredibly tired [...]," [1] Whedon would recall. "And so, even though people are constantly yelling at me and screaming on the Internet that I have to get them back together, we knew that there was gonna come a time where there wouldn't be as much of a place for Angel on the show, so it made sense to give him his own" (*JWC* 9). [2]

Stage Two was a single *Buffy* episode: Season 2's "I Only Have Eyes for You" (2.19 – written by Marti Noxon and directed by James Whitmore, Jr.), where David Boreanaz showed Whedon his real potential as an actor. The sixth episode in which David Boreanaz had played Angel's soulless worse half, the sadistic vampire Angelus, "Eyes" found Buffy and her former lover possessed by Sunnydale High poltergeist and forced to act out a decades-old, forbidden love and murder suicide between a teacher and a student. Boreanaz had really begun to come into his own as an actor while playing Angelus. Watching him deliver Whedon's lines in "Innocence" (2.14) –

> She made me feel like a human being. That's not the kind of thing you just forgive.
> Spike, my boy, you really don't get it! Do you? You tried to kill her, but you couldn't. Look at you. You're a wreck! She's stronger than any Slayer you've ever faced. Force won't get it done. You gotta work from the inside. To kill this girl you have to love her.

– it seems almost impossible that this could be the same handsome stiff of "Welcome to the Hellmouth." Impressed by his "subtle, interesting work" in "Eyes," Whedon became certain for the first time of Boreanaz's true star potential. In Whedon's estimation, Boreanaz was a different kind of performer and Angel a different kind of character from Gellar/Buffy: "He's intense, dark, a solid moral person you trust. Buffy was a constant underdog and open to everyone. Angel is someone you see from afar; he's more closed. The kind of attraction they emit is different, almost the opposite, which is why they made such a good couple" (*JWC* 15).

Two stages, of course, are never enough, and the third came with Whedon's realization that within the Buffyverse

> there was another story [...] about a different element, concerning redemption and past mistakes. The difficulty and moral mutability in searching for redemption for what you've done in the past is not an adolescent story at all. That was when I said, "We have a show. I have a star and he has a name and I have a reason to go somewhere else."

Angel would not be, in any chromosome of its multi-genre DNA, a teen drama.[3] The difference between *Buffy's* Angel and *Angel's* Angel is pronounced, as Laura Resnick shows in an incisive essay. On *Buffy*, he only has eyes for the slayer; on *Angel* a variety of women capture his attention, from the doomed waitress of "City of," to a princess from another dimension ("She" 1.13), to Cordelia, and, of course, Darla:

> Throughout much of *Angel's* second season, Angel is darkly, passionately obsessed with Darla, his female sire. He expresses this slightly Oedipal obsession in a variety of ways, including setting her on fire ("Redefinition" 2.11) and flinging her through a set of glass doors before spending the night having rough sex with her ("Reprise" 2.15). During the throes of his obsession, he abandons his job, he alienates his tiny handful of friends and he's an accessory to a massacre" ("Reunion" 2.10).

Given her impressive compilation of evidence, we cannot help but acquiesce with Resnick's rhetorical questions: "Now is this really a guy we want to see dating a cheerleader? If you knew *this* guy was climbing into a sixteen-year-old's bedroom window regularly, as Angel did on *Buffy*, wouldn't you call the cops? [...] *Angel's* Angel is *not* a suitable love interest for a high school girl" (19).[4]

On *Angel*, Whedon would observe, "we're dealing with the big, bad grown-up world and the people first entering it. We're looking at a lot of the things people go through: getting their apartments, trying to date outside the controlled environment of a campus, getting married. These rituals happen to people in their 20s." "[O]f course," Whedon promised – a promise he kept for five seasons, "they'll all be scary and horrible" (*JWC* 15).

Angel would be more adult than *Buffy*, more noirish (the story of a vampire must take place mainly in the "nice dark" [Whedon in the "City of" DVD commentary]), more superheroish (Batman is frequently evoked in the show – Doyle describes Angel's apartment as having a "Bat Cave air" in the first episode – and in commentaries[5]), more episodic (Whedon and company would battle The WB for five years over its wish that *Angel* be more an easily syndicated anthology show and his own "religion in narrative" faith in serial story-telling and seasons-long character development). The idea that Charisma Carpenter's Cordelia Chase would accompany Boreanaz's Angel to Los Angeles was the contribution of *Buffy* writer and director (and, in the next century, co-creator of *Grimm*) David Greenwalt, who would also head to the City of Angels (or "The City of Angel," as the title of the new show's first episode would imply), becoming Whedon's co-executive producer and showrunner.

Rhonda Wilcox and I have suggested that *Angel*'s noirishness might best be characterized by the painting technique known as chiaroscuro.[6] *Angel* "exhibits a different take on morality and a different sense of humor" from the "unrelievedly dark" world of film noir: "Most of *Angel*'s main characters are both heroic and seriously flawed. (They are also, thanks to both the writers and the versatile actors, capable of great humor [...].) They wound, kill, and commit moral incest. Yet time and again characters struggle to do right (in a very un-noirish fashion). Light and dark mix exquisitely [...]" (226).

On the consistently hilarious *Buffy*, Angel was almost never funny. (A scene like the one in "Lie to Me" [*BtVS* 2.7], written and directed by Joss Whedon, in which, during a visit to a vampire-wannabe club, an irritated Angel fulminates that "These people don't know anything about vampires. What they are, how they live, how they dress [...]," only to be confronted by a young man dressed identically to the vampire with a soul is the exception.) On *Angel*, however, as Wilcox and I observe, "Each of the characters" – including Angel himself – "is, to some degree or other, made more sympathetic by being made the subject of humor." *Angel* is full of decidedly un-noirish laughter, from the "comic-stylings of Wesley Wyndham-Pryce," to Angel's uproarious dance moves and awful karaoke singing, to Cordelia's sarcasm.[7]

Angel was also more cinematic than its parent show, as Tammy Kinsey shows in an incisive essay:

> *Angel* is an anomaly in television. Within the rubric of an essentially traditional narrative, we see many techniques common to experimental film and abstract art. Those who watch *Angel* are well acquainted

with the bright flashes of light, smeared images of motion, and odd articulation of space seen in many editorial transitions as well as in the visions. The meanings implicit in those brief moments are paramount to the experience of the series as a whole. These transitions compress and expand time, move us both forward and backward in the narrative, and reveal much information in little screen time. (44)

Whedon had yet to become the "brilliant independent filmmaker" (IGN-Film Force interview) of his youthful dreams, but he was, in collaboration with his *Angel* creative team, nevertheless expanding the increasingly cinematic "televisuality" that had, according to John Thornton Caldwell, characterized small screen style since the 1980s.

And yet the new child would cry quite a lot and require more than usual attention. Season 1 was all over the narrative map and only began really to find its way when Wolfram and Hart, the evil law firm run by the mysterious, never-seen "Senior Partners," emerged as a constant nemesis; Doyle, the Powers That Be's conduit to Angel,[8] was replaced by Cordelia Chase; and Wesley Wyndham-Pryce, *Buffy*'s failed Watcher-turned-rogue demon hunter rode into town. Both slayers, Buffy and Faith, also came to LA, resulting in excellent episodes like "I Will Remember You" (1.8) and "Five by Five" (1.18), as did Spike, who would stand on a rooftop watching Angel help the helpless and parody not only "Captain Forehead" ("Chosen," *BtVS* S 7.22) but *Angel*'s whole premise:

> How can I thank you, you mysterious, black-clad hunk of a night thing? (*low voice*) No need, little lady, your tears of gratitude are enough for me. You see, I was once a badass vampire, but love and a pesky curse defanged me. Now I'm just a big, fluffy puppy with bad teeth. (*Rachel steps closer to Angel, and Angel steps back warding her off with his hands*) No, not the hair! Never the hair! (*high voice*) But there must be some way I can show my appreciation. (*low voice*) No, helping those in need's my job, – and working up a load of sexual tension, and prancing away like a magnificent poof is truly thanks enough! (*high voice*) I understand. I have a nephew who is gay, so [...] (*low voice*) Say no more. Evil's still afoot! And I'm almost out of that Nancy-boy hair-gel that I like so much. Quickly, to the Angel-mobile, away!"

Doug Petrie is credited with authorship of the episode; but Spike's speech has "Whedon" written all over it.

In Season 2, the baby was crying less. With a new location for Angel Investigations in the Hyperion Hotel, Darla (Julie Benz), Angel's sire, returned from the dead to haunt him, Wolfram and Hart lawyers Lilah Morgan (Stephanie Romanov) and Lindsay McDonald (Christian Kane) becoming ever-more prominent, and new AI associates Charles Gunn (J. August Richards, introduced in Season 1) and The Host (Lorne – Andy Hallett) stirred into the mix, *Angel* Year Two would prove much stronger. A great *Buffy/Angel* crossover, "Fool for Love" (*BtVS* S 5.7)/"Darla" (2.7), made all the more powerful because the two shows aired back to back on Tuesdays in the USA, would be a season highlight.

By Season 3, *Angel* was sleeping through the night almost without a peep. Fred (Amy Acker), saved from Pylea (another dimension), had proven herself an asset to AI, the time-travelling Holtz (Keith Szarabajka), seeking revenge against Angel, and the return of an about-to-give-birth Darla carrying Angel's son, would be the main drivers of the narrative in a season thought by many to be *Angel's* best, even if Connor (Vincent Kartheiser – now best known as the loathsome Pete Campbell on *Mad Men*, a series created by fellow Wesleyanite Matt Weiner) – Angel's son, who grew to the age of 17 during a month in hell dimension, only to trap his father in a watery undead grave at season's end – wasn't exactly a fan favourite.

By the end of its third year, *Angel* had almost completely abandoned the anthology show plan, becoming serial to the core, a pattern that would continue, to the consternation of the suits, in Four, which many consider *Angel's* weakest season. In Four's arc Connor became more annoying and even appalling (when he slept with Cordelia); Wesley was ostracized; The Beast blotted out the sun; Faith was sprung from jail in order to defeat a newly released Angelus; Cordelia (possessed) went over to the Dark Side and gave birth to the deity Jasmine (Gina Torres); and The Senior Partners offered AI the chance to run Wolfram and Hart. The WB was slow to renew the series and only agreed to another year after 1) Whedon and company had recommitted to de-serialize Season 5 (make it "stand-alone-y" in Joss-speak [Stafford, *Once* 18]) and 2) an agreement was reached to import Spike from *Buffy*, where he had died in the series finale (a demand that irritated Whedon, given the careful ending of *Buffy* that he had worked hard to achieve (Stafford, *Once Bitten* 15).

Much has been made in recent years of the "reboots" of series like *Alias*, which in a January 2003 post-Super Bowl episode in its second season entirely threw out the show's basic premise and started over (unsuccessfully) in the pursuit of better ratings. But *Alias's* do-over was relatively mild in comparison to what *Angel* attempted in Season 5, as the show's heroes were given the keys to Wolfram and Hart and forced to come to terms in radical new ways with life in the gray. The idea for the reboot was Whedon's.

On *Angel* Whedon would author or co-author ten episodes: "City of" (1.1), "I Fall to Pieces" (1.4) and "Sanctuary" (1.19), "Judgment" (2.1), and "Happy Anniversary" (2.13) – all with David Greenwalt; "Waiting in the Wings" (3.13); "Spin the Bottle" (4.6); "Conviction" (5.1); "A Hole in the World, A" (5.15); "Not Fade Away" (5.22) – with Jeffrey Bell. But he would direct only six episodes: "City of," "Untouched" (2.4), "Waiting in the Wings," "Spin the Bottle," "Conviction," "A Hole in the World." Three season premieres (One, Two, Five) were written/co-written by Whedon, but only one season finale (Five's). Only two of the five season premieres (One and Five) and not a single season finale were directed by him. On *Angel,* he would direct other people's scripts (Mere Smith's "Untouched"), something he never did on *Buffy,* and allow others to direct his ("Sanctuary" and "Judgment" – Michael Lange; "Happy Anniversary" – Bill Norton; and "Not Fade Away" – Bell), which never happened on *Buffy* after "Welcome to the Hellmouth" and "The Harvest" (1.1 and 1.2).⁹ Whedon would also share showrunner duties during *Angel's* run: with David Greenwalt in Seasons 1 to 3, Tim Minear in Season 4, and Jeffrey Bell in 5. And in "Through the Looking Glass (2.21), he would, of course, appear on screen for the first time, playing the character of Numfar, performing, in unrecognizable makeup and with inspired silliness, the Dances of Joy and Honor. Not until his performance as a car rental salesman in *Veronica Mars* in November 2005 would he have such a marvellously apt role.

Whedon's diminished contribution as author and director and showrunner of record is perfectly understandable. Season 1 of *Angel* (1999–2000) overlapped with Season 4 of *Buffy. Firefly's* only season (Fall 2002), and a partial season at that, coincided with the beginning of *Angel's* Season 4. On 18 December 2002, five days after "Objects in Space," the final episode of *Firefly* to be aired, Joss and Kai's first child, Arden, was born.¹⁰ During *Angel's* Season 5, Whedon had already begun to work on the film of *Serenity.* Asked by *SciFi Weekly* early in the David E. Kelleyish/ multi-series phase of his television career, how he was managing the increased workload, Whedon candidly replied:

> I really have no idea. I am burned out already. David Greenwalt and I just stare at each other balefully and say, "What were we thinking?" I think my life is over, and that's just something I have to deal with. I don't know how it's done. Basically, it just means I

work harder. We were working 16 hours a day on *Buffy*, and now we work 16 hours a day, but more concentrated. It's more mentally exhausting. But it's not like you can let it slide. I still don't work on Sundays when I can avoid it. Now I'm actually firm about not working Sundays, since I'm so burned out after the week, more so than before. (*JWC* 14)

Asked by James Longworth (in 2002) how he planned to "keep *Buffy* and *Angel* from getting stale" in the years ahead, Whedon owned up to his diabolical master plan: "By dying of exhaustion" (*JWC* 61).

On *Buffy*, as we have already seen, Whedon had shown himself to be an adept showrunner, expert at both the episode and season level of developing and sustaining a "long haul" show and of discovering and nurturing trustworthy collaborators: "I work really hard [...] to surround myself with really smart people who can get a great deal done without me," he would tell James Longworth (*JWC* 60).

In a chapter of her monograph on the series in the Television Milestones series, Stacey Abbott offers an insightful reconstruction of *Angel* as the result of "the collective vision of Mutant Enemy." *Angel* began as the creation of *Buffy* folk – Whedon, Greenwalt, Noxon, Fury, Petrie, Espenson – but became a series under the more and more independent creative control of a new team that would include as well Minear, Bell, Jim Kouf (later to co-create *Grimm* with Greenwalt), Mere Smith, Elizabeth Craft and Sarah Fain (who would become showrunners of *Dollhouse* in Season 1), Drew Goddard (later director of *The Cabin in the Woods*) (for more on these individuals, see Appendix A). A *Buffy* character like Faith, crossing over as early as Season 1, would be more fully developed by *Angel* writers. Flashbacks, used brilliantly on *Buffy* by Whedon himself in episodes like "Becoming," Parts I and II, would become even more prominent in *Angel's* rich text, with Minear taking the lead as flashbacker-in-chief in episodes like "Somnambulist" (1.11), "The Prodigal" (1.15), "Are You Now or Have You Ever Been" (2.2), "Darla" (2.7). *Angel* thus became proof, as Jane Espenson would say (Abbott makes these her closing words): "It all begins with Joss. But it doesn't end there" ("Introduction" ix).

The End. As Joyce Millman details, *Angel* never completely recovered from its severance from its televisual sire. Its

richness and ingenuity couldn't insulate *Angel* from the fallout of *BtVS*'s leaving The WB in 2001, after a licensing fee dispute between series producer Twentieth Century Fox Television and The WB [...].

The departure of *BtVS*S robbed *Angel*, then entering its third season, of its lead-in audience and crossovers. During the next two years, The WB changed *Angel*'s time slot three times, frustrating fans without significantly improving ratings [...]." ("*Angel*," *Essential Cult Television Reader* 33)

When the WB announced the cancellation of *Angel* in February 2004, Joss Whedon posted his response on the Bronze Beta posting board: "I've never made mainstream TV very well. I like surprises, and TV isn't about surprises, unless the surprise is who gets voted off something. I've been lucky to sneak this strange, strange show over the airwaves for as long as I have [...]." In closing, Whedon waxed poetic, asking fans to recall Robert Frost's "The Road not Taken": "Remember the words of the poet: Two roads diverged in the wood, and I took the road less traveled by, and they CANCELLED MY FRIKKIN' SHOW" (http://www.bronzebeta.com/ Archive/Joss/Joss20040214.htm). He would never be able to make that "Angel-debates-socioeconomics-with-a-sturgeon season arc" he planned for the future (quoted in Stafford, *Once* 106).

Given that the termination was Whedon's second in two years (*Firefly* had been cancelled in December 2002), his bitterness is understandable. The *Survivor* reference was only one of many anti-reality television remarks Whedon would make. In May 2004, Whedon would tell the *Toronto Star*: "If I had created reality television I would have had a much greater influence, but then I would have had to KILL MYSELF" (quoted in Stafford, *Once* 24).

Coming when it did – five days before Angel would be transformed into an adorable puppet man/vampire in "Smile Time" and eleven days before Fred died into Illyria in "A Hole in the World" (written and directed by Whedon) – the cancellation was intended to give *Angel*'s creative team enough time to bring the series to a reasonable end. The series finale which Whedon would co-author with Jeffrey Bell (with Bell, not Whedon, directing), "Not Fade Away," would air on 19 May 2004, and was not wholly different from what had been originally envisioned as the season finale.

The 10 June 2007 final episode of David Chase's *The Sopranos* (HBO, 1999–2007), an *Angel* contemporary, set off (again) a cultural debate about the proper ending of a television series. Chase's choice to cut to black as Tony, Carmela, AJ and Meadow (once she finishes parallel parking) settle down to eat in a New Jersey diner in which they may or may not be about to be whacked, proved wildly controversial because it was inconclusive.

The cultural cachet of *Angel* was not, of course, prominent enough for its ending to cause a comparable stir, but "Not Fade Away" was a disputed finale. As we have seen already, Whedon has always been averse to cliffhangers, an aversion he shares with Chase, and yet the finales of both *Angel* and *The Sopranos* might be mistaken as cliffhangery.[11]

Whedon had clear goals in mind with "Not Fade Away" – as he explained to *Geek Monthly*.

> The final statement of the series means a great deal to me. I had written the final statement in my head knowing that it would work just as well as a season ender as it would a series ender. I always did every season of every series that way. The only time I ever did a cliffhanger was when [Buffy] first moved to UPN and we had a two-year pick-up, so we knew we were coming back.[12] But generally speaking, every season I expected to be cancelled, so every season finale was more or less the final statement I had to make on everything ever. And then it turned out to be that it really was the final statement. I had planned a Season 6, but obviously I knew [Angel was cancelled by the time we filmed it] or I would never have offed the characters that I did.[13]

Consequently, the showdown in the alley between Angel, Spike, Gunn and Illyria and Evil's advancing horde, Whedon admitted, took "on a resonance that it absolutely wouldn't have had, had there been another season." Perceived as a cliffhanger, the scene created some anger among fans. It was an ending which, like *The Sopranos'* "Made in America," or, to cite cinematic precedents, like *Butch Cassidy and the Sundance Kid* (George Roy Hill, 1969) and *Thelma and Louise* (Ridley Scott, 1991), may not have given us closure, but did make a statement:

> With *Buffy*, I needed closure, because she, poor girl, had earned it. *Buffy* is about growing up. *Angel* is really about already having grown up, dealing with what you've done, and redemption. Redemption is something you fight for every day, so I wanted him to go out fighting. People kept calling it a cliffhanger. I was like, "Are you mad, sir? Don't you see that that is the final statement?" And then they would say "Shut up."[14] (*JWC* 145)

Asked by Edward Gross early in the series' run if *Angel* had turned out better than anticipated, Whedon's answer, updating that earlier metaphor about a crying baby, is revealing:

I wouldn't say better, because the show I anticipate is always so staggeringly brilliant that it makes the Earth rotate in the other direction, but it has done what *Buffy* has done in that it has lived up to my hopes to be a decent show, and then it has shown me things that I hadn't expected. A work of art takes on a life beyond its creator, and when that happens, it's the most gratifying thing in the world. It's like raising a child who becomes a grownup and is suddenly talking to you. *Angel* has started to do that; *Angel* is talking to me now. It could have been just a nice solid formula show, and I think it's going to be something more than that.[15]

Firefly

It's the classic thing to have a preacher on board your stagecoach. I don't mean *Stagecoach*. I mean original idea of my own.

(Joss Whedon, *Serenity* 11)

In a fascinating collection of essays on *Firefly* and *Serenity*, Rhonda V. Wilcox and Tanya R. Cochran begin their examination of Whedon's first failed television show and the movie it improbably generated with a look at a moment from "Our Mrs. Reynolds" (1.6) – an episode written by Whedon. In the process of an attempted seduction of Wash, "the trickster" Saffron regales the pilot with a myth, supposedly her own, of "Earth that was":

[W]hen she was born, she had no sky, and she was open, inviting and the stars would rush into her, through the skin of her, making the oceans boil with sensation, and when she could endure no more ecstasy, she puffed up her cheeks and blew out the sky, to womb her and keep them at bay, 'til she had rest some, and that we had to leave 'cause she was strong enough to suck them in once more.

"By the time she has finished making a world with words," Wilcox and Cochran note, "Wash, that most Whedon-like of characters, can only respond, feelingly, 'Whoah. Good myth'" (1).

A wonderful moment dramatically, the scene, as the critics brilliantly explain, has even greater import for understanding Whedon as a creator:

Whedon has been making worlds for many years now, and in *Firefly* he takes us to the sky. In his space Western series (co-produced by Tim

Minear), characters use the contraction "'verse" for their universe. The pun should make us think of poetry, song; it should remind us that Whedon creates a world with words – as do we all, in a sense. The stories we tell ourselves about our lives, the ways we mentally shape our experiences – these stories construct our worlds for us, at least in part. Whedon wonderfully uses images and music, too, but here the foundation is words – the dialogue and the story. Perhaps this is what makes him pre-eminently successful in the long-term medium of television [...]. Whedon's *Firefly* still spins through the sky of our minds. (1)

Firefly would introduce us to a new Whedonverse, one far from present day "Earth that was" in space and in time. It is set 500 years in the future after the human race has relocated to a nearby solar system after abandoning a too-crowded home planet in order to perpetuate civilization on newly terraformed inhabitable worlds. It exists now in the "sky of our minds" because it existed only briefly on our television sets. "The Train Job," *Firefly's* unintended pilot, aired on 20 September 2002; on 2 December, less than three months later, it would be cancelled; on 20 December, "Serenity," the series' intended pilot, became the last *Firefly* episode actually broadcast.

Network interference with *Buffy* and *Angel* up to the time *Firefly* went into production had been minimal (discounting for the moment the WB's failure to continue *Buffy* after Season 5). The WB, it is true, had asked for a more attractive Willow, postponed the airing of "Earshot" and "Graduation Day, Part II," did not want Tara and Willow to kiss, and demanded less seriality on *Angel*, but Fox micromanaged *Firefly*. It rejected the planned pilot, demanding something more action-oriented (Whedon and Tim Minear came up with one, "The Train Job," over a weekend). It asked that Zoë and Wash not be married – not sexy enough they were convinced (Whedon refused and Fox demurred); it demanded that Mal be more of an action hero (without network interference, Whedon acknowledges, Mal would not have kicked Niska's muscle-bound henchman into the engine in "The Train Job" [Firefly: *The Official Companion* I 6]). It warned him to scale way back on the Western elements (the genre being no longer popular on big or small screens) in a series whose opening credits would introduce the name of each actor and its creator with a homage to the classic Western series' *Bonanza's* (NBC, 1959–73) "branding" graphics and end with an iconic image of the *Serenity* buzzing over a herd of horses![16] The budget for *Firefly* was even smaller than *Buffy's* or *Angel's* (Firefly: *The Official Companion* I 8). The handwriting was on the wall from the outset: "It wasn't like they were saying 'just tweak this' and 'just tweak that.' It was over before it began" (Sullivan).

As a vote of no confidence, Fox would schedule *Firefly* on Friday night, American television's graveyard. The odds against survival were great. As Keith DeCandido reminds,

> Fox's standards for success are considerably higher than they are for the WB or UPN – which are, in turn, higher than they are for cable or syndication. Shows like *Stargate SG-1* [1997–2007] and *The Dead Zone* [2002–] – not to mention *Deadwood* [2004–6] and *The Shield* [2002–8] – can afford to attract a smaller viewership because a show needs considerably fewer viewers to be successful on Showtime, Sci-Fi, USA, HBO or FX. These shows can thus afford to appeal to a more limited audience because that'll be enough to sustain them (56–7).

Nine years before, *The X-Files* had begun its nine-year run (1993–2002) on the same network on the same night. For at least two years, one of the great cult science fiction shows of all time would fare poorly in the ratings game, but Fox allowed it time to secure a fan base, and it would go on to become a huge hit, a cultural phenomenon, and a cash cow for Fox. *Firefly*, on the other hand, arrived at a time of "desperate networks," as Bill Carter would call them in a book that chronicled the turbulent first few years of twenty-first-century American television, when the sort of long-range thinking and patience that made Chris Carter's show possible simply no longer existed.

Firefly's from-the-outset precariousness did have an upside of sorts, as Whedon would later recall: he and his collaborators – including Tim Minear, stolen from *Angel*,[17] and Ben Edlund ("a sensibility that's so left of center" [Firefly: *The Official Companion* I 9]) – "were on our toes every second, because we figured the one thing we had to fall back on was quality. That's all we had. And quite frankly, the first episodes wouldn't have been as strong, as frantic about trying to save it [...]." To be sure, Whedon adds, such a situation is not and was not "the way I'd *like* to live my creative life" (Firefly: *The Official Companion* II 10).

Firefly's origin myth involves an often-delayed London vacation with his wife Kai. Whedon's plane book was Michael Shaara's *The Killer Angels* (1974), a fictional account of the pivotal American Civil War Battle of Gettysburg, but he read it against the grain and found a different kind of inspiration – "That's the show I want to make!" the man with two shows already on the air would think (*JWC* 67) – hatching an idea that would in a sense combine the influences of both Jeanine Basinger and Richard

Slotkin. Basinger, after all, was an authority on war films, having authored *The World War II Combat Film*, so Whedon must have been familiar with the potential of such a book as *Killer Angels*, though what really fascinated him about Shaara's work was "the minutiae of the soldiers' lives." Whedon had hatched a second, more Slotkinesque goal as well: "I wanted to play with that classic notion of the frontier: not the people who made history, but the people history stepped on – the people for whom every act is the creation of civilization" (*JWC* 67).

The first scene of *Firefly* to air – the saloon brawl and its aftermath in "The Train Job" – would capture perfectly the kind of show it was meant to be. As I have written elsewhere,

> a newcomer to the series is not likely to read the scene as science fiction. The [saloon] setting, in fact, invites the viewer to begin processing the narrative as a Western. When the characters begin to use a smattering of Chinese words as part of their colorful language, we are, of course, less certain of the genre locus. When, however, in an ensuing bar fight Captain Mal Reynolds is thrown through a window and the evidently holographic pane reforms behind him, we suspect we are not in Kansas anymore. And when, their backs against a cliff, Mal and company are saved from certain doom by a hovering spaceship the verdict is in: we are watching science fiction.

As I go on to explain, "The Chinese words, the holographic window, the spaceship – each is a 'novuum' in [Darko] Suvin's terms; the presence of each *estranges* us, undermines our expectations, requires us to adapt/expand our imaginative framework and, finally, to begin reading the narrative as science fiction" ("The Island's Greatest Mystery," 289–90).

Visiting the set just before his new series aired, Whedon – described as "bouncing on the tips of his sneakers" – would confess to Felicity Nussbaum that "Every once in a while, I'll just look up and say, 'My spaceship!'" *Serenity* was not the only aspect of *Firefly* Whedon was ready to brag about: "And did I mention there's a whore?" (*JWC* 64). (That Inara would be more like a geisha than a Western prostitute was the idea of Whedon's wife Kai [*Serenity* 11].)

When Ronald D. Moore and David Eick launched the reimagined *Battlestar Galactica* in 2004, much was made about its commitment to Moore's "naturalistic science fiction" in the series bible.[18] Whedon had already given us, in place of the "giant Sheratons" (*JWC* 89) so common to earlier science fiction film, a spaceship with armchairs instead of captain's chairs, apple peelers out of the creator's own kitchen (Firefly: *The Official*

Companion 1 25), toilets (in "Serenity" we actually watch Mal urinate[19]), ladders, and six shooters instead of ray-guns – two years before *Galactica*.[20] Whedon was going for "a gritty realism that wasn't an *Alien* ripoff"[21]; Steven Bochco and David Milch's "you are there[ish]" police drama *NYPD Blue* (ABC, 1993–2005) was a template.

The series was not envisioned as terribly futuristic or even as essentially fantastic. It was to be Whedon's first "nonlatex" show (*JWC* 67), with no aliens or nonhumans of any kind (its monsters – the fearsome Reavers – were degenerated *homo sapiens*). He had created a fascinating cast of "nine underdogs struggling in the moral chaos of a postglobalist universe" (*JWC* 65) – or, as Whedon himself would put it, "nine people looking into the blackness of space and seeing nine different things" (quoted by Erickson 168) – that would, because of his limited budget, spend most of their time onboard Whedon's prized spaceship. As early as "Our Mrs. Reynolds" (1.3), he was seeing his master plan – a show with fascinating individuals "just being themselves" (Firefly*: The Official Companion* II 9) – bearing fruit in an episode in which "you could just toss that pebble in the pond and the entire show could just be ripples" (Firefly*: The Official Companion* II 9).

If *Firefly* was latex-free, it was also intended to be relatively free of metaphor, at least for a Whedon show. As he would tell Shebytches.com, in both *Firefly* and *Serenity*, he "took away the metaphorical aspect" so prominent on *Buffy* and *Angel*. Still, this new 'verse's SFness brought with it a new kind of figuration: "science-fiction always opens you up to every ele[...] want, because the future is just the past in a ble[...] a straight-on metaphor, it was more an idea of, [...] the human experience that I've read about or felt [...] like after a war? And it doesn't matter which wa[...] at is it like for the people who lost?'" (*JWC* 141[...] shed up" every bit as much as "genre mashed up"[...] lose a collaborator as Jane Espenson didn't qui[...] s up to: "The notion that the only metaphor *was* seeing the future as another *then*, or as another *now*, seemed limiting [...]. I had missed the point. Joss was going for something real and direct with this show; something that didn't require a metaphorical lens to focus it. His most clearly 'sci-fi' television project to date was also going to be his most literal. And it was the stronger for it" (3).

Whedon was much more involved as a writer and director in *Firefly's* short run than he had ever been on *Angel*. He would author and helm not only the real and substitute pilots – "Serenity" (a two-parter) and "The Train Job" (co-authored with Tim Minear) – and "Objects in Space" as well. He would also write "Our Mrs. Reynolds" (directed by Vondie Curtis Hall) and co-write "The Message," again with Minear, who also directed. Of its 15 television hours, then, Whedon was credited as a writer or director in six.

The basic tenets of Whedon's "story is god" still held true in this new verse:

> What you do when you build a show is, you open as many doors as possible, and then don't look in all of them. And that goes for not just the audience, but you yourself. You have to control it, because some shows will just build mysteries without knowing where they're going and suddenly realize that that's what they're doing and they become unbearable. But you do want to open every avenue possible – romance, conflict, trouble, excitement, revelation – without deciding exactly what's going to happen, because the show's going to evolve; relationships are going to evolve; storylines are going to evolve. That's the way they work. (Firefly: *The Official Companion* II 8)

So it came as a terrible blow when Fox denied his ability to practise his narrative religion. Atypically, he admitted to having no idea how his first season was even to end (Firefly: *The Official Companion* II 11).

Asked by Bullz-Eye if, in the light of the afterlife of the cancelled *Firefly*, there had been any possibility of saving *Angel* as well – perhaps negotiating a Season 6 in some form, Whedon would reply

> You know what? There probably was a chance in hell. I look back and think back at all the people who fought so hard. I was so exhausted by what had happened with *Firefly* and with the *fifth* season of *Angel*, which I worked a lot harder on than I had expected to, [...] I could've maybe fought.

The whole process, Whedon recalls, bringing the funny even in his sadness, made "feel like [...] I have grown older – and, oddly, shorter" (perhaps this explain Kai's occasional tallerness). And yet

> It never occurred to me that I *could* fight. When the head of the network tells you you're cancelled, it never occurred to me to say, "Well, no, it's not!" And I kinda regret that. I just thought that the law had been laid down. Now, I look back and think, what care I for the law? I've broken it enough times, and I probably could've then, had I not been so tired.

Still, he remained proud of both *Angel* and *Firefly* – "swimmingly proud" (Firefly*: The Official Companion* II 13) of the latter, as proud as he was of his spaceship (and his whore). When it was cancelled, he immediately vowed to bring it back to life in some form. He was, after all, an experienced hand at calling entities back from the grave. He would not even need to search for an Urn of Osiris on eBay; no fawn would need to have its throat slit.

But television? The medium to which he had made such an important, lasting contribution? Asked by Daniel Robert Epstein in 2005 why his love affair with television had cooled ("Why don't you think it loves you lately?"), Whedon's response was hard to dispute: "Well when you have both your shows canceled you go 'Maybe they're kicking me out'" (*JWC* 135).

9 CREATOR OF *SERENITY*

In which a cancelled, cult television series becomes a shiny movie.

[T]o be creative you need to know a lot and cultivate special skills.
(Howard Gruber, "Breakaway Minds," 71)

ooooooooo

"You've got some storytellin' to do."

(Mal in *Serenity*)

You want your first film to be, let's say, not sucky [...].
(Joss Whedon, *JWC* 133)

This is part of the difference between the show and the movie, because the show was really about what is it to be the little guy, and the movie was, what is it like to be the little guy – in an awesome epic! Where you win! Because it's a movie!
(Joss Whedon, Firefly: *The Official Companion* I 6).

Looking back over his collaboration with Joss Whedon on *Buffy* and *Angel*, David Greenwalt would exclaim "What a film school this has been."

They call me a Hollywood veteran in my bio, and I'm about to turn fifty-two and I've been doing this for twenty-seven years, but I've never had so much fun, and I've never learned so much about film-making [...]. It's like the old studio days; I'd like to think in the 1930s, I would have been one of those studio guys making three movies a year. *And nowadays you can't learn anything in film-making. You can wait five years and make one film; what the hell can you learn from that?* (my italics)

Joss Whedon had waited considerably more than five years. He had made the aspiring-filmmaker trek to California in 1988 at the age of 23; filming of *Serenity*, the first film he would write *and* direct, began in June of 2004 as he was about to turn 40. In typical Whedon fashion, however, *Serenity* would be, in sharp contrast to Greenwalt's rhetorical question, a learning experience, offering a master class in cinematic art but providing career counselling as well that would, by a circuitous path, "with wandering steps and slow," lead Whedon back to television before he returned to film directing, this time helming the third biggest-grossing film ever.

"As a youth, what I wanted to do with my life was make summer movies for a studio." *Serenity* would take Whedon within ironic sight of that dream – "making early-fall movies for a studio" (*JWC* 128). *Serenity* would be a new classroom for the film studies auteur Whedon – "when I made *Serenity*, they let me do the thing. They helped me, they guided me through it. It was my first movie, and the people at Universal were amazingly supportive at the same time as being instructive, but at the end of the day, I did my thing" (*JWC* 148) – but it's not as if he enrolled with no prior knowledge of his own. Read through the fascinating pre-production notes included in Serenity: *The Official Visual Companion* – "A Brief History of the Universe, circa 2507 A.D.," "Joss on Frame/Lens/Perspective," "Joss on Light," and "Joss on Music" – and you will see that he had already given a tremendous amount of thought to his first outing as a director.[1] These so-called "Mee-mos" – "memos," the self-deprecating auteur would explain, being "too small a thing to contain that much pretension" (*Serenity* 6) – written "in a frenzy of late night inspiration" in order to facilitate his "understand[ing of] the work I was about to undertake even as they confused and frightened everyone around me" (*Serenity* 6), expose "an unfiltered look into the mind of a filmmaker" (*Serenity* 6) and establish Whedon as a director who has very specific ideas about every aspect of film art, from lighting to scoring. We also have the long interview in the official *Serenity* book and Whedon's DVD commentary, all of which provide us with an extensive understanding of Whedon's intensions, frustrations and compromises as he tried to make his movie "not sucky."

Whedon would find film much more "fluid" than television – would be regularly "surprised, more than I ever have been in TV." Everything about the production "talks back to you and it does that while you're still making it. TV doesn't do that until you're done" (Topel, CHUD Interview). Which explains why he found making *Serenity* such a learning experience.

Serenity is stamped, of course, with many of Whedon's already established signatures, developed as a television auteur (see Chapter 14). It brings the funny *and* the naughty – even in the midst of horror and tragedy. Soon after Wash has died and with a horde of hungry Reavers at the door, Kaylee responds to Simon's deathbed admission that not having sex with her was his biggest regret with "Hell with this. I'm going to live." It gives us one of Whedon's biggest finishes yet: a huge battle in space, a crash landing, a siege, River's "My turn" slaughter of the Reavers. River's dream sequences are visually enthralling and advance the tale. United by Mal's ambitious "aim to misbehave" and the loss of two of its members, *Serenity's* rag-tag family becomes even more closely knit – even Jayne signs on – and the ship itself even more of a home (even if it is falling apart). It empowers its women: River emerges as a superhero, and even Inara gets to wield a weapon. Its fight scenes – with Summar Glau (soon to become a terminator in *The Sarah Connor Chronicles* [Fox, 2008–9]) doing 95 per cent of her own stunt work – are the best Whedon has ever done. The devil is definitely given his due: great pains were taken to make The Operative an understandable, anything but "mustache twirling" (Whedon in the DVD commentary), though always menacing villain; and Mal himself was substantially darkened (he shoots three unarmed men in the course of the film) because Whedon "didn't want his arc to be going from hero to hero because I wasn't making *Air Force One*" [Wolfgang Petersen, 1997]" (DVD commentary).[2] No less than two beloved characters are killed (Wash, Book). The patois of *Firefly* carries over, though it is somewhat less prominent. A 4-minute-30-second uninterrupted tracking shot (one-er) introduces the ship and its crew following the film's deft opening exposition.[3] The theme of redemption is key. Like *Firefly*, its multiple generic allegiances remain apparent.

Stacey Abbott has already offered a discerning analysis of the complexities of Whedon's endeavour in "'Can't Stop the Signal': The Resurrection/Regeneration of *Serenity*." *Serenity* is a film, Abbott remarks, that stands as a kind of ororboric (snake biting its own tail) moment, "the point where Whedon's television and cinema career came full circle." For the transformation of *Firefly*, with the enthusiastic push of the fervent Browncoats who, collaborating with its maker, kept this new 'verse alive, "into a big-screen science fiction/action film" marked "a reversal of his reconception of the horror/comedy film *Buffy the Vampire Slayer* [...] for television" (227).[4] A failed movie becoming a masterful, and long-running television series; a failed, cancelled television series becoming a successful movie – obviously not sucky.

The new challenge was, however, formidable. Whedon was making "a movie with a title that sounds vaguely Buddhist; that doesn't have an easily sellable premise; that doesn't have a single bankable star" (*JWC* 116), and he needed to create a film for two audiences, "both faithful to the series" and its die-hard fans who had played a major role in getting the film made in the first place, and "decidedly cinematic and accessible to the uninitiated" (Abbott 228–9). If *Firefly* had survived and become a long-running series, the basic story of *Serenity* – the revelation of River's true capabilities and the origin of the Reavers – might have been pursued at the end of the second season (Firefly: *The Official Companion* II 11), and not surprisingly, Whedon would characterize the challenge of writing *Serenity* as being akin to writing an entire season of *Firefly* and then condensing it into a single film (*Serenity* 36). It was as if movie storytelling only allowed "the bullet points" to be told (*Serenity* 18). He would describe the task as the toughest he had ever faced as a writer – "You have to service the fans and make it for people who'd never seen it, which means not repeating or contradicting anything you've done before and yet having all this information that there just has to be" (quoted by Abbott 228–9). That ranking, that-degree-of-difficulty score, we should note, was made before he tried, and failed, to write Wonder Woman.

Abbott makes an excellent case that *Serenity* is "more regeneration than resurrection" (Abbott, "'Can't Stop'" 2," 229), and this was necessitated by distinct narratological differences in the two media:

> While a television series can operate with different character-based narrative strands that may occasionally interact but generally run alongside each other, a film needs to integrate its narrative strands towards a single conclusion – in this case, unlocking and revealing the secrets trapped within River. This serves to resolve the trauma of her character – she tells Simon that she's "all right now" – and enables Mal to take a noble stance and win a battle against the Alliance. (231)

As Whedon remarks in a response (quoted as an epigraph above) meant to be hilarious (and it is) but which also reveals his belief in a kind of media-specific narratological determinism, "the show was really about what is it to be the little guy, and the movie was, what is it like to be the little guy – in an awesome epic! Where you win! Because it's a movie!" "Much the way Mal realizes he's a hero," Whedon explains, "the movie realizes, 'I'm a movie!'" Well aware that "people don't love a great debate flick" (*JWC* 116), Whedon supplied, in subservience to movie business dictates, the sort of action scenes and big ending his film would need to have a big opening weekend and bring fans other than *Firefly* cultists into the tent. He built it; but they didn't come. *Serenity* barely covered its production cost of $38,000,000 in worldwide box office.

Abbott argues, rightly I think, that *Serenity* nevertheless succeeds as cinematic art in a way that, for example, the *Star Trek: The Next Generation* films, which she describes as "often feeling like extended episodes rather than cinematic features," did not (231). *Serenity* remains "a character drama," that never allows the special effects tail to wag the narrative dog. (Abbott quotes *Firefly* and *Serenity* visual effects supervisor Loni Peristere's remark that "Joss always works that way: his effects are integrated into the story, but they're not the story" [232].)

For Abbott, no aspect of *Serenity* is more revealing than Whedon's use of close-ups, especially of River: "Rather than objectifying River's face," the "elaborate sequence" in which she pronounces, for the first time, the name "Miranda" (an echo of *Citizen Kane*'s "Rosebud" [Wilcox, "I Don't Hold," 161]) "serves to privilege her subjectivity – again highlighting how Whedon places spectacle at the service of characterization and story, and, *in so doing, interweaves the stylistic conventions of film and television.*" (my italics; 236)

In a revealing interview with Mike Russell, Whedon reflects on the experience of making *Serenity*. Asked if filmmaking was more or less stressful than TV making, his answer was "*as* stressful," which came as a surprise to the rookie:

I thought it would be less stressful. I thought I'd be golfing in between takes and writing sonnets. Two things have not worked in my favor. One is, although I don't have three shows to run – and believe me, nothing will ever be as hard as that was – the movie takes up your attention in a way that three shows do. All of the creative energy that you're usually pouring into telling 20–40 stories a year, you're pouring into one. And you find you need it.

Filmmaking inspires/requires an obsession with minute detail: "You wake up in the middle of the night and you go, 'His pants are too baggy!' And it's important. You have [to] watch everything so carefully because every mistake you make is gonna be forty feet high. Whenever you think, 'Well, maybe that's good enough,' I say to myself, 'Cinerama Dome'" (*JWC* 83). (Recall that Whedon's longing to be a filmmaker, as opposed to a television auteur, had been driven by the desire to have the time and money and energy to "create everything that's in the frame" [*The Watcher's Guide* 2, 323].)

Whedon was, of course, worrying about much more than the cut of Mal's pants. He had never appreciated before the tremendous pressure placed on language in film and found the realization that no wasted words are permissible daunting (*Serenity* 18), and 59 minutes into his customarily brilliant and revealing DVD commentary, Whedon discloses his hidden agenda for his "intimate epic" (*Serenity* 19). "If there's anything

I've tried to convey" – and he could be speaking of his entire body of work as much as of *Serenity* – "it's that nothing is simple."

> One of the things that I did with this movie, always, was try and hide the intent of everything I did [...]. I didn't want the Evil Empire with Darth Vadar [...]. It's the same in the music, trying to hide [...] not make it sound bombastic and manipulative but hitting everything. Trying to hide the cinematography, making it look beautiful without making it look licked. Making everything bigger than life while *pretending that it's actual size and only really, toward the end of the movie, admitting that we're actually in a movie.* This is the mandate that we worked with, and it's a very, very fine line to walk and made everybody's job really hard, and *I don't think anybody really liked me by the end of this, and that includes me. I don't think I will be working with myself again. We didn't get along.* (*Serenity* DVD commentary; my italics)

If, like Alvy Singer (Woody Allen) in that wonderful moment in *Annie Hall* (1977) in which Marshall McLuhan conveniently appears from outside the frame to confirm his take on the media guru's work, Stacey Abbott could call upon this testimony of Whedon himself that she is absolutely correct in her assumption that *Serenity* indeed "interweaves the stylistic conventions of film and television."

DVD commentaries often disclose juicy details concerning behind-the-scenes tensions and conflicts, and, not to disappoint, Whedon reveals a doozie: that in the future he "won't be working with himself again." He jests, of course, riffing on/parodying often-heard reports of "creative differences" between producer/director/star, and yet it's not hard to find a degree of actual confession in such funny. After all, in point of fact, he did not, as a movie director, work with himself again until he secured the momentous assignment of Marvel's *The Avengers*. Wonder Woman was stillborn; *The Cabin in the Woods* was filmed (with Drew Goddard, not Whedon, directing); *Goners* remained in development hell. Joss Whedon returned to television to make *Dollhouse*.

Asked by JoBlo.com if, in the aftermath of making his first movie, he could now go back to television, Whedon's answer is very different from his "Maybe they're kicking me out":

> I am totally prepared to go back to TV. Not 24/7 as I did in the first years of *Buffy*, but now I've learned enough about surrounding yourself with the right people and delegating that I can actually run a show without ruining my life. TV is a medium that I love in a very different

way than I love movies. The things that I can't do in this movie [*Serenity*] are the smaller moments, the long protracted interaction, *the things that make TV really fascinating, watching people change over the years*. I've waited my whole life to make movies, but movies don't do that. (*JWC* 83; my italics)

10 VISITING THE *DOLLHOUSE*

In which yet another promising television series proves both controversial and doomed.

How do [the creative person's] purposes evolve? What determines his high level of aspiration? How does the process of self-criticism work? How does the creative person grow so that he can continue to assimilate the criticism of others without surrendering his own evolving vision?

(Howard Gruber, "And the Bush Was not Consumed," 278)

ᴼᴼᴼᴼᴼᴼᴼᴼᴼᴼ

For as much blame as Fox warrants for *Dollhouse*'s rough takeoff – the scrapped pilot, the uncertain early episodes, the Friday death slot – the network deserves credit for producing a show this ambitious and allowing it to air all but one episode for two seasons, despite deadly ratings. This wasn't a *Firefly* situation, where Whedon needed a movie to tie up loose ends. This was a complete series, and we should be grateful for what we got.

(Scott Tobias, Onion TV Club)

At a Paley Center "Inside Media" evening (15 May 2009) devoted to Joss Whedon's "brilliant but cancelled" fourth television series *Dollhouse* (Fox, 2008–9) the show's creator – tongue characteristically, firmly planted in cheek – wonders out loud about the origins of his diegetic surrogate Topher Brink, the geeky scientist who programmes the Actives: "That Topher – what's wrong with him? He just creates these character people and then he just puppets them around, and he thinks it's OK to do that. Who's he based on? What monster?" Neither Whedon nor his cast and crew knew then that *Dollhouse* would, to pretty much everyone's surprise, be renewed a month later. (Whedon would later characterize the extension as a mistake: "Fox forgot to cancel my show [...]. Very awkward. They looked and said, 'Oh, this is our bad. We forgot to cancel your show. You're going to have to make more'" ["Whedon on *Horrible* Nomination"].)

In the series finale (29 January 2010), however, the jury was still out on the driven-nearly-mad-by-guilt, neural-apocalypse-causing Topher, as the following exchange makes apparent:

> Paul Ballard: The point is Topher thinks he can flip it. Create a pulse to restore all the wiped minds.
> Zone: Yeah? He also thinks he's a little teapot short and stout.
> Adelle DeWitt: Topher Brink is a genius! And you will keep a civil tongue in this house or we'll put your tongue in a stew. ("Epitaph Two: Return" 2.13)

Shakespeare, John Keats once insisted in an 1819 letter, "led a life of allegory: his works are the comments on it." Whether we understand Joss Whedon – who would turn to adaptation of the bard's *Much Ado About Nothing* for relaxation after wrapping *The Avengers* – as an allegorical monster or genius,[1] *Dollhouse* is not likely to make or break his reputation.

In 2005, Whedon would ruminate darkly on his experience with television:

> You know, when I was at the height of my success, I was squashed like a cockroach by the very company who had benefited the most from that success [...]. The fact of the matter is, there is no track record in TV. Nobody cares about a track record. With the exception of about one or two guys, you just can't get something on because you're you. And in some ways that's good, because you should always have to fight for something; that's how you find out that you believe in it. But in some ways it's bad, because you can be squashed like a bug when you're actually doing it right. So it's not so much that I got over TV as I began to feel the TV landscape had gotten over me. And maybe that'll change. (Matheson)

Whedon's decision to do *Dollhouse* should not be read as an indication that the climate of television had necessarily changed. The Aristotelian "material cause" of *Dollhouse* was practically Whedon's long-term development deal with the bug-squasher itself, Fox. Before *Dollhouse* had aired, *Entertainment Weekly's* Jeff Jensen had noted that Fox had gone out of its way to acknowledge its previous rocky relationship with Whedon and support his new venture.

Whedon's possible misgivings about his new project were nevertheless apparent in the aired *Dollhouse* pilot's opening scene in this exchange between Adelle DeWitt (Olivia Williams), the Dollhouse's boss, and potential recruit Echo (Eliza Dushku):

DeWitt: We can offer you a clean slate.
Echo: Did you ever try to clean an actual slate? You always see what was on it before. ("Ghost," 1.1)

Writing in *Salon*, Heather Havrilesky had already noted the possible metacommentary on Whedon's pact with Fox implicit in the metaphor: that the new show's relative lack of Whedonian signatures might well be the result of the network's scrubbing of its creator's customary cult-engendering eccentricity.

With an origin myth that includes a sit-down at lunch with career-in-the-doldrums Dushku (*Buffy*'s bad girl slayer Faith), desperate for a project, *Dollhouse* was never pure Whedon from the outset. The idea he came up with (according to some versions during a visit to the men's room) was a science fictioner set in a (literally) underground Los Angeles company, a division of the ultra-sinister Rossum Corporation, offering for-hire for very large fees "secret agents," dolls, both male and female, able to take on almost any role or task after being reprogrammed by futuristic neurological technology. Originally intended to be a network-friendly, relatively free-from-seriality, episodic series (where have we heard this before?), *Dollhouse* was to give us Dushku (Echo) performing a different Active each week, thereby showcasing her acting talents.

From the beginning, however, *Dollhouse* was a troubled show. Its "rough takeoff – the scrapped pilot, the uncertain early episodes, the Friday death slot" – singled out by Tobias (see the epigraph above) was a disconcerting development but basically *déja vu* all over again: had not *Firefly* faced the very same obstacles? More significantly, complaints, troubling in regard to a show from "Joss Whedon: Feminist,"[2] were heard from the beginning about the show's questionable messages: were not the dolls being sold into sexual slavery in some episodes?, critics understandably asked. In *Wired*, Adam Rogers would memorably characterize *Dollhouse* as "an icky *Fantasy Island* with gunfights and psychosis" (174).[3] Many found fault as well with Dushku's acting, and some of the stand-alone stories were lame, to say the least. But the remainder of the ensemble cast was uniformly excellent, especially Williams as Adelle DeWitt; Harry Lennix as Boyd Langston, Echo's "handler" (and eventually much more); Enver Gjokaj and Dichen Lachman as prominent dolls Victor and Sierra; and Fran Kranz as Topher.

Being a Whedon show, *Dollhouse* became, of course, much more than merely episodic. Echo faced her weekly challenges – as, to name only a few, a crisis negotiator ("Ghost"), back-up singer/bodyguard ("Stage Fright" 1.3), burglar ("Gray Hour" 1.4), blind cult member

("True Believer" 1.5), a dead woman ("Haunted" 1.10), an FBI agent ("Vows" 2.1), a mother ("Instinct" 2.2), a college student ("Belle Chose" 2.3). But in multi-episode story arcs we also followed investigation of the Dollhouse's improbable existence by rogue FBI agent Ballard (Tahmoh Penikett); met the mysterious psychopath Alpha (Alan Tudyk) ("Omega" 1.12; "A Love Supreme" 2.8); learned about the backstories of Echo/Carolyn, Victor and Sierra ("Needs" 1.8; "Belonging" 2.4; "Stop-Loss" 2.9); tracked the crusade of Senator Daniel Perrin (Alexis Denisoff) to expose the Dollhouse ("The Public Eye" 2.5; "The Left Hand" 2.6); ascended to the mysterious and frightening "Attic," a nether world for failed Dolls and Rossum Corporation enemies ("The Attic" 2.10); and visited other Dollhouses and discovered Rossum's insidious schemes and ambitions ("Echoes" 1.7, "Getting Closer" 2.11; "The Hollow Men" 2.12).

By his own admission (in the Paley Center discussion and elsewhere), Whedon had put two women in charge, *Angel* veterans Sarah Fain and Mere Smith, in order to help deflect criticism, and, when they left the series after Season 1, replaced them with another pair of female showrunners: Michele Faszekas and Tara Butters (creators of the cancelled CW show *Reaper* [2007–9]). Whedon's own credited involvement, however, was minimal.

One of the greatest, most innovative writers/directors in the history of the medium, he would write *and* direct only two episodes – "Ghost" and "Vows" (2.1), the initial outings of both seasons – and write the very meta "Man on the Street" (1.6), perhaps the best-aired episode of Season 1. Purported prior to airing to be a *Dollhouse* "game-changer," it was the first in which Whedonian wit was prominently featured (my favourite: Patton Oswalt's Bill Gatesey character talking about a judge who will "throw the Kindle" at Paul Ballard for his intrusion). On *Entertainment Weekly* online, Ken Tucker would cogently observe:

> So it turns out, Joss Whedon is operating at a different speed than most current makers and consumers of TV. At a time when everyone wants to make snap judgments of new shows, and when television content creators feel pressure to make their concepts immediately understandable/irresistible, Whedon chose to lull us into thinking *Dollhouse* was going to remain a series about Eliza Dushku looking as though someone had hit her over the head with a shovel every week whenever she wasn't dolled up like a boy-toy having ferocious sex with a "client."

Whedon had done this before, of course. Season 5 of *Buffy* had many perturbed by the introduction of a little sister for the Slayer, but then, after getting her ass kicked by Glory, we learned, in "No Place Like Home" (5.5), as we were told by a monk dying in Buffy's arms, that Dawn was the Key, and we gasped.

Whedon would also supply the story for and direct the unaired "Epitaph One," available for the first time on DVD. Overseas distribution of *Dollhouse* had required 13 episodes, but Whedon and company had only contracted for 12. So on the fly they gave us – for lagniappe – a dark tale set in an apocalyptic future, a nightmare world in which the Dollhouse's wiping technology has gone global, basically zombifying the human race. Shot on a Fox-placating shoestring budget, it stands as a splendid example of television's astonishing ability to do more with less, to transform necessity into genius. "Epitaph Two: Return" (2.13), the series' satisfying finale, would, of course, return to *Dollhouse*'s future tense.

Whedon's interviews and DVD commentaries have always been self-deprecating, but his work on *Dollhouse* took his disparagement to new levels. The opening sequence of "Ghost," which gives us a motorcycle chase scene (actually shot, Whedon acknowledges, by David Solomon) and Dushku dancing wildly in a skimpy dress, leads the director to observe: "I'm like Michael Bay but not so good at shooting," and a subsequent scene showing us the Dollhouse's co-ed shower finds him commenting sarcastically "I'm some kind of genius man."

If *Dollhouse* seemed to transpire a bit outside the known Whedonverses, it is possible with 20/20 hindsight to see it nevertheless as the beginning of a trend. In his dialogue with Drew Goddard in *The Cabin in the Woods: The Official Visual Companion* Whedon admits to an end-of-the-decade new favourite theme:

> I think for me, ultimately, so much of our behavior is socialized and programmed and so much of it is self-destructive and useless and cruel, and so much of our society is more and more in the hands of a few very rich, very corrupt people, or very well-meaning people who have no business controlling the lives of others. It doesn't matter if they're corrupt or well-intentioned – the point is, we are all controlled, we are all experimented upon, and we are all dying from it […]. So the person who is experimented upon is me, it's everyone, and it's constant. So I guess it's a bit of an obsession. (19)

This obsession, so apparent in *The Cabin in the Woods*, first surfaced in *Firefly* (e.g., the machinations of The Alliance). *Dollhouse* – a series produced contemporaneously with *Cabin's* conception and filming – explored it to the fullest.

What was *Dollhouse*? As unsatisfying as it sometimes was to even ardent Whedon proponents like the present author, it is hard to disagree with Tobias's assessment (in the epigraph) that even Fox "deserves credit for producing a show this ambitious and allowing it to air all but one episode for two seasons, despite deadly ratings," and, unlike *Firefly*, it had its chance. But then again, it could have been so much more. In the "Defining Moments" featurette on the Season 2 DVDs, Whedon acknowledges that he had originally pitched at least six seasons of *Dollhouse* stories to Fox.

Watching it again, beginning-to-end, over a few days' time, I found it substantially more satisfying than I had when parsed out over a couple dozen Fridays, almost ready to agree with Noel Murray's assessment of *Dollhouse*'s whole arc: "It's as though *MacGyver* gradually morphed into *Battlestar Galactica*." I am going to tuck it away – perhaps in "my drawer of inappropriate starches" – and watch it yet again one day soon.

11 NOT MAKING WONDER WOMAN

In which Whedon fails at his potentially greatest challenge.

[T]he completion of one project often opens the way to [...] such a change in the focus of attention from the newly achieved pinnacle to the next morass. But which morass?

(Howard Gruber, "The Evolving Systems Approach," 7)

ᴏᴏᴏᴏᴏᴏᴏᴏᴏᴏ

I in no way want this to be a slam on Warner Bros., but the fact of the matter is, it was a waste of my time. We never [wanted] to make the same movie; none of us knew that.

(Joss Whedon, Gopalan)

How many more times do I need to be told that the machine doesn't care. The machine is not aware of what is in your heart as a storyteller.

(Joss Whedon, *JWC* 100)

In the IGN-Film Force interview Whedon discloses his career master plan: "I was going to be a brilliant, independent filmmaker who then went on to make giant, major box office summer movies."

IGN-Film Force: So, Spielberg...
Whedon: Spielberg by way of George Romero or Wes Anderson, or a
    strange combination of the two [...]
IGN-Film Force: Commercial success with artistic integrity intact
    [...]
Whedon: Exactly!

Joss Whedon's 2005 agreement to write and direct a Wonder Woman movie for Joel Silver and Warner Brothers would have skipped one of the stages envisioned in the conversation above. With only one movie on his resumé, the recently completed, relatively small-budget *Serenity,* and with no Romeroing or Wes Andersoning as preparation, he would leap into a "giant, major box office" summer blockbuster. The temptation was probably irresistible, as I have already suggested (see p. 14): a chance to upgrade his "nobody" status, become a figure to reckon with (not "that Sweden guy") and upgrade his entertainment industry cachet from cult to mainstream; the opportunity to work with the producer of a movie (*The Matrix*) he has often cited as his all-time favourite; the enticement of a budget, substantially larger than *Serenity*'s, that would permit him "to create everything that's in the frame"[1]; the chance to do "the next thing"[2] (*JWC* 51).

It was not the first such temptation, or even the first possibility of becoming a Marvel Boy expatriated in the DC Universe. An unorthodox expert on what constitutes a perfect Batman film,[3] Whedon, encouraged to make the effort by both his agent and wife (Kozak), had pitched a new Caped Crusader film in December 2002, a pitch, he would tell *Time*, he still holds "dear," though *Memento* director Christopher Nolan would make the winning pitch, resulting in 2005's well-received *Batman Begins*, the hugely successful *The Dark Knight* (2008), and *The Dark Knight Rises*, a summer blockbuster competitor with Marvel's *The Avengers* in the summer of 2012.[4] Whedon would learn that the cherished assignment went to Nolan on the same day *Firefly* was cancelled (*JWC* 100).

Whedon had also written an outline for a film version of *Iron Man*, the 1960s-era Marvel superhero created by Stan Lee, Larry Leiber, Don Heck and Jack Kirby, sorely tempted by "that cool shiny suit." Though New Line's response was positive, Whedon failed, for clear and decisive reasons, to pursue involvement: "I just didn't want to be in production, in development with a studio. I had the TV shows going [*Angel, Firefly*], and I just thought, 'This is not the time for this.' [...] I just suddenly had a flash of, 'This is going to be a long period of development. This is not going to happen'" (*JWC* 158). "Why I didn't figure that out about Wonder Woman," Whedon would add, "I cannot say." Jon Favreau's *Iron Man* movie (its screenplay attributed to no less than four authors) was released in the Spring of 2008 to very positive reviews and $100,000,000 opening weekend box office. Whedon had foreseen he would be envious: "I get jealous of anyone who gets to do cool stuff. That's never not the case. It's part of being ambitious" (Robinson, *Onion AV Club* 2007). We can assume his prophecy came true. Whedon and Robert Downey's Iron Man would, of course, meet again.

When Brian Singer opted out of the third X-Men movie in order to make *Superman Returns* (2006), the Internet was abuzz with talk about Whedon, already contributing to the franchise with his *Astonishing X-Men* comic books, becoming a natural successor, and in August 2004, while shooting *Serenity*, he would tell comingsoon.net that he would love to take on the project (Weil). Whedon faced scheduling difficulties, however, and when the contracts were signed, it would be Michael Bay-lite Brett Ratner who would go on to make the $210,000,000 *X-Men: The Last Stand* (2006), a film that owed a great-deal to Whedon's comics and would gross a disappointing $234,360,014 in the USA.[5]

As early as 2001, there was also talk of a fifth *Alien* film, a possibility Whedon found intriguing despite the certainty it would open old wounds. "[W]e'd been in talks about *Alien 5*," he would tell Tasha Robinson in the first *Onion AV Club* interview. Although the hunger was clearly there as well for a visit to Gotham, and a third *X-Men* film would have been a more natural match, in Whedon's mind Wonder Woman was an entirely different matter from *Iron Man* despite the latter's Marvel-ness. "[U]nder the impression that it was already being made"; impressed by producer Joel Silver's "freight train" momentum (Legel, Comic-Con Interview); beguiled by the prospect of becoming the Amazon Princess's Tim Burton (Batman)/Bryan Singer (X-Men)/Sam Raimi (Spider-Man); attracted by another opportunity to give life to a female superhero, Whedon took the job, though admittedly "never actually a huge fan" (*Time*). How could he not?

During over a year and a half in Wonder land Whedon would offer in a variety of interviews barely disguised pleas for help and more than a little obfuscation. Adam Rogers would later report, not entirely accurately, that "his script [...] got trapped in development hell" (194), it was a hell dimension largely of his own making. While the mythos of Batman is "a slam dunk" (as he told Whitney Matheson),[6] Wonder Woman was not as three-dimensional. A character "without a definitive story. Or even without a definitive version,"[7] she was also one of the few superheroes not associated with a city: "She doesn't have a town, she has a world," Whedon would observe (*JWC* 147). Still, Whedon admitted being impressed by her "great recognizability" (Matheson) and expressed his hope to make her real: "I really feel her. Let's face it: She's an Amazon, and she will not be denied" (Grossman).

She was, of course, denied, and during his time in Hell, Whedon nevertheless remained aware of inherent problems, especially "the scariest trap of the superhero film: the second half." Making hour two "emotionally resonant and surprising," Whedon would confess (complete with a *Mad Max* reference),

> is the thing that makes me stare at my computer all day and weep. Structurally, it is not as hard as *Serenity*, but if I am lazy for even a

heartbeat, it'll show, and it'll show wide and it'll show big. And your mistakes, man are they large in the cinerama-dome. It's different than TV.

The central problems of developing the screenplay – identified by Whedon retrospectively as "the meaning, the feeling, the look, the emotion, the character, the relationship with Steve Trevor" in his interview with Tasha Robinson (*JWC* 146) – presented the veteran screenwriter and script doctor a formidable challenge, though he claimed he knew precisely how to approach each crux. He loved the bracelets and had reimagined their origins. He was considering inclusion of an invisible jet, and was certain she would not fly under her own power ("She might jump. There could be some hopping" [*JWC* 98].) He was determined to eliminate "the star spangled adult diapers" (*JWC* 134). He knew she was *not* going to look like *The Matrix's* Trinity (Carrie-Ann Moss) (*JWC* 98). "The idea was always that she's awesome, she's fabulous, she's strong, she's beautiful, she's well-intentioned [...]" (*JWC* 146), and yet it would be, when all was said and done, a fish-out-of-water" story (*JWC* 46).

Whedon's penchant for female empowerment tales made him seem a natural to do a Wonder Woman film, but the character was not his and could not be made to live in a 'verse of *his* making. Created by William Moulton Marston (1893–1947), the psychologist and inventor who gave us the lie-detector, Wonder Woman was more like Whedon's grandfather's superheroine, and her karma was hardly clean. Marston himself had led an anything-but-normal life for his time – he lived in a quasi-polygamous relationship with his wife and another woman – and his comic book creation found herself in S&M situation with astonishing regularity (see Daniels, *Wonder Woman: The Life and Times of the Amazon Princess* and Jones, *Men of Tomorrow* 205–11).

Throughout his time with Wonder Woman, Whedon was bombarded with one question in particular: who would play her? He had reached an agreement with Silver and company early on not to pursue casting until a script was in place (Matheson), but he did offer a quintessentially Whedonian response: the role was Morgan Freeman's, until he turned it down (Nguyen). Later, the question would become so annoying that Whedon would skip the 2006 Comic-Con so he wouldn't have to answer it (or any question about Wonder Woman).

After a seemingly good start, the situation deteriorated as he began to realize, with a sense of "déjà vu all over again," the real nature of the state of affairs:

At first it was great, like 'hey, they're letting me run with it.' But then I figured out it was like *Firefly* – they were letting me run with it because they didn't like *any* of it. There was really no feedback because nobody knew what it was I wasn't giving them. I asked them point blank, because I'm always adaptable and collaborative. It seemed like nothing landed with them at all.

(Legel)

Asked by Matheson in December 2005 to disclose confidential information and reveal how much of Wonder Woman was "already written," Whedon would claim "I'm very close," and yet, after he had withdrawn entirely from the project, he would confess to The *Onion AV Club* in August 2007 that there was no draft at all:

It took me a long time to break the story structurally to my satisfaction. When I did that, it was in an outline, and not in a draft, and they didn't like it. *So I never got to write a draft* where I got to work out exactly what I wanted to do. (*JWC* 146; my italics)

Why the dissembling?[8]

Later, with greater candour, Whedon would insist, in a post-Wonder Woman conversation with *Entertainment Weekly*, that not only his involvement in that fiasco but the making of *Serenity* as well were highly detrimental to his great love of writing.

I had a lot of trouble writing – not just writing [Wonder Woman], but writing *at all*. Part of it had to do with having just finished *Serenity*. I ran into James Gunn, who'd just done his first film, *Slither*.[9] And he was like, "The director in me killed the writer in me." And we fell on each other. It was like finding a support group. After you direct and edit something, you just realize everything is negotiable. The line that you died for, you pull without hesitation because [the script] seems a little long. He was like, "Every time I sit down to write I think, *Is this even going to make it in?*" And you can't write like that.

(Gopalan)

In an interesting meeting of minds with fantasy master Neil Gaiman during his time with the Amazon Princess, Whedon would tell *Time* that "In my head, it's the finest film ever not typed yet" (Grossman), but it never did get typed or even move beyond an outline. "I never wavered for a second," he would tell The *Onion AV Club* in his most candid discussion of the failed project.

> I knew exactly what I wanted to do. It was really just a question of housing it. I would go back in a heartbeat if I believed that anybody believed in what I was doing. The lack of enthusiasm was overwhelming. It was almost staggering, and that was kind of from the beginning. I just don't think my take on Wonder Woman was ever to their liking.

"I got chills when I think of some of this stuff," Whedon recalls, "but apparently I was the only one who was chilly" (*JWC* 146). "[I]n a year and a half no one had ever asked me what Wonder Woman was about," Whedon would confess at Comic-Con (Legel, Comic-Con Interview). "I asked Joel Silver, point blank, 'Well, if they don't want what I'm doing, what do they want?' he said, 'They don't know.'" The "blind date" didn't lead to marriage (*JWC* 147).

You will recall Whedon's valedictory comment on the Wonder Woman debacle (quoted in the prologue above): "I'm a moron. I'm a complete dweeb. I don't get it, I never get it. Every time, I think everybody's lovely, and it's all going to work out, and I've never been right. For some reason, I can't get that right, can't figure that out. I think I'm getting better. I think I'm mean now. You're going to see a whole meaner person, now" (*JWC* 148). A quintessentially Whedonian boast – part Xander facing down Jack O'Toole in the basement of Sunnydale High in The Zeppo (*BtVS* 3.13, part Tara entreating her beloved Willow to be "strong like an Amazon" ("The Body" 5.16), part Wash navigating through the chaos of Alliance and Reaver craft in *Serenity* "like a leaf on the wind" – and followers of the master hope it to be true, well except for the meanness part. Indeed it does seem a much better strategy than his announced tactic earlier in the Wonder Woman morass: "I don't yell, I do the other thing. I lower my voice. It's very scary. You don't want to be there when I lower my voice" (*JWC* 135).

Whedon's intimidating lowered voice must have proved persuasive, for in April 2010 he would become the man in charge, both writer and director, of Marvel's much ballyhooed *The Avengers*. *Entertainment Weekly*'s announcement of the assignment would capture how the news was received by many: "Joss Whedon to Direct *The Avengers*?: Existence of God No Longer in Doubt."

12 NETWORKS OF ENTERPRISE

In which Whedon's many collaborative endeavors, inside and outside the system, are chronicled.

[A]t any given moment in history, not one but many environments are available, and the creative person both chooses and constructs a milieu that suits the needs of the enterprises in question. The creator's external environment is not a given and resources are not "gifts" – they are the ever-changing results of constant work.

> (Howard Gruber, "The Evolving System at Work," 7)

In the course of a single day or week, the activities of the person may appear, from the outside, as a bewildering miscellany. But the person is not disoriented or dazzled. He or she can readily map each activity onto one or another enterprise.

> (Howard Gruber, "The Evolving System at Work," 13)

One point that emerges repeatedly in these studies [of creative individuals] is the incredible density of thought. Every idea seems to be implicated with innumerable other ideas in an intricate network.

> (Howard Gruber, "And the Bush was not Consumed," 289).

ooooooooooo

Since I was near death from too much creating, I decided I needed to fulfill my kidhood dream of writing a book on top of everything else.

> (Joss Whedon, "Foreword" to *Fray*)

Jeph Loeb has long been a prominent figure in the world of comic books – the author (usually working with artist Tim Sale) of such graphic novels as *Superman for All Seasons, Superman | Batman: Public Enemies,* and *Challengers of the Unknown Must Die*! Loeb has likewise worked in television, as an executive producer for series like *Smallville* (WB, 2001–) and *Heroes* (NBC, 2006–), where he served as superhero informant for the supposedly comic book naïf Tim Kring.

In "Citizen Joss," Loeb introduces *Fray*, the first comic book creation of Joss Whedon. Loeb recalls his friend's initial announcement of his plan:

> He told me he was going to write a comic book for Dark Horse called *Fray*. "Write a comic book," I thought I heard him say. Here was a man who had not one, not two, not three, but four series in some form of production, was about to have his first child. (Actually his beautiful wife was doing the having. When you're talking about Joss, it's important to clarify the possible from the impossible.)
>
> Innocently, I asked him, "Why?" As with most things Joss takes on, he responded, "I think it would be fun."

As Loeb's title indicates, the moment made him recall a certain "black and white film about a bald guy," Orson Welles's *Citizen Kane* (1941), in which the titular young millionaire playboy announces "I think it would be *fun* to run a newspaper."

Fun – a word we have heard often in these pages. "For the creative person," Howard Gruber observed in an interview, "the greatest fun is the work. I think you have to take notice when Darwin says he read Malthus [*An Essay on the Principle of Population*] 'for amusement'" ("Breakaway Minds," 65). One of Gruber's important discoveries about creative individuals is their ability (referred to in Chapter 8 above) to maintain equilibrium among an often diverse "network of enterprises," to "easily handle seemingly different but intimately related activities" ("Breakaway Minds," 71).

Like the "tangled bank" of which Darwin speaks in the final paragraph of *The Origin of Species,* a kind of ecology governs the mental space of creative individuals, who tend to be like those jugglers who somehow succeed in keeping an impossible variety of spinning plates balanced without any falling to the floor. Creative persons "choose tasks that fit different moods and needs," but their plate-spinning is no mere act and decidedly not an end-in-itself. It "provides an organization of goals" which, in turn, enables the individuals to "set different levels of aspiration" ("The Evolving System at Work," 13).

The particular enterprises, sometimes exhibiting an "astonishing longevity" – "at any given time some enterprises may lie dormant" ("And the Bush Was not Consumed," 293) – "includes a scheme for replenishing [...] with new tasks if ever the original stock nears completion" ("The Emergence of a Sense of Purpose," 17). That the network is often organized into "subunits," as Gruber observes, "helps to diminish the effect of disruption, but each unit must be strong and stable so that it can endure until work is resumed" ("The Evolving System at Work," 12).

"[W]hen the running off of a plan comes up against obstacles," Gruber notes, "new procedures must be invented. How the individual decides whether to struggle with such difficulties or to shift to some other activity is regulated by the organization of purposes as a whole" ("Cognitive Psychology, Scientific Creativity, and the Case Study Method," 315).

It goes without saying that, like many a creative individual's, the career arc of Joss Whedon has been fraught with difficulties, but he kept the plates spinning, chose his tasks carefully, and refused to surrender. In over two decades of creative work to date, his "bewildering miscellany" has included writing, directing and showrunning television series (often more than one at a time), writing a musical, script doctoring, writing and directing movies and (more recently) directing other people's shows, acting, authoring comic books (his own and others) and creating an online musical. In the face of failures and obstacles (as Gruber hastens to remind "The creator's external environment is not a given" ["The Evolving System at Work," 7]), Whedon has continued to work, to evolve and have fun.

Collaborating:
In which Whedon plays well with others.

[P]eople with different networks of enterprise can and must collaborate.
(Howard Gruber, "The Evolving System at Work," 12)

Part of the difficulty of achieving a creative outcome arises from the need to make it compatible with human purposes, The creative person may very well start with a wild idea. Soon enough it becomes familiar and, within a private universe, no longer seems wild. But to be effective the creator must be in good enough touch with the norms and feelings of some others so that the product will be one that they can assimilate and enjoy. Even the person who is far ahead of the times must have some community, however limited or special, with whom to interact.
(Howard Gruber, "The Evolving System at Work," 14–15)

It goes without saying that, working in inherently collaborative media like television, film and comic books (as we will see in the next section), Joss Whedon's creative achievements are not solely his own, and his network of enterprises involves the significant contributions of others. No one is quicker to acknowledge this than the ever-generous Whedon, who is unfailingly magnanimous in praise of his team – actors, writers, directors, set designers, grips, pencillers, inkers. In the Academy of Television Art and Sciences panel discussion (included on the Season 6 DVD set [Disc Three]), Whedon observes that when things are working well on the set, even the dolly grip feels like he is telling a story.

That Whedon plays well with others does not mean he is not demanding. When it comes to his first love of writing, for example, he has always been a taskmaster. As he told James Longworth in 2002:

> When we came into it [*BtVS*], I hired a staff. It took me four years to get a really, really solid staff. If I don't like something, if it's not right, I'll rewrite it. And I've rewritten a dozen scripts from the words, "fade in" on this show. I've written half or three-quarters of the scripts. Now I have a staff where that's happening much, much less, because they are really solid.
>
> (*JWC* 60)

Admittedly "undisciplined," "very lazy" and "a big procrastinator," Whedon has never been anxious to do more than needs to be done.

> If somebody else is getting it right and is embodying what the show should be, I don't need to do it. I've worked for producers [he's talking about you, Roseanne Barr] who need to do every goddamn thing, no matter what. If you turn in a perfectly good script, they're going to rewrite it anyway, just so they could be the one to have written it. I do not like to create work for myself, and if somebody is getting it right, I like them to know it. So I'll never rewrite anything that I don't have to.
>
> (*JWC* 61)

It Was Joss

With *The Sopranos* [HBO, 1999–2007] in mind, Robert J. Thompson and I have argued that the approach to writing a series in which one central intelligence authors nearly every episode, thereby assuring "a greater degree of aesthetic continuity and allow[ing] [...] the same kind of single vision that we associate with more traditional art forms"[1] nevertheless has a downside, "[inviting] the burnout of the auteur and the exhaustion of the narrative premise." The model we advocated instead as "the most effective one for telling artistically mature stories in a continuing series" is one in which a showrunner serves as "the final rewriter of every [...] script, [...] farming out most of his episodes to other writers." On *The Sopranos* the result was a series

> enriched by the subtly different voices that various writers bring to the series. Chase's refusal to hog all of the scripts for himself provides a degree of multivalent complexity to the universe he has created. At the same time, Chase's stewardship assures that the show takes advantage of the unique ability of a television series to tell stories that develop character and accrete detail over long periods of real and narrative time.
>
> (Lavery and Thompson, 22–3)

For the most part Whedon adhered to such a model, and yet ...

Whedon has discussed the Writers Guild of America's decision to give sole screenplay credit for *Speed* to Graham Yost (an early poster, still in his possession, showed Whedon to be the writer), recalling that Yost once said to him "You would have done the same thing" – i.e., taken sole credit if it was offered.[2] Then and now, Whedon disagrees, citing (1) his willingness (at John Lasseter's request) to allow the animators writing credits on *Toy Story*; (2) "entire episodes of *Buffy* that [he had] written every word of that my name is not on" (*Joss Whedon Conversations*, 97). Which episodes those are I do not know, but again and again in DVD commentaries Whedon's collaborators – Marti Noxon, Jane Espenson, David Fury, Doug Petrie, Drew Goddard, Drew Z. Greenberg, Tim Minear, Jeffrey Bell – own up to his uncredited contributions to their episodes, their scripts.[3]

Having Kendra (not yet identified as a second vampire slayer) witness Buffy kissing the still-in-vamp-face Angel at the skating rink was Whedon's idea, not Marti Noxon's, the credited author of "What's My Line," Part I (*BtVS* 2.9), as were other memorable moments in the two-parter: the ever-naughty Whedon came up with Willy the Snitch's query to Kendra and Buffy: "Has either of you girls considered modeling? I have a friend with a camera? Strictly high-class nude work. You know, art photographs. But naked," as well as Kendra and Buffy's in-tandem lines "Two slayers." "No waiting."

Extra-monstrous vampire Zachary Kralik's need for pills – and hence need for the (holy) water that will kill him towards the end of "Helpless" (*BtVS* 3.12) – was suggested by Whedon to the episode's writer David Fury, and Whedon penned the quintessentially Whedonian deeply moving/incredibly romantic/hilariously funny exchange in the same episode, in which Angel recalls the first time he ever saw Buffy (we saw it too in "Becoming," Part II [*BtVS*S 2.22]):

> Angel: I watched you, and I saw you called. It was a bright afternoon out in front of your school. You walked down the steps ... and ... and I loved you.
> Buffy: Why?
> Angel: 'Cause I could see your heart. (gets up) You held it before you for everyone to see. And I worried that it would be bruised or torn. And more than anything in my life I wanted to keep it safe ... to warm it with my own.
> *Buffy looks up into his eyes for a long moment, then leans into him, and they embrace, holding each other close.*
> Buffy: That's beautiful. Or taken literally, incredibly gross.

The delightful, and revealing, conversation between soon-to-be-invincible Mayor Wilkins, the vampire Mr. Trick, and soon-to-be-dead (killed by Faith) Deputy Mayor Alan Finch about favourite comic strips in "Bad Girls" (*BtVS*S 3.14) –

> Mayor Wilkins: (smiles up at Trick) Do you like *Family Circus*?
> Trick: I like *Marmaduke*.
> Mayor Wilkins: (disgusted) Oh! (shivers) Eww! He's always on the furniture. Unsanitary.
> Trick: Nobody can tell Marmaduke what to do. (grins) That's my kinda dog.
> Allan: (smiling eagerly) I like to read *Cathy*.

– was Doug Petrie's idea originally, but Whedon resurrected it from the trash and wrote the final draft. Whedon made other important contributions to the episode as well. Though Petrie was the author of this, Wesley Wyndham-Pryce's (Alexis Denisoff's) maiden voyage, it was Whedon who nailed the mission statement for his character: "He thinks he's Sean Connery. In reality he's George Lazenby."[4] Wesley and Giles's discussion of the latter's "Watcher Diary" – written by Whedon. Having Faith steal things from a sporting goods store (instead of a museum)? – Whedon.

Jane Espenson's insightful and candid commentary on "Earshot" (*BtVS*S 3.18) points out numerous uncredited Whedon contributions: the already mentioned English class discussion of *Othello*, and Buffy's brilliant, mind-reading insights; the moving/romantic/funny (again) exchange between Buffy and Angel: "Angel: In two-hundred-forty-three years, I've loved exactly one person. Buffy: Ohh … it is me right?"; the idea (executed by Espenson) that Oz's overheard ponderings should be "Nietzschean."[5] ("No one else exists either. Buffy is all of us. We think. Therefore, she is.")

The ingenious "Mary Sue" episode "Superstar" (*BtVS*S 4.17),[6] also written by Espenson, was in fact, as she readily admits, Whedon's original idea, and in the writer's room he described its idiosyncratic teaser in its entirety.

The idea of having Dawn's diary serve as a frame for "Real Me" (*BtVS*S 5.2) was Whedon's idea, not David Fury's. So, too, was the establishment of Harmony as the episode's hapless Big Bad.

In "I Was Made to Love You" (*BtVS*S 5.15), Xander's rhetorical question from inside the puffy suit in which Buffy embraces him – "This is the day you choose to hug me?" – was Whedon's line in another Espenson-authored episode. So, too, was this later exchange as Xander and the-distraught-over-her-failed love-life Buffy dance at a celebration of spring party:

> Xander: How you doing, having o' the fun?
> Buffy: You know, I am. Dancing with you is way better than trying to hook up with some good-looking guy.
> Xander: I think I liked it better when you were kicking me in my puffy groin.

And Whedon suggested other additions to the episode:

- That, post-"Ted" (*BtVS*S 2.11), the whole Scooby Gang – even newcomer Tara – immediately recognize April's true nature ("Buffy: So, what do you guys think she is? I mean, this may sound nuts, but I kinda got the impression that she was a … Tara: Robot. *Everyone nods in complete agreement.*)
- A memorable exchange between Warren and the Slayer: "Buffy: Warren, this is important. Is she dangerous? Warren: She's only programmed to be in love. Buffy: Then she's dangerous."
- And, of course, the closing scene, in which Buffy returns home to find her mother dead on the couch (repeated as the teaser of the next episode, "The Body," written and directed by Whedon himself).

From first to last, Season 6 of *Buffy* would not be without Whedon's uncredited contributions. Dawn's poignant snuggling with the Buffy Bot in "Bargaining" (*BtVS* 6.1) was not Marti Noxon's idea but Whedon's, as was Xander's *faux-brave* insistence that he is a "powerful man-witch himself" later in the episode. The famous yellow crayon, the memory of which saved the world in "Grave" (*BtVS* 6.22), was not David Fury's invention but Whedon's (Academy of Television Arts and Sciences panel).

It was Whedon's suggestion to director David Solomon to shoot the hilarious flashback to Anya's origins in "Selfless" (*BtVS* 7.5) "like a bad movie." The stunning "Mrs. Xander Harris" song in the same episode, a flashback to the time of Sweet's visit to Sunnydale (in "Once More with Feeling") – Whedon wrote in one night to fill a felt need in Drew Goddard's screenplay, and he also added Xander's absurd suggestion that they might be dealing with a "copycat spider demon." The same episode's moving final scene, as Anya and Xander go off in opposite directions, perhaps for ever – again Whedon's idea, not Goddard's.

It will surprise no one that the following exchange between Holden and Buffy in "Conversations with Dead People" (*BtVS* 7.7) –

Holden: Oh my god!
Buffy: Oh your god what?
Holden: Oh, well, you know, not my God, because I defy him and all of his works, but – does he exist? Is there word on that, by the way?
Buffy: Nothing solid.

– was written not by Goddard but the "angry atheist" Whedon.

In "The Killer in Me" (*BtVS* 7.13), Drew Z. Greenberg wanted to have Willow punish the two boys at The Bronze by magically making them gay until Whedon pointed out that they would not want to suggest that homosexuality should be considered a punishment." (Whedon "would have been a great gay guy," Greenberg observes.)

The really creepy teaser of "Dirty Girls" (*BtVS* 7.18), an episode also written by Goddard,[7] the one that introduced evil former priest Caleb as The First's henchman as he picks up a Potential hitchhiker – was conceived and written by Whedon.

On *Angel* Whedon would continue to make significant anonymous contributions. In Espenson's "Rm W/A Vu" (*Angel* 1.5), Whedon suggested Doyle's telephone-answering mangling (first of many) of Angel Investigations' "We help the hopeless" into "We hope you're helpless."

If it had been up to the writer (and Executive Producer) of "Are You Now or Have You Ever Been" (*Angel* 2.2) Tim Minear, the "*Titanic*" shot with which we enter the Hyperion Hotel in the 1950s would have been pulled; Whedon insisted it be kept in and also suggested that the episode (and its metaphors) be moved from the 1940s (as Minear had originally intended) to the McCarthy-era.

It was Whedon who hatched the basic idea – that the AI team go "over the rainbow" into its own Oz – for the three-part finale of Season 2 ("David Greenwalt," 160).

In "Billy" (*Angel* 3.6), Whedon would write two memorable scenes in which evil Wolfram and Hart lawyer Lilah has a dialogue with, first, Angel ("That's a very dramatic entrance, except for the part where you can't enter") and then Cordelia (Lilah: "So? You know me." Cordelia: "Please, I *was* you – with better shoes").[8] Whedon also cut back on the episode's over-the-top *The Shining*-ness.

Whedon, not Fury, wrote that filler scene in "The House Always Wins" (*Angel* 4.3) in which Wesley has a would-be erotic conversation with Lilah while simultaneously dealing with a delivery man.

When Wesley tries to burn Lilah's contract with Wolfram and Hart ("Home," *Angel* 4.22), it was Whedon's idea (not Minear's) to have it magically reappear in her file.

The (rather anti-climatic) return of Spike to corporeality in "Destiny" (*Angel* 5.8) was suggested by Whedon, as was Angel and Spike's contest to be the Shanshu prophecy's one, true vampire with a soul.

It was Whedon's idea to include the video of Doyle, a character who had died in Season 1's "Hero" (*Angel* 1.9), in *Angel*'s 100th episode ("You're Welcome," *Angel* 5.12), and he would write the guaranteed-to-bring-tears final scene between Angel and Cordelia that ended the episode.[9]

On *Firefly*, too, Whedon would make uncredited contributions. The idea of Shepard Book terrifying River with his crazy hair in "Jaynestown" (*F*, 1.4) – not Ben Edlund's but Whedon's (*Firefly Companion*, Vol. 2, 14). In "Safe" (*F*, 1.7) he would write the scenes in which Jayne goes through Simon's possessions and welcomes Simon back onboard *Serenity* (*Firefly Companion*, Vol. 1, 126). He made major contributions to the origin stories of "Out of Gas" (*F*, 1.8) and suggested changing its final act break so that the commercial breaks would come after the scavengers enter *Serenity* with guns. The frequent references in "War Stories" (*F*, 1.9) to Shan Yu the "psychotic dictator/warrior poet" who "wrote volumes on war, torture, the limits of human endurance" were Whedon's invention, not Cheryl Cain's, as was the torture device (Whedon acknowledges his debt to "the machine that goes 'Ping'" in *Monty Python's The Meaning of Life* (Terry Jones, 1983)

(*Firefly Companion,* Vol. 2, 105). It was Whedon, too, who would insist that Wash carry a bigger gun into battle as the crew embarks to rescue Mal from Niska.

Directing Other People's Shows, Cameoing

Whedon's collaborative nature has manifested itself outside of his own 'verses in various ways. He has written for two comic book series, *X-Men* and *Runaways,* created by others (as I will discuss later); directed two episodes of *The Office* (NBC, 2005–) and one of *Glee* (Fox, 2009–); and done a cameo for one of his own favourite shows, *Veronica Mars* (UPN, 2004–7).

In response to Tasha Robinson's question about his motivation for such projects (*JWC* 154), Whedon explains "I love working with other people's characters if they're characters that I care about." His role as an on-assignment director of *The Office* came about because he was "an insane fan." "[I]t was really fun for me to direct an episode, because I had very strong opinions about what everyone was going to be doing in the background, based on all of their history. It's helpful when you're a geek."

Whedon already had connections to *The Office.* He knew Greg Daniels, the American version's creator and showrunner, through his wife Susanne, who had played a major role in putting *Buffy* on the WB, and via Jenna Fischer, the wife of former employee and friend James Gunn, and had his own office near the show's headquarters. These connections, and the show's practice of inviting prominent directors in as guest star helmers,[10] led to an impossible-to-reject invitation to direct an episode, "Business School" (3.17) in which Jim Halpert (John Krasinski) convinces his gullible Dunder Mifflin nemesis Dwight Schrute (Rainn Wilson) that a bat's bite has transformed him into a vampire.

"God, it was fun," Whedon recalls. Even as a "visiting director" he would make substantial contributions to the episode:

> They wanted my notes on the draft before they went into the rewrite. There was a lot of physical stuff, especially when the bat appears, that I got to pitch. I got to pitch a ton of stuff. Some of it, they were like, "Great!" Some of it, they were like, "Hmmm … try it." The physical stuff made it in pretty well, and there was some stuff where I was like, "We're not going to shoot this, we don't have time, and I know that it's not going to work." They're incredibly open with their actors, and they're shooting improv.

He would ask the art department to redo Pam Beesly's (Jenna Fischer) artwork for the exhibition that ends the episode. He found the experience "open and collaborative" and, still the company man he was when *BtVStM* was ruined, tried to remain "completely respectful of their process and their world." "I'm just going to do my best." "Obviously, as a director on that show, all you want to do is hide. If anybody notices that it was directed, you've kind of failed. They gave me way more freedom than I can remember giving people […]. I'm not going to lie about it" (*Onion AV Club* 2007). Whedon would return to direct "Branch Wars" (4.10), which aired in November of 2007.

The main attractions of doing a *Glee* episode for Whedon were no doubt the combined prospect of doing another musical and of working again with Dr. Horrible himself, Neil Patrick Harris, and "Dream On" (1.19) turned out well. Noting the episode's prominent use of characteristically Whedonian "one-ers," Todd VanDerWerff (*Onion TV Club*), for one, judged it to be one of the best if not the best episode of a series known for its unevenness.

Having already written an enthusiastic endorsement ("Ace of Case," in *Entertainment Weekly*) of a series often cited as *Buffy's* heir apparent and that he himself described as "a teeny bit flawless,"[11] Whedon's "guestage" as a supercilious employee-of-the-month rental car salesman in *Veronica Mars's* "Rat Saw God" (2.6) must have seemed a no-brainer. Spoofing his nerd image, Whedon plays Doug, a straight-arrow, by-the-book, Lariat Rental Car "company man" who has the following exchange with Veronica (Kristen Bell), who is trying to acquire information about the driver of a certain vehicle:

> Veronica: Hi. I'm hoping you can help me.
> Douglas: Well, the good news is, that's just what I'm here for.
> Veronica: Looks like I totally got the right guy. (*Veronica, turning on the charm, points to Douglas's "Employee of the month" picture behind him. He grins inanely.*)
> Veronica: Okay, here's my thing: my friend, she rented the coolest car from you guys, and some of us were going up to see the Staind show, and I wanted to find out what it was so that I could rent one for us to roadtrip.
> Douglas: Okay, what's the name?
> Veronica: Margot. Schnell. Margot with a "t," Schnell is –
> Douglas: It means fast. In German.
> Veronica: Wow. You speak German?
> Douglas: "Jawohl." Okay, uh, that's a LeSabre.

Figure 9: Whedon Cameos in *Veronica Mars*

Veronica: And what did they call that awesome color? It was …
Douglas: White? That's called white.
Veronica: Yup.
Douglas: Yeah. That particular car is rented right now, but I can get you a Regal with moonroof in teal for two-fifty a week, not including tax and liability, which'd be a great way to go and see Stain.
Veronica: Duh. Stain-duh. Gosh, that is more than I thought. Um, you wouldn't happen to have anything more like … forty?
Douglas: [*severely*] No.
Veronica: [*abashed*] Oh.

A bit later we hear Douglas chewing out an underling (YouTube has a hilarious outtake of the entire rant):

Douglas: Okay? I'm here, I'm *double me*, there's two of me.

It's almost as if he were about to name a certain fast food franchise in that other California city, the late Sunnydale. Whedon's contribution is solid and memorable and for fans of the Whedonverses an intertextual delight.

Anybody who thinks that Drew and I are not Hadley and Sitterson clearly never met us.

> (Joss Whedon, The Cabin in the Woods: *The Official Visual Companion* [hereafter *CWOVC*], 13)

I never thought writing it by myself. I thought, "This is something I want to do with Drew." Drew, since he has been working for me, has been a dear friend and one of my greatest collaborators. And so *Cabin* was never meant to be anything other than a collaboration. And *Une Film de Drew Goddard*.

> (Joss Whedon, *CWOVC*, 19)

Hadley: We're not the only ones watching, kid.
Sitterson: Got to keep the customer satisfied.

> (*The Cabin in the Woods*, *CWOVC*, 99)

Marty: Giant evil gods.
Dana: Wish I coulda seen 'em.
Marty: I know! *That* would be a fun weekend.

> (*The Cabin in the Woods*, *CWOVCI*, 151)

The most "remarkable thing" about Whedon's first full-fledged excursion into the horror film," according to Clark Collis in *Entertainment Weekly*, "is not that it took three years to arrive on screens but that its pair of creators thought anyone would let them make it in the first place." (11).

The Cabin in the Woods, a film first conceived in 2007 (Collis 11), greenlit in 2008, completed in 2009 but not released until the spring of 2012 – only a month before Marvel's *The Avengers* – was not, of course, the first Whedon had written (or co-written) directed by another. In a way, the horror film was a throwback to the 1990s when Whedon was script-doctoring or when directors like Kuzui and Jeunet botched his screenplays, but this time he was working with a long-time collaborator and friend, and the movie they made together was a true collaboration between Whedon and his "dear friend and one of [his] greatest collaborators" Drew Goddard.

Goddard had joined the writer's rooms of *Buffy* and then *Angel* in their final seasons, writing or co-writing such memorable episodes as "Conversations with Dead People" (*BtVS*S 7.7 – with Jane Espenson) and "Lies My Parents Told Me" (*BtVS*S 7.17 – with David Fury) and "The

Girl in Question" (*Angel* 5.20). He would go on to write/co-write some of the best episodes of *Lost,* including the brilliant time travel episode "Flashes Before Your Eyes" (3.8, 2/14/2007 – co-authored by *Lost* co-creator Damon Lindelof) and author the screenplay of the giant-monster-destroys-New York movie *Cloverfield* (Matt Reeves 2008).

In an invaluable dialogue "Into the Woods: Joss Whedon and Drew Goddard on the Making of the Film" in *The Cabin in the Woods: The Official Visual Companion* we learn a great deal about the inspiration for and division of labour on the film. We learn more than ever before about Whedon's horror film tastes. "I've loved all of the great horror films," he recalls.

> I watched *Nosferatu* many times – the original – as a child, so from the very start, and then the Universals and Jacques Tourneur [*Cat People, I Walked With a Zombie, Night of the Demon*] and Val Lewton [*The Body Snatcher, Curse of the Cat People*] in the Forties and the giant monsters of the Fifties. I watched everything. And of course, the really disturbing films of the Seventies and early Eighties – all the greats of my youth, *Halloween, A Nightmare on Elm Street*, all that stuff. Then I started to not like horror right around the torture porn era. But even during that, there have been great flicks like *The Descent* that have restored my faith. That's a classic horror movie.
>
> (9[12])

Cabin was born out of Whedon's discontent with both the genre's increasingly clichéd formula –

> How many times do they have to drop the knife? How many times do they have to split up? How many times do they have to start acting like assholes?

and its increasing inhumanity –

> Now [in most current horror films] they are just fodder – now it's always about the villain, what inventive villain can we make, because that's the action figure, and then we'll throw some expendable teenagers at them, and they get more and more expendable and more love is put into the instruments of torture and no love at all is put into the dialogue polish [...]. I absolutely can't stand movies where people don't do what any sane person would do. That doesn't mean panic.

Panic is fine; people panic. But when they make obviously idiotic decisions, then it makes me not only crazy but angry.

(11)[13]

Intended to counter these trends,[14] to object to the "unseemly," "weird," and "really, really creepy" preoccupation, now in command of the horror genre, "with youth and sex, and at the same time this very puritanical desire to punish it" (42), the idea for the film – originally hatched by Whedon – was "exactly what the movie is, which is, you play your normal horror movie – five kids go to a cabin in the woods – and you find out that everything they're doing is being manipulated from downstairs, and eventually they get downstairs and fuck shit up" (10).

An admitted homage to Sam Raimi's *Evil Dead* films, *Cabin* is also deeply (pun intended) indebted to H.P. Lovecraft. The horrors in which the kids are ensnared is part of an annual sacrifice intended to placate the ancient ones deep in the earth. (Recall that Whedon had previously visited this Lovecraftian abyss in "A Hole in the World," an episode he wrote for *Angel's* final season. See note xx above.) Thus Lin corrects the superficial assumption of the new security guard Truman that the movie's monsters are "like something from a nightmare [...]." "No," Lin counters, "they are something that nightmares are from. Everything in our stable is a remnant of the old world, courtesy of ... [pointing down] ... you know who" (91). And The Director (Sigourney Weaver, making her first appearance in a Whedon film since *Alien Resurrection* in 1997) explains to Marty and final Final Girl Dana: "The gods. The sleeping gods; the giants that live in the earth, that used to rule it. They fought for a billion years and now they sleep. In every country, for every culture, there is a god to appease. As long as one sleeps, they all do" (149).

Although *Cabin's* path from idea to screen was slowed by MGM's bankruptcy (a financial morass that likewise slowed much more upscale projects like *The Hobbit* and the new Bond film *Skyfall*), the $30,000,000 film was built to survive the movie business. As Collis reveals, Whedon and Goddard, "aware studio executives might be tempted to tinker with their script's unusual plot machinations," strategically "travel[ing] as far down the development path as they could before shopping the project around." Their plan, as revealed by Goddard, was ingenious: "We did the budgets, figured out the schedule. We did all the legwork and said, 'This is the package, take it or leave it.' Because this is the type of movie that can easily get killed by committee. Luckily, people got it" (11).

Goddard and Whedon wrote by taking the few pages of the script already completed and secreting themselves away in a rented "bungalow"

(Goddard upstairs, Whedon down). Unlike the "hours of gossip and chatting and personal stories" typical in a television writer's room (13), they would set daily tasks and talk/think about nothing but story during their full immersion. For the most part they kept to their appointed labours, later working over each others drafts, but on at least one occasion they traded off assignments, and Goddard's account of the exchange speaks volumes about Whedon's imagination. "I remember one day, I was working on the cellar scene," Goddard recalls,

> but I knew that when Dana came to reading the diary itself, like I said Joss loves prairie folk, and I thought, "I bet he's going to want to write this," so I yelled downstairs, "Hey, do you want to write the diary?" And he goes, "Yeah, I do," and then – I'm not kidding you – six minutes later, he ran upstairs with it, this full page, this beautifully written horror diary of a prairie girl. I was like, "How did you write that that fast?" And he's just like, "Some things I was born to do." [laughs] He cranked that diary out faster than I've ever seen anyone write anything. I couldn't write my own name repeatedly as fast as he wrote that diary. It was amazing.
>
> (17)

After several changes of mind about who should direct (19–20), Whedon, now better and wiser at delegating authority post *Dollhouse*, surrendered first director's chair for the Canadian (shot in Vancouver) production to the rookie helmer but greater "horror aficionado" Goddard. He would candidly admit that, too late, he came to realize that "producing a movie is kind of like ordering celery while your date has steak" (19–20), but second unit duties were numerous, the experience of producing – which was less time-freeing than he hoped (he still found himself "a little cross-eyed with exhaustion" [26]) and a bit too "adult" ("I had [to] be more of a grown-up," Whedon recalls, "than I care to stomach" (38) – was nevertheless educational,[15] and Whedon in the end had no real regrets.

He and Goddard "never had any major disagreements. We disagreed about some things, but in general, if it was a matter of the aesthetic of a scene, Drew is extremely collaborative and he knows how much I'm invested in the story, and we're old friends. He listens" (38). In his "Afterword" to *Cabin*'s visual companion, Whedon would, with characteristic humour, have this to say about his partner in horror: "Drew Goddard is one of my favorite living souls. Tall, handsome, good-hearted. He's like the Chris Hemsworth [Curt in *Cabin*; Thor in Marvel's *The Avengers*] of people. Untouchable. And of course therefore a villain. No one revels more in evil, in destruction, in chaos. Yet, on the sly, this guy is more decent, conflicted, self-abnegating and just plain neurotic than, well, me. You want to make a horror movie, you call Drew Goddard. You want to make a horror movie that contains a meditation on the human condition asking questions about our darkest selves that you know going in cannot be answered [...]. You call Drew Goddard" (172).

"[Y]ou know you've done *something* right," Clark Collis observes, "if your film gets thumbs up from both *Fangoria* and NPR.org." As of this writing, *Cabin* has also grossed a respectable $58,401,848 worldwide. But in the Whedon Spring of 2012, the movie *Cabin*, like the cabin in the movie, was destroyed, obliterated, by an emerging giant: Joss Whedon's *The Avengers*.

Comic Book Author:
In which a childhood dream comes true as the comic book geek authors such comics as *Fray*, *Astonishing X-Men*, and *Buffy* Season 8.

The work I do on *Buffy* in particular is influenced by comic books in that everybody is bigger than life, and I really think of the *Buffy* group as sort of a superhero team. To me, it's actually like they all have their own costumes and their own powers [...]. It's a very comic book aesthetic, like a lot of work I do.

(Joss Whedon – Ervin-Gore)

Q. [Y]ou may be the first director to have the latest issue of his comic book come out the same week as his feature-film debut.
Whedon. It's pretty cool. It's pretty cool. I ain't lyin'.

(Joss Whedon, *JWC* 125)

That's also the trouble with comics characters. If you read them at a certain age, they worm their way into your psyche. They live in your head. They are as real as anybody else in there, and you care about them.

(Neil Gaiman)

It's perhaps a cruel irony that comic books simultaneously confer outsider status and offer supplication to the outsider.

(Sean Howe, quoted in Koontz 53)

In "Gifted and Dangerous – Joss Whedon's Superhero Obsession," Roz Kaveney presents a strong argument for why our understanding of his work in comic books "should be as central to our sense of the artistic personality of Joss Whedon as any of his television and movie scripts, as well as something we enjoy as much." At the same time, Kaveney makes the case that "his comics obsession is the source of much of what is strong in his work, as well as some of his weaknesses" (202).[16]

Whedon discusses the history of his relationship with comics on several occasions – in his NPR interview with John Ridley, for example (in which he reveals the *Electric Company* origin of his Marvel boy-ness) and in his foreword to *Fray*. In the latter he confesses that "girls and comics" – more specifically "girls in comics" – were a pre-eminent early teen interest. He and BFF Chris Baal were disappointed by the dearth of "interesting girls young enough for a twelve year old to crush on" and found themselves at odds in their "pathetic – I meant to say 'rich' – fantasy lives" over the objects of their imaginary loves, most prominently Kitty Pryde. "Literally no character in comic books means more to me than Kitty Pryde" ("Spotlight Interview with Joss Whedon"). Since childhood, he has remained convinced he had a shot with her: "If she could be in the X-Men, there was no reason a short, skinny, not-overly-hygienic New Yorker whose mutant power seemed to be the ability to whine amusingly couldn't join up too. (And possibly win her over, since Colossus – not that bright.)" Not surprisingly, when given the chance to author his own *X-Men* comics, Whedon would make his beloved Kitty a central figure and even find a way to resurrect his onetime rival Colossus.[17]

A "Marvel boy" whose comic book obsessions over the years have included not only Spider-Man (especially "in the Ross Andru" [1927–93] days [1973–8]) and Chris Claremont's X-men (1975–91), but Jim Starlin's *Warlock* (1979, 1982–3, 1991, 1992–5), Frank Miller's demythologizing of Daredevil (1981–93) and Batman (*The Dark Knight Returns* [1986], *Batman Year One* [1987]) and *Sin City* (1991–9) (Ervin-Gore); Brian Michael Bendis's *Powers* (2000–4), Warren Ellis's *Planetary* (1999–2008) and *Ultimate Galactus* (2004–6) ("Foreword" to *Fray*; "Joss Whedon: The Pull List"). When Whedon, in the DVD commentary for "Conviction" (*Angel* 5.1) describes Angel's encounter with the SWAT team as "pure *Punisher*" he reveals yet another Marvel comic with which he is clearly familiar (also co-created – with Gerry Conway – by Ross Andru).

Whedon's own sense of superhero comic book aesthetics is particularly strong and articulate. He finds much of the genre "just really, really poorly written soft-core," characterized by weak narrative and lame imagination:

I miss good old storytelling. And you know what else I miss? Super powers. Why is it now that everybody's like "I can reverse the polarity of your ions!" Like in one big flash everybody's Doctor Strange. I like the guys that can stick to walls and change into sand and stuff. I don't understand anything anymore. And all the girls are wearing nothing, and they all look like they have implants. Well, I sound like a very old man, and a cranky one, but it's true.

(Ervin-Gore)

Such concerns would, of course, inform Whedon's bottom line when he came actually to write his first comic book, *Fray*:

I had come to Dark Horse with pretty much one stipulation: No cheesecake. No giant silicone hooters, no standing with her butt out in that bizarrely uncomfortable soft-core pose so many artists favor. None of those outfits that casually – and constantly – reveal portions of thong. I wanted a real girl, with real posture, a slight figure (that's my classy way of saying "little boobs"), and most of all, a distinctive face. A person.

Whether *Angel: After the Fall*, with its often lurid depictions of Illyria, Nina and Gwen, offers us "real girls" is an open question, as a spirited debate on Whedonesque makes dramatically clear.

Working in comics has its pros and cons for Whedon. Compared to television, comics offer greater possibilities for realization, giving the maker "license to go down every alley your brain can think of." With *Buffy* Season 8 in mind, he notes that

Willow's been on a mystical walkabout, you can actually show that. Instead of, "Well, she can talk about it in the magic shop for seven pages, because that's the money we got." You can pursue every thread, emotionally and visually, in a way that you just can't on TV.

(*JWC* 144)

"Writing the first issue," Whedon would admit to Roger Ash, "was different from anything I've ever done," and yet the screenwriter and television auteur immediately recognized both striking similarities to and differences from his earlier work:

you're looking for the big moments, you're looking for the big emotions, and you're constantly saying these guys are overacting. It's different in the sense that you have to choose a still picture that will convey what usually you would have movement to convey. When you're taking off in the air or landing, which one is the one you need to show? How much do you need to convey visually? How much can you do in one panel? That's different and pretty exciting just because it's new. (*JWC* 19–20)

Still, comic art lacks heft, is in need of more umph, more reality, more ... "juice." "[O]n TV, you're on TV," Whedon reminds. "There's actors, the people who created the characters with you, that everybody loves [...]." Comic art is different:

> The hard part about writing comics is *creating juice*. Let's say I'm trying to create a love interest for Buffy. People are like, "It's Angel!" "It's Spike!" [...] But to create somebody in the comic who has anything like the juice of somebody who was on the show, that's an insane challenge. It's going to be really tough. That goes for the Big Bad, as well. A villain that people care about, who they've only seen as a drawing, is, again, a challenge.
>
> (*JWC* 144)

The "control freak" in Whedon admits to fantasizing about writing *and* drawing/inking his own creations – "I really wish I could just do it myself, but I obviously can't. I would rather do everything myself" (Ervin-Gore). Still, comics do give him total control over his characters, who never challenge his authority, "never say, 'Oh, I don't think I'd say that in boldface,' or 'I don't think I'd wear this.' They just sort of do whatever I tell them" (Robinson, *Onion AV Club* 2001).[18]

Whedon has been involved in a variety of comic book projects.

Buffyverse Sequels and Prequels:
Fray (2001–3); *Tales of the Slayers* (2002)

Whedon had evidently been contemplating writing a novel (see the "Foreword") when he embarked on *Fray*.[19] Finding himself "too busy writing *Buffy* to think about writing about *Buffy*," and reluctant to tamper with Faith-based continuity (the second Slayer would play an important role in latter seasons of both *Buffy* and *Angel*), he settled on "telling a story far enough in the future that it wouldn't – couldn't – interfere," a narrative about "a new Slayer, and a new world for her to live in." With modest goals –

I wasn't out to reimagine, or predict, the future. I wasn't out to challenge the reigning Gods – [Alan] Moore [b. 1953], [Warren] Ellis [b. 1968]; [Garth Ennis] [b. 1970], and the gang – in terms of storytelling (My visions of the future are always pretty much the standard issue: The rich get richer, the poor get poorer, and there are flying cars.)

– he went for a "simple story about a really cool girl."

That girl is Maleka Fray, a brave, strong, talented thief (she works for a criminal fish named Gunther), five centuries into the future, who discovers, with the assistance of a demon named Urkonn, her real place in the long-forgotten Slayer line, while simultaneously finding reconciliation with her estranged cop sister and doing battle with her presumed dead twin, now an evil and ambitious vampire.

In Roz Kaveney's estimation, *Fray* is "an astonishingly assured piece of work" (219). With an encyclopedic knowledge of comic book history and aesthetics, Kaveney identifies Whedon's debts: *Fray's* deft use of repetition of a "panel in a different context to demonstrate the ongoing nature of traumatic past incidents" – that was Moore's influence; the ability to marshal an ensemble of support characters? – learned from Claremont (220). Fray's mastery of the vertical world of the city? Spider-man and Daredevil are her teachers – and Whedon's (221).[20] Kaveney also praises the book's "balance between fast storytelling in multiple panels and splash pages full of an appropriate sense of wonder" (219–20).[21]

In his conversation with Roger Ash (for the Westfield Comics website), Whedon tells how *Tales of the Slayers* came to be (*JWC* 20–1). During the filming of "Fool for Love" (*BtVS* 5.7), the episode, written by Doug Petrie, that gives us Spike's backstory, including his killing, in flashbacks, of two slayers. A conversation with "comic book nut" Petrie resulted in the hatching of a plan to do "a compendium of stories of slayers throughout history." Petrie immediately claimed the rights to the tale of Nikki Wood – the African-American 1970s slayer, and mother of Principal Wood – killed by Spike on a subway car.) Once Dark Horse Comics bought the pitch, Whedon discovered "that practically my entire staff wanted to do it." Amber Benson (Tara) would write "The Innocent," about a French Revolution-era slayer; Jane Espenson offered a Jane Austenish slayer in "Presumption"; the slayer in David Fury's "The Glittering World" was Native American; Rebecca Rand Kirshner's "Sonnenblume" concerned Buffy's forerunner in Nazi Germany; Petrie's Nikki tale was entitled "Nikki Goes Down." Every tale would have a different artist.

Whedon himself would author three pieces: "Prologue," another look at the First Slayer (originally introduced in "Restless" [*BtVS*S 4.22]); "Righteous," about a Dark Ages chosen one; and another glimpse of Maleka Fray in "Tales." The first two exhibit Whedon's strong sense of dark irony. Using demon strength given to her through Shadowmen magic, the First Slayer saves her village from demons only to find herself banished – because she is part demon. (The subject would be revisited, of course, in *Buffy*'s final season ["Get It Done" 7.15; aired 18 February 2003].) "Righteous" is told, in verse, by the watcher of a deeply religious medieval Slayer who saves her walled town from the vicious vampire St. Just only to find herself burned at the stake as a witch:

> That girl has power like none before
> 'Tis evil, by Saint Paul
> She walks with Darkness, Satan's whore
> She's here to damn us all.

To "bring that wanton woman down" seems the only option if ever her contemporaries hope to "please" their "heavenly sire." Her watcher, however, has other plans: angry over the ungrateful execution of his charge, he opens the gates to allow the enemy within. In "Tales," futuristic, post-apocalypse flying-car-era Maleka Fray, wielding a certain magic scythe, battles "Lurks" (vampires) without the aid of a watcher and ignorant of the whole Slayer tradition, until she fortuitously discovers a library of Watcher Diaries and begins to understand the history of her chosenness.

Other Franchises:
Astonishing X-Men (Marvel, 2004–6); *Runaways* (2007–8)

Joss Whedon's authorship (along with artist John Cassaday) of the third volume (issues 1–24) of *Astonishing X-Men* is a quite different achievement from *Fray* or *Tales*. For the first time in comic book form he took over someone else's franchise[22] – a 'verse of great scope and complexity[23] already "written by everybody that can write, and drawn by everybody who can draw" ("Spotlight Interview with Joss Whedon").[24] His own signatures are nevertheless identifiable throughout: the prominence of his beloved Kitty Pryde; prominent Big Bads (Ord the Breakworlder, Cassandra Nova); a triumphant chosen family; a "Spin the Bottle"/"Tabula Rasa"-style reversion of characters to an earlier period in their lives (the feral

Beast and childish Wolverine of "Torn"); the moving death of a major character (Cyclops's temporary end in "Unstoppable").[25]

Kaveney notes that what makes *Astonishing X-Men* distinctive from the work of such earlier series authors as Claremont and Grant Morrison "is that Whedon is a rather funnier writer than either of them" and "his comics dialogue [...] is closer to sounding like spoken dialogue [...]." "Whedon does what he does," Kaveney concludes, "with great élan" (223). *Astonishing X-Men* would garner Whedon a great deal of praise: *Wizard* magazine would, for example, name "Gifted" its Book of the Year. The major complaint levelled during Whedon's time in charge concerned the slowness of its publication: some issues were delayed by months, and eventually Marvel went to a bimonthly rather than monthly schedule. Whedon, after all, had a day job, and Cassaday, too, was dividing his time with other projects.

Whedon's six-issue role as author of the Marvel comic *Runaways*, taking over from its creator Brian K. Vaughan, presented the opportunity for yet more Whedon-style "fun": "I'm actually having the time of my life," he would tell Tasha Robinson (*JWC* 153). Working with artist Michael Ryan, he would produce a truly entertaining volume, full of pop culture references (other Marvelverse characters, including The Punisher and Daredevil's Kingpin put in an appearance), great fight scenes, time travel paradoxes (a major chunk of the story takes place in 1907 New York and involves a childhood version of Marvel's *The Avengers*), and witty dialogue.

Whedon ended up doing *Runaways* because he had already been talking to Vaughan about involvement in then-still-possible *BtVS*S movies.

> I had been reading his stuff and hanging out with him, and I was just a big fan and a friend, and I thought he really got it. He had some ideas about Faith, and we sat down to dinner, me, him, Tim Minear, and Drew Goddard. He threw out these ideas about Faith, and we were all like, "Dang, he's kicking it. He's really going to bring something to the table." Literally, because we were at a table.

Vaughan would begin, starting in Season 3, writing for *Lost* (ABC, 2004–10), following in the footsteps of fellow School of Whedon members Goddard and David Fury, but his Faith ideas stayed on the table, and he would have the opportunity to use them as one of the authors of *Buffy the Vampire Slayer* Season 8. In turn, but not really as a trade (as some reports had it), Whedon agreed to do *Runaways*, from which Vaughan and the original artist Adrian Alphona were stepping down. After his usual protest of being too busy, Whedon reports, he "lost sleep for an entire night, thinking that they were so cute and I loved them so much," and finally agreed (*JWC* 153).

This story of a different kind of chosen family – the titular characters are the blended children of super villains now trying to go straight – seems a natural for Whedon, and it shows on every page. If a movie of *Runaways* is being contemplated, Whedon could be a natural choice to write/co-write and direct.

Continuations of and a New Edition to the Whedonverses: *Buffy* Season 8 (2007–8), *Angel: After the Fall* (2008), *Serenity: Those Left Behind* (2005), *Serenity: Better Days* (2008); *Sugarshock!*

Given the enthusiastic fan bases for *Buffy*, *Firefly* and *Angel*, it was probably inevitable that they would not simply fade away when they came to an end in (respectively) May 2003, December 2002 and May 2004. The media was full of speculation about possible spin-offs, major motion pictures and made-for-TV movies, reincarnations,[26] and in one instance, the feature film *Serenity*, the wishful thinking came true. But another option, in another medium, existed, of course: the possibility of comic book reincarnations. When *Buffy the Vampire Slayer* Season 8 (hereafter *BtVS*S8) debuted, it was by no means clear how long it would run. We found Tasha Robinson asking Whedon "Do you intend for *Buffy* Season 8 to be completely open-ended, or do you have a specific arc in mind?" Whedon's answer was clear: "It has a specific arc and an ending. It will be open-ended in the sense that there could be a *Buffy: Season Nine*" (*JWC* 143–4). Eventually, *BtVS*S8 would have a 40-issue run (14 March 2007–19 January 2011), and Season 9 has indeed begun.

Whedon would run the entire enterprise very much like a television showrunner/executive producer, writing some of it himself, overseeing a diverse group of authors – many of them Buffyverse veterans like Jane Espenson, Doug Petrie, Drew Goddard, Steven S. DeKnight, Drew Z. Greenberg – and illustrators. Comic books veterans and Whedon collaborators like Brian K. Vaughan and Jeph Loeb also contributed to a fascinating and quite massive project, a worthy addition to the *Buffy* canon, giving us a giant Dawn; a resurrected Warren; the truth about The Immortal; 1,800 Slayers; a new version of The Initiative; a powerful – and able to fly! – Willow; a much-more-than-a-carpenter Xander; the return of Dracula and Ethan Rayne; a courageous and self-determined Faith; a Buffy with Daniel Craig fantasies who has her first lesbian relationship and experiences a time-warping encounter with Fray. *BtVSS*8 would, of course, kill a major character, perhaps the most heart-wrenching of all Whedon's murders: Buffy's watcher Rupert Giles; and it would, like any season of *Buffy*, offer a Big Bad, "Twilight," in the end revealed to be Angel, who takes Giles's life and not only seeks to destroy all the Slayers but put an end to magic.

A major direct contributor to *Buffy* Season 8, Whedon was not directly involved in *Angel: After the Fall* (hereafter *AAF*). The possibility of revisiting the Angelverse, of returning to that alley where Angel, Gunn, Illyria and Spike faced impossible odds, had long been considered, although many fans did not want to see what they considered a perfect ending compromised. It was not, however, until Whedon read *Spike: Asylum,* an IDW comic written by Brian Lynch, with art by Franco Urru, and then happened to meet the author in a restaurant, that it became a reality. Together, Lynch and Whedon laid out, in a long breakfast meeting, the basic story of *AAF*, which would include some elements of Whedon's original ideas for the sixth season of *Angel* that never happened. In the *AAF* graphic novel, we find the appropriate phrasing "Plotted by Joss Whedon and Brian Lynch." (Lynch's acknowledgement likewise deems Whedon the project's "watcher.")

We know from an interview with Lynch on the Comic Book Resources website about several specific Whedon contributions. After reading an early outline, Whedon encouraged Lynch *not* to play it safe; it was Whedon who suggested that the narrative begin with the aftermath of the final battle from "Not Fade Away," delaying the conflict until later; Whedon who solved the dilemma of how to depict Connor in *AAF* – Lynch would change him into a non-conflicted superhero; Whedon who would raise the possibility that, instead of slaying the dragon, as he planned to do in "Not Fade Away," Angel would train the magical beast.

Whedon's involvement in two *Firefly/Serenity* limited series – *Serenity: Those Left Behind* (hereafter *STLB*) and *Serenity: Better Days* (hereafter *SBD*) – was more central. Working with Brett Matthews, another Wesleyan graduate who had been his assistant on all three of his television series and written the "Heart of Gold" episode of *Firefly*, Whedon gives us two stories about Mal and his crew taking place in the time between the events of *Firefly* and *Serenity*. Though neither is terribly memorable, the art (by Will Conrad, with covers on *SBD* by Adam Hughes) is lovely, the banter almost series quality, the action exciting, the capers capricious. Badger, the Hands of Blue, Dobson (not dead) put in significant appearances. Because this Whedonverse came to an untimely end, *STLB* and *SBD* are nevertheless poignant in a way *BtVS*S8 and *AAF* are not, like missing fragments of a previously unknown history.

Working again with Darkhorse, in collaboration with illustrator Fábio Moon, Whedon would add another 'verse to the Whedonverses with a 2007 one-off online comic. *Sugarshock!*, Whedon scholar Elizabeth Rambo has observed, "may be Whedon's least known work, even though it won an Eisner Award for Best Web Comic" but "deserves more attention than it has received." "[W]hile Whedon's script draws on familiar genres, including science fiction and manga," Rambo argues convincingly that: the result is both *sui generis* and quintessentially Joss Whedon. *Sugarshock!* may seem like a bit of fluff made up primarily of verbal play, wacky non sequiturs both visual and verbal, and quirky characters, but the darker sides of Whedon's 'verses are here as well: violence, betrayal, and loss – within a comedic framework [...]."[27]

For all of Whedon's love of comics, his early twentieth-century prolific involvement with them stands as a subsidiary enterprise in which he invested, and kept alive, his imaginary energy in the wake of *Firefly/ Serenity* and the Wonder Woman failure. His return to television with *Dollhouse* (see Chapter 10) was not entirely motivated by aesthetic reasons. "[T]he paychecks [for TV work] don't make your family laugh," he notes. Because he "would like my children to eat solid food, and possibly go to grade school, let alone college, Whedon did not see himself becoming a full-time comic book artist (Robinson, *Onion AV Club* 2007).

Now that authoring comic books and mastering a new kind of showrunning have been added to Whedon's list of fun things, it seems likely he will continue to work in the medium as time permits. He has insisted he will be returning to the *Fray*verse ("MySpace Comic Books"), and how will he be able to resist all the temptations likely to present themselves in the years ahead?

Working Outside the System:
In which Whedon, in pursuit of a new business model, goes independent to create the web series *Dr. Horrible's Sing-Along Blog* and a homemade Shakespeare adaptation of *Much Ado About Nothing*.

I'm interested in being an Internet Roger Corman. He's responsible for a slew of the greatest directors of the last couple decades, because he was the only B-movie system that there was. Now the whole world can be that system.

(*JWC* 174)

All the roles I play must be hidden from the world.

(Joss Whedon, *Dr. Horrible's Sing-Along Blog*: *The Book*, 8)

Dr. Horrible's Sing-Along Blog. In the wake of the 5 November 2007–12 February 2008 Writers Guild of America strike – during which Whedon walked the picket lines – another Whedon venture debuted, not in movie theatres, not on television, not in a comic book but on the Internet. *Dr. Horrible's Sing-Along Blog* (hereafter *DHSAB*) premiered, free (for a limited time) on the web, posted, one act at a time, 15, 17 and 19 July 2008. *Dr. Horrible* then disappeared (midnight 20 July), available only on iTunes until its release on DVD in December.

In a letter available on the website, Whedon offers, in his inimitable way, *Dr. Horrible's* origin myth:

Once upon a time, all the writers in the forest got very mad with the Forest Kings and declared a work-stoppage. The forest creatures were all sad; the mushrooms did not dance, the elderberries gave no juice for the festival wines, and the Teamsters were kinda pissed. (They were very polite about it, though.) During this work-stoppage, many writers tried to form partnerships for outside funding to create new work that circumvented the Forest King system.

Frustrated with the lack of movement on that front, I finally decided to do something very ambitious, very exciting, very mid-life-crisisy. Aided only by everyone I had worked with, was related to or had ever met, I single-handedly created this unique little epic. A supervillain musical, of which, as we all know, there are far too few.

In other words, during the Writers Guild of America strike – of which he was a stalwart and outspoken supporter, Whedon hatched a scheme to create, with the help of scores of others, including his brothers Zack and Jed, Jed's fiancée Maurissa Tancharoen, School of Whedonites Ben Edlund (uncredited),[28] David Fury and Marti Noxon, Whedonverses actors Nathan Fillion and Felicia Day (Vi on *BtVS*S Season 7), and Neil Patrick Harris (*How I Met Your Mother* [CBS, 2005–], *Doogie Howser* [ABC, 1989–93]), a musical-comedy about a would-be mad scientist named Billy (Harris) – with a "Ph.D. in horribleness," he aspires to become Dr. Horrible – in love with Penny (Day), a woman he meets at the laundromat,

Figure 10: Dr.
Horrible hears about
his application to
join the Evil League
of Evil

who pursues membership in the "Evil League of Evil," while battling his
nemesis, idiotic, cheesy superhero Captain Hammer (Fillion). *DHSAB* is
set in a world populated by superheroes with a variety of powers (mention
is made of "the Mayor's dedication of the Superhero Memorial Bridge")
and supervillains (the "thoroughbred of sin" Bad Horse, Dead Bowie,
Fake Thomas Jefferson, Fury Leika, Professor Normal, Johnny Snow and,
of course, Moist (Simon Helberg), Billy's "evil, moisture buddy," a friend
indeed when anything needs to be "dampened or made soggy").

Anything but horrible, *DHSAB*, clearly indebted to Sondheim's *Sweeney
Todd* (1979), was a complete success. The music and the acting are both
delightful and hilarious, the production values and special effects amazingly
good (considering the low budget). That was the master plan, after all:

> to make it on the fly, on the cheap – but to make it. To turn out
> a really thrilling, professionalish piece of entertainment specifically
> for the internet. To show how much could be done with very little.
> To show the world there is another way. To give the public (and in
> particular you guys) something for all your support and patience. And
> to make a lot of silly jokes. Actually, that sentence probably should
> have come first.

Here and throughout his letter, Whedon shows himself to be conscious, even hyper-conscious, of *DHSAB*'s role in the development of what Henry Jenkins has called "convergence culture" and the advent of "transmedia storytelling."

DHSAB was quintessential Whedon: naughty, hilarious, cultish, exhilarating, genre-bending, virally memorable – especially its catchy music and Sondheim-goes-geek patter lyrics: a near-perfect manifestation of the "loser aesthetic" identified by Richard Burt and elucidated by Matt Hills (*Fan Cultures*) that has been Whedon's TV auteur signature in *Buffy*, *Angel* and *Firefly*. And, needless to say, it was inherently collaborative.

Horrible would eventually be released on a loaded DVD (including a unique sung commentary track: "Commentary, the Musical"), at which time *DHSAB*'s cast and crew got paid, proof positive of Whedon's strategy to "turn *Dr Horrible* into a viable economic proposition as well as an awesome goof" that he hoped would "inspire more people to lay themselves out in the same way." "It's time for the dissemination of the artistic process. Create more for less," Whedon would proclaim. Tired of struggling against the men in suits, bored with "there's no business like show business" clichés, he has now established himself as a major figure out to change "the face of Show Friendliness."

With his usual humility and generosity, Whedon refused to take much credit for *DHSAB*: "I would like to say I directed this thing, and occasionally I told the camera where to be, but every one of these guys showed up so dialed in that I was just like, 'I'm happy to be here.'" (*Dr. Horrible's Sing-Along Blog: The Book*, 78).

In the wake of *DHSAB*'s resounding success, Whedon found himself doing interviews not with the *Onion AV Club*, *Geek Monthly* and *Salon*, but the Wharton School of Business (*JWC* [175–83]) and *Forbes Magazine*. At the time of writing, a sequel is definitely in the works.

In October 2011, soon after wrapping up filming of *The Avengers*, *The Hollywood Reporter* and various Internet sites reported that Whedon had "relaxed" after completion of the massive project by shooting, at his house in Santa Clara, California, his own script of Shakespeare's *Much Ado About Nothing*. Featuring several veteran Whedon performers – Alexis Denisof (*BtVSS*, *Angel*, *Dollhouse*), Nathan Fillion (*BtVSS*, *Firefly*, *Serenity*, *DHSAAB*), Clark Gregg (Marvel's *The Avengers*), Amy Acker (*Angel*, *Dollhouse*), Sean Maher (*Firefly*, *Serenity*), Fran Kranz (*Dollhouse*, *The Cabin in the Woods*), Reed Diamond (*Dollhouse*), Tom Lenk (*BtVSS*, *Angel*, *The Cabin in the Woods*) – *Much Ado*, we learned, would be released by

"Bellwether Pictures," a new "micro studio" Whedon had established with his wife Kai Cole as co-head.

The chosen name, like most of Whedon's use of language, is both intriguing and revealing. According to Dictionary.com a "bellwether" is

1. a wether or other male sheep that leads the flock, usually bearing a bell.
2. a person or thing that assumes the leadership or forefront, as of a profession or industry: *Paris is a bellwether of the fashion industry.*
3. a person or thing that shows the existence or direction of a trend; index.
4. a person who leads a mob, mutiny, conspiracy, or the like; ringleader.

But from The World English Dictionary, we also learn that a "bellwether" may likewise be understood as "a leader, esp one followed unquestioningly." A good word, is it not, for a Joss Whedon enterprise?

In *Why Buffy Matters* (2005), Rhonda Wilcox makes frequent, revealing comparisons between Whedon's foundational creation and the work of William Shakespeare, but she could not have known that eight years later he would actually write and direct the Bard's work for the big screen, thereby demonstrating conclusively that the subject of this book is never more Shakespearean than when he's doing Shakespeare.

When, after its wide release in June 2013 and just before this book went to press, I finally had the opportunity to see *Much Ado* at an art cinema in Nashville, Tennessee, the black and white, literally homemade, low, low budget comedy seemed to more than justify the high praise it had already secured from screenings at venues like the Toronto International Film Festival. Whedon had found a way, using his own School of Whedon ensemble, to splice his narrative DNA with Shakespeare's: word play, humour mixed with pathos, expertly choreographed physical comedy, the battle of the sexes, engaging camera movement in, around and through Whedon's own architecturally unique, uncommonly beautiful home (designed by his wife) – these signatures all flourish and delight. In an early review, Nikki Stafford, author of superb *Buffy* and *Angel* guidebooks, took special note of how Whedon "knew the strengths of each of his cast members" and used them expertly. Fillion's Dogberry is a much more likeable idiot – "though it be not written down, yet forget not that I am an ass" – than his Captain Hammer, though equally as clueless and, in combination with Lenk's Verges, gives us a comedy duo worthy of its own sitcom. Of course, *Much Ado* also offers pleasures meant solely for those cultists who speak fluent Whedon. Was that not a Burnt Boyboy, an odd doll that had a prominent cameo in "The Body" (*BtVS*S 5.16), visible on a shelf in the children's bedroom assigned to Benedick and Claudio? And what a delight it was for *Angel* fans to see Fred (now in the form of Amy Acker's Beatrice) and Wesley (now Denisof's Benedick) finally united.

I cannot be certain if Jan Kott's path-breaking book *Shakespeare, Our Contemporary* (1964) – which argued that the bard shared a *Weltanschauung* with Samuel Beckett and the absurdists – was on Whedon's reading list at Winchester or Wesleyan (it was published in the year he was born), nor was he the first director to restage one of his plays in our day (recent updaters include Baz Luhrmann [*Romeo and Juliet*, 1998] and Michael Almereyda [*Hamlet*, 2000]), but Whedon's strong faith in Shakespeare's timeliness is unmistakable. When Stephen Colbert asked Whedon, "Why go slumming with Shakespeare?", he responded that *Much Ado* is "very human, very much what we are going through now." When Colbert inquired if the Beatrice and Benedick relationship was similar to the formulaic "will they or won't they" storyline of film and TV romance, Whedon responded without hesitation: "It's the original will they or won't they."

Much Ado will not be the only work to come out of Bellwether, for under its aegis we will also be offered such future projects as the movie *In Your Eyes* (to be directed by Brin Hill) (Puchko), the *Horrible* sequel ("*Dr. Horrible* Sequel"), and *Wastelanders*, a planned webseries Whedon has developed with comic book legend Warren Ellis (Pantozzi).

13 MARVEL'S *THE AVENGERS*

In which Whedon finally has the opportunity to make a blockbuster, smashes box office records, and becomes a major filmmaker.

> The fact that creative work is difficult and therefore spread out over months and years has consequences for the organization of purpose. In order to make grand goals attainable, the creator must invent and pursue subgoals. Delays, tangents, and false starts are almost inevitable. The creative person must therefore have some approach to managing the work so that these inconclusive moves become fruitful and enriching, and at the same time so that a sense of direction is maintained. Without such a sense of direction, the would-be creator may produce a number of fine strokes, but they will not accumulate toward a great work.
>
> (Howard Gruber, "Inching," 265)

ooooooooooo

> So I'm writing, I'm editing, I'm shooting. I can't sleep. I'm like, great, it's just like running a TV show.
>
> (Joss Whedon on filming *The Avengers*, quoted by Rogers, 198)

Readers of this book to this point are unlikely to disagree with Adam Rogers's observation (in *Wired*) that, at the beginning of the second decade of the twenty-first century, "It began to seem as though Whedon's intellectual aspirations – the result of a film-major/unofficial-gender-studies-minor education at Wesleyan in the paradigm-subverting days of the postmodern mid-'80s – were getting in the way of success" (194). But then Whedon's *The Avengers* became the frakking third highest-grossing film of all time! How?

"New organs of perception come into being as a result of necessity," the mystical Sufi poet Jalaal al-Din Rumi (1207–73) once observed enigmatically. "Therefore, increase your necessity so that you may increase your perception."

In an interview for the second volume of the official *Watcher's Guide* (2000), Joss Whedon, then a relative newcomer to showrunning (*Buffy* had just completed its fourth season) and yet to direct his first movie (*Serenity* was still five years away), would comment on the educational value of making television and then wonder aloud about what it might be like to make movies instead of TV:

> I think everybody who makes movies should be forced to do television [...]. Because you have to finish. You have to get it done [...]. [Y]ou've got to do it right and do it fast [...]. So TV is a good thing [...]. Ultimately, you want to move on from that. You just want to say, "Okay, now I want to do something where I have the time to create everything that's in the frame. Everything." And that's sort of where I'm starting to be. I'm getting to the point now where I'm like, "Okay, I've told a lot of stories. I've churned it out." I just feel like I want to step back and do something where I can't use the excuse of "I only had a week." (Holder, Mariotte, and Hart, 323)

With Marvel's *The Avengers*, Whedon would have the opportunity – and the budget ($220,000,000, almost six times larger than *Serenity*'s $38,000,000) – "to do something where I have the time to create everything that's in the frame."[1] And, of course, he had much more than a week, but, as we shall see, Marvel's *The Avengers*' magnificent success – an exemplary case of the cumulative "great work" Gruber spoke of (see the epigraph above) – still owed much to the "necessity" under which it was created.

Writing in *Wired* before *The Avengers* had been released, Rogers would reveal the limitations Whedon had agreed to before taking on the assignment in March 2010.

> Marvel went for his angle – with some restrictions. Whedon would have just 92 days to shoot, and the postproduction schedule was going to be brutally tight. The company told him the villain had to be the evil god Loki, from *Thor*. Execs said the movie had to have a big fight among the Avengers. They wanted a set piece in the middle that tore the team apart somehow. And there had to be an epic final battle.

Whedon, still at heart a "company man," readily acquiesced. "I was like, great, you just gave me your three acts," Whedon would tell Rogers. "Now all I have to do is justify getting to those places and beyond them" (196, 198). Jettisoning the existing *Avengers* screenplay (Zak Penn still gets a writers credit),[2] Whedon quickly overcame, thanks to the necessities by which he was bound, the sort of writer's block that had precluded writing a Wonder Woman script.

Whedon remained undeterred even as Marvel nixed early drafts of the script. According to Rogers, Whedon fought for retaining Black Widow (Scarlett Johansson) as a central character when the studio recommended she be eliminated, insisting that "without her the Helicarrier was going to feel like a gay cruise" (198).

Prior to and during shooting, virtually every journalistic piece on the highly anticipated movie asked the same question: how could Marvel Studios take such a huge risk, putting a tentpole film – the culmination of *Iron Man* and *Iron Man 2* (Jon Favreau, 2008, 2010), *The Incredible Hulk* (Louis Letterier, 2008), *Thor* (Kenneth Branagh, 2011), and *Captain America* (Joe Johnston, 2011) and predecessor to *Iron Man 3* (Shane Black, 2013), *Thor: The Dark World* (Alan Taylor, 2013), and *Captain America: The Winter Soldier* (Anthony and Joe Russo, 2014) – in the hands of an unproven director?

It would not be the first time, of course, as Rogers would note, that a superhero movie was put in the hands of a relative unknown: Christopher Nolan (*Batman Begins*, *The Dark Knight*, *The Dark Night Rises*; Bryan Singer (*X-Men* [2000], *X-2* [2003]); and Sam Raimi (*Spider-Man 1* [2002], *2* [2004] *and 3* [2007] were "art-house," "quirky" and "small-scale" before taking on their "comic book epics" (196). (Branagh and Favreau likewise come to mind.)[3] Besides, Whedon brought other credentials to the director's chair, as this book has endeavoured to show: his unimpeachable prowess as a cult auteur – Jeff Bercovici would observe with delicious irony that "Whedon has the kind of credibility that only comes from repeated failure" (*"Avengers* Director Joss Whedon"); his card-carrying status as a Marvel geek and comic book author (of *Astonishing X-Men*); his extensive experience as a television creator.

As pre-eminent television critic Maureen Ryan, who had learned how to watch Whedon on the small screen, conclusively demonstrates, what made Marvel's *The Avengers* a titanic success had its origin in Whedon's work in TV: "the film itself is a celebration of everything we ever loved about Whedon's small-screen work. The things that he did really well in *Buffy the Vampire Slayer*, *Angel*, *Dollhouse*, *Firefly* and *Dr. Horrible's Sing-Along Blog* are the things he did very well in *The Avengers*." Whedon's long-term followers, Ryan reminds us,

> know that he excels at creating mismatched groups that haltingly form ad-hoc families – fractured families with lots of internal tensions, of course. Most shows (and movies) have enough trouble creating just

one or two compelling characters, but in Whedon's work, there are usually a half dozen characters, each with his or her own baggage and agenda. The ways in which each person works out their personal issues and comes into conflict with, or assists in, the mission of the group as a whole – well, those kinds of rich, knotty dynamics drove the best episodes and arcs in the Whedon canon.

Amazingly, given the drastically truncated story time available to a filmmaker, Whedon found a way to distil his proven narrative schema for exhibition at the multiplex.

Enhanced, for those who saw them, by the expectations established for each of the superheroes by the movie's backstory predecessors, not to mention the "assembly instructions" laid down through the recurring roles of SHIELD, Agent Coulson, Nick Fury and Tony Stark, especially in those mini-episode-closing credit sequences, Marvel's *The Avengers* had an advantage not available to, say, *John Carter* (Andrew Stanton, 2012) or *Battleship* (Peter Berg, 2012), and Whedon himself had a hand in establishing multi-film continuity (including an uncredited revision of the *Captain America* script),[4] but what Whedon as both writer and director accomplished in Marvel's *The Avengers* was unprecedented in still another way:

> *The Avengers*, for all its exultant clobbering time, actually deepened most of the characters in important and exciting ways. That's where Whedon's other area of expertise came into play: He makes us relate to the specially chosen and the superpowered because he shows them experiencing self-doubt, self-loathing and fear.
>
> Yes, these men and women are exalted and special, but they're vulnerable too. That's what makes us love them, and Whedon has always understood that.
>
> (Ryan)

As Whedon himself would tell Andrew O'Hehir, *The Avengers* is "kind of an old-fashioned movie. It's not a cavalcade of sensation. There's a ton of stuff in it and we really put them through the wringer, but at the end of the day, it's a human story that I feel people can relate to on a lot of levels."

Though not as impressive as the "REALLY fine [meal], with truffles and s#!+"-enabling box office receipts, the response of the critics to Marvel's *The Avengers* was for the most part positive. On NPR's *Fresh Air*, for example, high-brow critic David Edelstein, while admitting he sometimes "find[s] a lot of Whedon's banter self-consciously smart-alecky," vouches his "love" for "how he can spoof his subjects without robbing them of stature" and identifies, with all the brilliance of a true Whedon *aficionado*, that "the heart of *The Avengers* clearly isn't the predictable, whiz-bang computer-generated battles between good and evil, but scenes in which our superheroes hang out, spar with words as well as weapons, and weigh the merits of individualism versus teamwork. It's not unlike Howard Hawks's iconic gunfighters taking one another's measure in *Rio Bravo*." "Prepare yourself, earthlings, Edelstein warned (correctly): "For the next few weeks, we'll all be living in the Whedonverse."

Of course, not everyone loved Marvel's *The Avengers*. The snarky Walter Chaw, writing for the Film Freak Central website, and Rene Rodriguez, the *Miami Herald*'s film critic, for example, both savaged the film, and their caustic takes are revealing about Whedon's place in contemporary culture.

For Chaw, *The Avengers* is both "completely inoffensive" and "agreeably stupid" and Whedon's "definitive artistic statement":

> It's a giant, loud, sloppy kiss planted right on the forehead of a fanboy contingent that will somehow find jealous dork solidarity in the largest product excreted this year by a Hollywood machinery that's the playground now of Whedons and Apatows and Farrellys, where it used to be the domain of John Fords and Sam Peckinpahs and Von Sternbergs. Not a full-grown man among them, they're drunk on power and nerd cred, making references to their references and amazed that someone like Scarlett Johansson returns their calls.

This is, of course, more *ad hominem* insult than critical discernment, and Chaw does not let up, insisting, all-knowingly, that the film "finally, has no inner life – there's nothing to explore here, except maybe the ways that men express their insecurities in the avatars they create," and privy, in a way the author of these pages would envy if it had any basis in reality, to Whedon's mental state: "[W]henever [*The Avengers*] threatens to be about something – like when Bryan Singer or Chris Nolan direct a superhero movie – *Whedon reveals he lacks the confidence* to be much more than the operator of the world's most expensive amusement park ride." (my italics) Predictably Chaw would praise the ambitiousness of Nolan's *The Dark Knight Rises* two months after *The Avengers*.

Like Chaw, Rodriguez claims special access to *The Avengers*' director's creative process, able to discern that "Whedon, who seems *to have gotten in over his head*, struggles to keep this unwieldy movie spinning. He is so preoccupied with the sheer physicality of the thing that he doesn't have time to step back and consider the larger picture. He drowns in the details" (my italics). *The Avengers*, Rodriguez concludes doesn't "add up to anything. This is a long, talky, clunky movie [...]. From Whedon, you expected more than spectacle [...]."

It is difficult to understand how Rodriguez, one of Michael Bay's most caustic detractors (see page 9 above), missed *The Avengers* "extras." Take note that the educated-by-television Maureen Ryan was not so oblivious, nor were Charlie Jane Anders ("Several Reasons Why *Avengers* Kicks Ass [That You Haven't Already Heard]" for *io9*) and others who catalogued the many pleasures Marvel's *The Avengers* offers. I will limit myself here to identifying only a few signature moments that contribute to Whedon's creative portrait.

Figure 11: Another Whedon T-shirt

In the Whedon Spring of 2012, just before the release of both *The Cabin in the Woods* and Marvel's *The Avengers*, the T-shirt above (Figure 11) went on sale on the Internet. Just after *Avengers* hit the theatres, Blastr posted a slide show: "Tara, Wesley and 13 other Joss Whedon deaths that broke our hearts." Included on their late-lamented list, of course, was the most recently deceased, SHIELD Agent Phil Coulson, Captain America trading card collector, who stood up to a god, accusing him of lacking conviction, whose death at the hands of Loki brought the Avengers together, giving them (with assistance from Nick Fury) something to avenge.

On the Helicarrier, just after Loki has been captured and imprisoned (and Tony Stark takes note that one of the crew is playing Galaga on his computer), the assembled Avengers speculate about the significance of their enemy's magical staff. When Captain America observes that it bears a certain resemblance to a Hydra weapon, Nick Fury responds that, whatever its origin, it was capable of transforming both Hawkeye and Dr. Selvig into Loki's "personal flying monkeys." The reference is lost on the often-too-literal and unearthly Thor, but Captain America is quite delighted that he "gets" the allusion to *The Wizard of Oz* (Victor Fleming, 1939), a motion picture he evidently saw back before America entered the war (back when he was still just Steve Rogers).

It has been part of the argument of this book that Whedon is a "film studies auteur," drawing on his encyclopedic knowledge of film history and genre to both write and direct. Marvel's *The Avengers* is a prime example. We know from a variety of interviews that a rewatch of *Black Hawk Down* (Ridley Scott, 2001) had made him want to do a war film and Robert Aldrich's *The Dirty Dozen* (1967) had provided a kind of template for *The Avengers*. As was established earlier, Whedon's mentor Jeanine Basinger has written a definitive "anatomy of the genre": *The World War II Combat Film* (1986).[5]

Marvel's *The Avengers* likewise offers numerous examples of what might be called the "popular culture sublime" (PCS), moments so self-consciously redolent with iconic characters, character traits, symbols, technology and weaponry that the response of the knowing viewer/fan becomes a kind of imaginal transcendence. Could any filmmaker other than Whedon have given us the sublimity of the entire sequence in which Thor abducts Loki from the *S.H.I.I.E.L.D.* jet and then does battle on the ground, first with Iron Man (who gets a power boost from the Norse god's lightning) and then Captain America. It is impossible to conceive a more PCS moment than Thor's hammer slamming down, icon to icon, on the Captain's shield.

Writing for the CHUD website, Joshua Miller would confess to another PCS moment.

> My adult-ness was powerless to Hulk in *The Avengers*. When he was on screen my decades stripped away and I was left a 10-year-old boy, drooling with pure, guiltless, innocent joy. It was almost a religious

experience. When Cap takes charge of the Avengers during the final battle, barking orders to our other heroes, then turns to a seething Hulk and says, "Hulk ... smash" I *literally* teared up – from happiness![6]

Even the film's harshest critics agreed that *The Avengers'* Incredible Hulk far surpassed all previous TV/movie incarnations of the "other guy" – as Bruce Banner deems him in the film. Mixing action and humour has long been a Whedonian signature, and the Hulk brings both the PCS and the funny in equal measure. His below-decks chase of Black Widow, his thunderous smackdown with Thor, his punch-out of a Leviathan, his skyscraper-scraping save of Iron Man after his free fall from the vortex are unforgettable; but so too are his comic moments: being told (as Banner) after plummeting from the sky that, in the opinion of a security guard (played by cult actor Harry Dean Stanton), he has "a condition"; his just-for-the-hell-of-it decking of Thor; his hilarious, cartoonish pummelling of the-full-of-hubris Loki ("Puny god!") – a scene that at a screening I attended received the longest sustained laughter I have ever experienced in a movie theatre.

If all the above stand as quintessentially Whedonesque, it still must be said that *The Avengers'* "increased perception" is the result of Whedon's restraint, his acceptance of necessity. "In over his head"? Nothing could be farther from the truth. Whedon knew precisely what he was doing. When the first edit of the movie came in at over three hours, what ended up on the cutting room floor was core Whedonstuff (as Rogers reported):

> The darker aspects of the dysfunctional team dynamic: out. A quiet scene with Captain America trying to absorb the craziness of modern-day New York: out. And so on [...]. "You don't have to say what you're trying to say. You can just do it, and then people will feel it," Whedon says. "The more I hone this and just focus on the Avengers as they relate to one another, the better it works. *That's painful*, but it's a reality. (199; my italics)

Painful ... "Pain is where I hang my hat," Whedon had told Jim Kozak with Marvel's *X-Men* in mind (*JWC* 102), but in making Marvel's *The Avengers* he had internalized the pain – and the necessity – and spun them into gold.

It should not surprise us that Whedon was slow to sign on for the inevitable *Avengers* sequel. "You know, I'm very torn," Whedon would tell the *Los Angeles Times* just before the *Avengers'* debut. "It's an enormous amount of work *telling what is ultimately somebody else's story*, even though I feel like I did get to put myself into it. But at the same time, I have a bunch of ideas, and they all seem really cool" ("*Avengers*: Joss Whedon talks sequel"). As he spoke, shooting for *Much Ado about Nothing* was already complete. At ComicCon in July 2012, Whedon would remain undecided. Less than a month later, however, came the news that he had agreed not only to helm *Avengers 2*, with its already-established-in-the-closing-credits-of-the-first-film Big Bad Thanos, but also to develop Marvel properties for television (Kit), including Marvel's *Agents of S.H.I.E.L.D.* series, now on ABC's Fall 2013 schedule and featuring (somehow) the late Phil Coulson. In May 2013, rumours that Whedon's new ventures would earn him $100,000,000 led Whedon to post a denial on Whedonesque, but a subsequent investigative piece on Forbes.com confirmed that he could well earn such an amount, though over a five-year period.

14 JOSS WHEDON, AUTEUR

In which Whedon's auteur signatures are identified, described and accounted for.

[Images of wide scope are] quasi-perceptual, in some way linked to something that really exists. But no thing is exactly like anything else, nor is it often conveniently like anything else in all the ways we might need for some particular scientific purpose. For this reason, a versatile repertoire of images is valuable for exploring the properties of the phenomenon that interest us.

(Howard Gruber, "Cognitive Psychology," 317–18)

It is a good guess that the creative individual departs from existing norms in a number of ways. This multiple deviance has as a first consequence the extreme rarity of any particular combination [...]. . a novel organization of the person's resources must emerge.

(Howard Gruber, "The Evolving System at Work," 6–7)

ooooooooo

There's a lot of very very beautiful footage from myself, the great auteur. I can actually make a very expensive location look as though we are shooting in front of a black curtain. A lot of your hack directors can't do that.

(Joss Whedon, "City of" DVD Commentary)

Allow me to begin with a compilation clip – in words (I know, I know, but this is a book after all):

- In the Sunnydale Mall, Buffy fires a borrowed rocket launcher at the uncomprehending Judge ("What's that thing do?"), blowing him into a thousand pieces (asked to pick up what's left, Cordelia protests "Our jobs suck!") ("Innocence," *BtVS* 2.14).
- In an alley in Galway, Ireland, the year 1753, a beautiful, mysterious blonde stranger, Darla (Julie Benz), asks a young Irish ne'er-do-well named Liam to close his eyes, reveals herself to be a vampire, and

chows down on her prey's neck as he falls to his knees. Slicing her own breast open with a sharp finger nail, she then forces Angel to feed on her, plunging his face into her cleavage, thereby siring, in a "whole big sucking thing," the vicious vampire Angelus. Down the alley, a carriage rumbles by on the main thoroughfare as if nothing unusual had happened (from "Becoming," Part I, 2.21).

- At The Bronze, Willow and Tara, celebrating the latter's birthday, hold each other tightly as they dance, the camera pulling back to reveal that the two witches are literally floating in the air ("Family," *BtVS*S 5.6).

- Buffy dashes through the halls of Sunnydale High School, the Mayor, now a giant snake, in close pursuit, smashing through walls, arriving finally in the library, where the ascended demon discovers a pile of explosives awaiting him. His last words before he and the whole high school are destroyed: "Well gosh!"

- Angel, still a fish out of water in his new role as head of Wolfram and Hart, picks up his phone to order "a cup of coffee or something" and experiences his usual confusion with modern technology:

> Phone Menu Voice: You have reached ritual sacrifice. For goats, press one, or say "goats."
> Angel (*hastily presses the button, pauses, tries again by pressing a different button*): Hello? … Can I get a cup of coffee? Or if there's blood – (*Angel presses the button to hang up, but he's switched to the previous line.*)
> Phone Menu Voice: To sacrifice a loved one or pet, press the pound (*Angel hastily presses the button to hang up, holding it down longer this time. He stares at the phone*). ("Conviction," *Angel* 5.1)

- Dressed in an SM outfit, uneasily, uncomfortably pretending to be her "skanky" vampire double from an alternate reality, Willow, bothered by the unusual tightness of her outfit and distracted by the sight, captured in a downward glance, of her own décolletage, exclaims "Gosh, look at those!" ("Döppelgangland" 3.16).

- Standing on a bridge at the Greater Well, its keeper Drogyn shows Angel and Spike a seemingly bottomless pit ("Angel: How far does this go down? Drogyn: All the way. All the way through the Earth") lined with the coffins of the Old Ones, from which Illyria has been disinterred. "There's a hole in the world," Spike observes. "It seems like we ought to have known" ("A Hole in the World," *Angel* 5.15).

- In a scene right out of a 1950s musical Xander and Anya perform a "retro-pastiche" number, singing and dancing, talking and not talking, of a "penis that got diseases from a Chumash tribe," the aging face of David Brinkley, and their hopes and fears for future marriage – all in their jammies ("Once More with Feeling," *BtVS* S 6.7).
- As Buffy (in a flashback voiceover) explains her plan to extend the power of the Slayer to all Potentials in the world ("From now on, every girl in the world who might be a slayer will be a slayer. Every girl who could have the power will have the power, can stand up, will stand up. Slayers every one of us. Make your choice. Are you ready to be strong?"), a montage of shots shows them coming into that power: a Japanese girl stands up at her family dinner table; an abused girl stops the blow of her abuser; a baseball player gains new confidence as she faces the next pitch ("Chosen," *BtVS* S 7.22).
- In a dream playground, oversaturated with light, Giles and Spike, dressed in matching tweed suits and vests, swing away happily trying to outdo each other, while the Watcher proclaims "Spike is like a son to me" and solicits greater exertion from his apprentice: "A watcher scoffs at gravity," he insists ("Restless," *BtVS* S 4.22).
- A ballerina (Summer Glau), under the magical thrall of an infatuated count/warlock, performs *Giselle* as she has for over a hundred years before a snoring, drooling Cordelia and an enthusiastic Gunn ("These guys are tight, and I am trippin' out") ("Waiting in the Wings," *Angel*, 3.13).
- In a long take, as she waits for the arrival of Giles, Buffy walks away from her mother's corpse on the sofa in the living room; throws up; goes to the door and looks out, her face flooded with light – sounds of life faintly audible in the distance; arrives in the kitchen where she tears off too many paper towels and returns to soak up her vomit – a kind of Rorschach image forming on the towels ("The Body," *BtVS* S 5.16).
- In a frame tale, narrator Lorne sings "Memories," the theme song from *The Way We Were*, and then regales his audience with a little story about youth, love and a spell gone awry ("Spin the Bottle," *Angel* 4.6).
- At episode's end, we see River as she carefully observes a ball (from a game of jacks) in her hand (the ball looks very like the moon we saw in the opening scene) and then throws it, the camera following it down, then through the levels of the *Serenity*, and out into space, where it finds the bounty hunter Jubal Early, now just an object in space, floating, as he has the last words: "Well, here I am" ("Objects in Space," *Firefly* 1.10).

- As a stoner and a final girl wait at the edge of the abyss, he apologizes: "I'm sorry I let you get attacked by a werewolf and then ended the world."
- A security guard finds a naked Bruce Banner, no longer Hulked-up, lying on the floor of an abandoned warehouse and has some questions for the man who fell out of the sky:

> Security Guard: Are you an alien?
> Bruce Banner: What?
> Security Guard: From outer space, an alien.
> Bruce Banner: No.
> Security Guard: Well then son, you've got a condition.

Joss Whedon, of course, wrote and or directed each of these moving, funny, beautiful, profane scenes and many more in the 30 plus episodes of television and two films he has helmed to date.

Directors are nearly always invisible in television, traditionally thought to be a writer's and producer's medium. Not surprisingly, given the anonymity of the television director, even the most die-hard fan, the most devout Whedonphile, can, in the course of 15 seasons of television (on four different series), employing scores of directors, lose track of who gets credit for a plethora of wonderful moments. We would do well to remind ourselves that it was Whedon who directed not only those "clips" I have shown above but such moments as Buffy's "I'm sixteen years old. I don't wanna die" confrontation with Giles and Angel in "Prophecy Girl" (Whedon's maiden voyage as a director); who oversaw Buffy's seductive dance with Xander in "When She Was Bad"; who helmed the wonderful irony of "Lie to Me's" ending; who guided David Boreanaz's transformation into a deliciously sadistic Angelus in "Innocence"; who was in charge when Angel hears Drusilla's confession in "Becoming," Part I, and Angel tortures Giles (and imagines using chain saws), and Spike wants to save the world in "Becoming," Part II; who orchestrated Willow's Barry White-assisted failed seduction of Oz and the snowy California Christmas morn that saves Angel in "Amends"; who staged Mayor Wilkins's unsettling confrontation with the Scoobies in the school library in "Graduation Day," Part I; who led that "empowering lemon bun" Wicca group in "Hush"; who sanctioned the longest lesbian kiss in TV history in "Restless"; who had Buffy break the ribs of her mother's corpse in "The Body"; who masterminded that confrontation between Tara's family and the Scooby Gang at the end of "Family"; who approved Giles's non-heroic murder of Ben (and Glory) in "The Gift"; who encouraged

Angel to push Russell Winters out of the window in "City of"; who found a way to rejuvenate (literally) head boy Wesley and über-bitch Cordelia in "Spin the Bottle"; who took us on a tracking shot tour of an Angel-led Wolfram and Hart in "Conviction"; who gave us the tear-jerking Fred and Wesley death scene in "Hole in the World"; who introduced us to the fascinating crew and passengers of a "Firefly" class spaceship and to the unseen but terrifying Reavers in "Serenity"; who threw Mal through a holographic saloon window in "The Train Job"; who gave us a creepy Sartrean bounty hunter in "Objects in Space"; who interviewed random Los Angelians about the existence of the "Dollhouse" in "Man on the Street" and showed us the after-effects of a "neural apocalypse" in "Epitaph One"; who choreographed Billy and Penny's poignant "My Eyes" duet in *Dr. Horrible*; who assembled the Avengers for Shawarma in an *Avengers* post-final credits sequence.

In a remarkable essay on "Television/Sound," Rick Altman demon-strates the dominance of the soundtrack in our "viewing" of television. TV only pretends to be visual. In reality, we listen to TV, we heed the voices that give us most of the medium's information, while "throwing their voice," like a ventriloquist, onto the "dummy" of the visual, which distracts only enough for us to be oblivious to the audio's manipulation. I cannot prove that Whedon has read Altman's essay, but we do know that on the DVD commentary for Season 4's "Hush," an episode which is, of course, mostly silent, Whedon – already being told by the ventriloquists at Fox that his show had "too much visual information" – confesses his desire to make the episode in order to put an end to his self-characterized drift as a TV director: afraid he was about to become a television "hack," Whedon was convinced that he was rapidly succumbing to TV's tendency to lapse into "radio with faces."[1]

I would not like the task of proving pre-"Hush" Whedon to be a hack director – "Innocence" (Whedon's own all-time favourite episode of *Buffy*[2]), "Becoming," "Amends," "Döppelgangland" are not the work of an uninspired toiler in the television mines. But what comes after "Hush" – is quite extraordinary: a celebration of television: the medium turned on its head *and* inside out, made ready for new forms of narrative experimentation, imaginative invention concocted out of boredom with the same old. "The Body," "Once More with Feeling" on *Buffy*, "Waiting in the Wings" and "Spin the Bottle" on *Angel*; "Objects in Space" on *Firefly* – these are watershed television from a new breed of television auteur. And, as we have already seen, Whedon would parlay what he had learned creating for the small screen into the stupendous big screen success of Marvel's *The Avengers*.

The American critic Andrew Sarris, who played a key role in translating the auteur theory into an American idiom, thought of auteurism's goal as the conversion of "film history into directorial autobiography." American intellectuals interested in the movies began to think and talk and understand the movies through the specially ground lenses provided by the auteur theory. "Over a group of films," Sarris insisted in what amounts to his foundational principle, "a director must exhibit certain recurrent characteristics of style, which serve as his signature. The way a film looks and moves should have some relationship to the way a director thinks and feels" (Sarris, 586). The auteur theory was ready to accept, of course, that "Just as not every conductor is a Leonard Bernstein, so not every director is an Alfred Hitchcock" (Dick, 147), and under its influence not all directors became maestros – those individuals Sarris categorized as "Pantheon Directors" – but many shed their anonymity. The works of a wide variety of directors were catalogued, in some cases exhaustively. And it was not only the movies of these directors that came in for greater scrutiny. The writings of auteurs and available interviews with them concerning their film aesthetics and methods were also put under the microscope, as Whedon's have been in these pages.

I want to offer here a retrospective overview, a roadmap, arranged alphabetically, of 20 key Whedonian signatures.[3]

The Whedonian

Atheism. In "Who Are You?" (*BtVS* 4.16), vampires take control of a church with the intention of feeding on the parishioners, and their leader takes the opportunity to pontificate:

> It's hard to believe. I've been avoiding this place for so many years, and it's nothing. It's nice! It's got the pretty windows, the pillars ... lots of folks to eat. Where's the thing I was so afraid of? You know, the Lord? He was supposed to be here. He gave us this address.

On *Firefly*, in "The Train Job" (1.3), Mal speaks with a new passenger on *The Serenity*, Shepherd Book, a clergyman:

> Mal: Well, what about you, Shepherd? How come you're flyin' with us brigands? I mean, shouldn't you be off bringing religiosity to the fuzzy-wuzzies or some such?

Book: Oh, I got heathens aplenty right here.

Mal: If I'm your mission, Shepherd, best give it up. You're welcome on my boat – God ain't.

Both of those scripts are Joss Whedon's.

Whedon does confess to relying on the iconography of the Judeo-Christian tradition: "That's what I was raised with. As much as I learned Greek myths and as much as I read Marvel Comics and watched *The Prisoner*, I grew up around Christianity and Judaism and those are the prevalent myths and mythic structures of my brain" (*JWC* 76).

Asked point-blank (*JWC* 39) if he believes in God, Whedon answers unequivocally: "Not a jot," and he tells Felicity Nussbuam on the set of *Firefly*, "I'm a very hard-line, angry atheist [...]. Yet I am fascinated by the concept of devotion" (*Joss Whedon Conversations* 68).[4]

Bringing the Funny. The term "the funny" appears three times in *Buffy*, twice in Whedon's own scripts. In "Becoming," Part 1 we find Buffy saying "Relax, Will, I was making with *the funny*"; and Giles uses the phrasing in "Amends" in an exchange with Angel (who in the previous season had killed his love Jenny Callendar and later tortured him): Angel: "I need your help." Giles: "And *the funny* keeps on coming."[5] In "slayer speak," as Michael Adams, notes, it serves as a synonym for "humor" and stands as one of the prime examples of the tendency of adjectives to become nouns in the Whedonverses (33–4, 180). Whedon brings the self-deprecating, ironic, absurd, patalogical, tautological, tongue-in-cheek, disarming, unconventional, understated, "punderful," new-twist-on-old-clichés, macabre, wicked, mock-literal, parodic, silly funny in almost all his writing.

In "The Harvest" (1.2), Cordelia explains why "Senior boys are the only way to go."

> Guys from our grade, forget about it, they're children [...]. But senior boys, hmm, they have mystery. They have ... what's the word I'm searching for? Cars! I just am not the type to settle. Y'know? It's like when I go shopping. I have to have the most expensive thing. Not because it's expensive, but because it costs more.

In "Prophecy Girl" (1.12), the Master is shocked to see Buffy, whom he has just murdered. To his "You're dead," the Slayer replies: "I may be dead, but I'm still pretty. Which is more than I can say for you." The Master still refuses to accept reality:

Master: You were destined to die! It was written!
Buffy: What can I say? I flunked the written.

In "When She Was Bad" (2.1), the principal of Sunnydale High tells Giles of his disgust at the Fall return of the student body:

Snyder: I mean, it's incredible. One day the campus is completely bare. Empty. The next, there are children everywhere. Like locusts. Crawling around, mindlessly bent on feeding and mating. Destroying everything in sight in their relentless, pointless desire to exist.
Giles: I do enjoy these pep talks. Have you ever considered, given your abhorrence of children, school principal was not, perhaps, your true vocation?

In "Lie to Me" (2.7), Buffy tries to hide her secret identity from old boyfriend Ford after killing a vampire in an alley.

Buffy: Um… uh, there was a, a cat. A cat here, and, um, then there was a-another cat … and they fought. The cats. And … then they left.
Ford: Oh. I thought you were just slaying a vampire.
Buffy: What? Whating a what?

In "Innocence" (2.14), Willow fulminates about Xander's betrayal after she has caught him kissing Cordelia:

Willow: I knew it! I knew it! Well, not "knew it" in the sense of having the slightest idea, but I knew there was something I didn't know. You two were fighting way too much. It's not natural!
Xander: I know it's weird …
Willow: Weird? It's against all laws of God and Man! It's (*disgusted*) Cordelia! Remember? The, the 'We Hate Cordelia' club, of which you are the treasurer.

In "Döppelgangland" (3.16), Anya laments her sorry state to D'Hoffryn now that she is no longer a vengeance demon:

For a thousand years I wielded the powers of The Wish. I brought ruin to the heads of unfaithful men. I brought forth destruction and chaos for the pleasure of the lower beings. I was feared and worshipped across the mortal globe. (*disgustedly*) And now I'm stuck at Sunnydale High. (*despondently*) Mortal. Child. And I'm flunking math.

Later in the same episode a frustrated, angry Anya bemoans Willow's failed attempt, through witchcraft, to find her necklace, and Willow has a suggestion: "Well, did you try looking inside the sofa in Hell?"

In "Graduation Day, Part I" (3.21), Mayor Wilkins prepares for his ascension by ingesting the loathsome Spiders of Gavrock and offers a review of the experience, and an additional bonus side-effect, for his vampire body guards:

> Mmm. My god, what a feeling. The power of these creatures. It suffuses my being. I can feel the changes begin. My organs are shifting, changing, making ready for the Ascension. Plus these babies are high in fiber. And what's the fun in becoming an immortal demon if you're not regular, am I right?

When interrupted, unannounced, by a vampire bringing news of Faith's battle with Buffy, he is irate at the lack of decorum: "We don't knock during dark rituals?"

In "The Freshman" (4.1), Willow rejects the idea, suggested by Buffy's (demonic) roommate that the Slayer has run away:

> Buffy wouldn't just take off, th-that's just not in her nature. Except for that one time she disappeared for several months and changed her name, but there were circumstances then. There's no circumstances.

In "Restless" (4.22), Xander explains his philosophy of life with the help of Buffy (playing in a sandbox) and Giles and Spike (on playground swings):

> Xander: (*in playground*) You gotta have something. (*Looks at Buffy*) Gotta be with movin' forward.
> Buffy: (*like a proud little kid*) Like a shark.
> Xander: Like a shark with feet and … much less fins.
> Spike: (*like a proud little kid*) And on land!
> Giles: Very good!

In "Lessons" (7.1) Giles inspires Willow with wonder at his botanical knowledge after he identifies the "flora kua alaya" Willow has just summoned through the earth from Paraguay:

Willow: Is there anything you don't know everything about?
Giles: Synchronized swimming. Complete mystery to me.

In "Chosen" (7.22), Buffy reports on her final battle with Caleb, who had in an earlier episode blinded Xander's left eye:

Willow: Did you find out anything about the scythe?
Buffy: It slices, dices, and makes julienne preacher.
Giles: Caleb?
Buffy: I cut him in half.
Willow: All right!
Xander: Hey, party in my eye socket and everyone's invited. (*everyone stares at Xander*) Sometimes I shouldn't say words.

Whedon's movie work brings the funny as well, often without the need for comic dialogue. Take, for example, the Betting Board (Table 6) in *The Cabin in the Woods*, listing all the possible monsters on which Sitterson and Hadley's colleagues can make a wager:

Table 6: The Betting Board in *The Cabin in the Woods*

Werewolf	The Scarecrow Folk
Alien Beast	Snowman
Mutants	Dragonbat
Wraiths	Vampires
Zombies	Dismemberment Goblins
Reptilius	Sugarplum Fairy
Clowns	Merman
Witches	The Reanimated
Sexy Witches	Unicorn
Demons	Huron
Hell Lord	Ruatch/Wendigo/Yeti
Angry Molesting Tree	Dolls
Giant Snake	The Doctors
Deadites	The Redneck Torture Family
Kevin	Jack O'Lantern
Mummy	Giant
The Bride	Twins

This should make for a terrifying visual, and in a sense, it does, but the horror is undercut by such odd inclusions as "Angry Molesting Tree," "Unicorn," "Sugarplum Fairy" and "Kevin."

The Avengers, too, offers many a non-verbal laugh. Hulk's previously mentioned response to Loki's arrogant "I am a God! I am not going to be bullied by a ..." rant, for example, or Agent Coulson's impatient, annoyed waiting on the phone while Black Widow extracts herself from her tied-to-a-chair interrogation.

Whedon's signature funny, we should note, is ever-present in other venues than his television and movie work. It can be found on numerous occasions in most Whedon interviews, in his DVD commentaries, in his prose writing. In her talk at the third *Slayage* conference, Jeanine Basinger observed that Whedon treats interviews as narratives – as further opportunities to tell stories. The same might be said for all of Whedon's modes of expression: very funny stories are Whedon's *modus operandi*.

The Big Finish. Whedon has demonstrated a real flare for the Big Finish. Since *Buffy* and *Angel* seasons customarily culminated in major battles, and since he often directed season finales, Whedon would have lots of practice: he was the maestro for the final showdown with The Master in "Prophecy Girl," for the defeat of Angelus and Acathla in "Becoming," Part II, for the First Battle of Sunnydale High in "Graduation Day," Part II. He would command the fatal-to-Buffy vanquishing of Glory and saving of Dawn in "The Gift"; the CGI-enhanced Second Battle of Sunnydale High in "Chosen." Television does not really offer a conducive canvas nor the necessary budget for a director to work on such a scale, and yet Whedon has managed again and again to pull off such scenes memorably. Not surprisingly, his big screen work likewise features big finishes: the "intimate epic" *Serenity*'s final showdowns – Mal against the Operative; the crew, and their secret weapon River, against the Reavers (a mismatch, as it turns out); the massive Battle of New York at the end of *The Avengers* (a conflict estimated by a disaster expert to have caused $160,000,000,000 worth of "real world" damage [Zakarin, *"Avengers* Damage"]).

Cross-Cutting. From his debut as a director in "Prophecy Girl," which ends with the Hellmouth opening in the SHS library as Buffy comes to the rescue, Whedon shows himself adept at cross-cutting, a staple of movie narrative since *The Great Train Robbery* (Edwin S. Porter, 1903). As Willow works the re-ensoulment spell, Buffy tries to prevent Angelus from sucking the world into hell, literally (in "Becoming," Part II). In "Hush," Willow and Tara work their first spell together, while Buffy and Riley battle the Gentlemen and their footmen. All parties converge on The Bronze to the tune of "Walk Through the Fire" in "Once More with Feeling." In "Waiting in the Wings," Angel finds a way to free the Count's hold on the ballerina, while Wesley, Gunn and Cordy do battle with the rapidly multiplying Tragedy/Comedy henchmen. In "A

Hole in the World," Angel and Spike jet to the Deeper Well, hoping to save Fred, while Wesley spends his final moments with the woman whose body Illyria will steal by the end of the episode. The entire crew of *The Serenity* works together to escape from the pursuing Reavers in "Serenity," Part II.

Dream Sequences. Whedon has shown a special flare for directing dream scenes: the dream funeral in which Buffy discerns Jenny Calendar's secret identity in "Innocence"; Angel's many dream flashbacks (some shared with Buffy) in "Amends"; the Faith's apartment "human weakness" dream in "Graduation Day," Part II; the four astonishing dream sequences in "Restless"; Darla and Angel's erotic oneirics in "Untouched"; River's dream/nightmare at the beginning of *Serenity*. Whedon's approach to dreams is not to treat them, in the style of, say, David Lynch in *Twin Peaks*, as excursions into the fantastic. His dreams are magically real, full of the stuff of mundane reality, including all the cheese. Not surprisingly, Cynthia Burkhead's book *Dreams in American Television Narratives: From Buffy to Dallas*, prominently features Whedon's dreamwork.

Emotional Realism. As Rhonda Wilcox and I showed in *Fighting the Forces*, "emotional realism" has always been the cornerstone of Whedon's work:

> Everything is grounded in the audience's identification with what they are going through. Whedon tells [David] Bianculli about appearing in a chatroom after "Innocence" (2.14), an episode in which Angel breaks the curse which had given him a soul by having sex with Buffy, becoming again the fiendishly evil Angelus. When a young woman responded on line by confessing to Whedon that "this exact same thing happened to me," Whedon explains, he knew he was accomplishing precisely what he had hoped for with the series.
>
> (xxiv)

For all his interest in things fantastic, from *Roseanne* to *Firefly* and *Serenity* and Marvel's, "ultimately, the thing that interests [Whedon] the most is people and what they're going through" (*JWC* 4).

Mere coolness is not an acceptable *raison d'être* in the Whedonverses:

> Everything that we pitch, everything that we put out there, whether or not it works, is based on the idea of: The audience has been through this. A normal girl goes through this. A normal guy deals with this.

You know, it's issues of sexuality, popularity, jobs. Whatever it is, it's got to be based in realism. We can't just say, you know, "The warship's come and, you know, they transmogrify, the – blah, blah, blah." We can't do that. We can go to some pretty strange places, but at the start, we always have to be about, "How does the audience relate to having done this themselves?" (*JWC* 8)

On the *A&E Biography* entry on *Buffy* we find Whedon hyperbolically acknowledging: "I don't know from science. I never took any science. I don't know how things work. I can barely tie my shoes.[6] But I understand emotions."

Family. As Jes Battis has shown, at the heart of all Joss Whedon's shows are "chosen families." "Whether they are at the forefront of a trend to replace the biological family on television with a radical substitute, or simply fantastic imaginings of families that could be," the families of the Whedonverses offer us "systems of kinship" that are "complex, enduring and full of hope, [...] new constellations of belonging, and new ways of living in the world" (165).

"I'm very much more interested in the created family than I am in actual families," Whedon would tell the *New York Times*. Driven in part by narrative practicality,[7] the signature Whedonian depiction of "the created family as being more lasting and more loving" derived as well from "telling stories about family that often hit on the traditional patriarchy as being kind of lame-o" (*New York Times*). "[A]ctual families don't get along [...]," Whedon confides to Ervin-Gore. "It's always the ones you build yourself that work the best, when people build bonds together because they actually need and love each other." As Mal tells the cynical Saffron in "Our Mrs. Reynolds" in *Firefly*, espousing the Whedonian family values in the show's signature language: "I got people with me, people who trust each other, who do for each other and ain't always looking for the advantage."

Female Empowerment. In talking about his still-in-development film project *Goners*, a laughing Whedon confesses to Tasha Robinson that "there may be some female empowerment in it at some point" (*Joss Whedon: Conversation*, 149). As he told MSN in 2003,

I will say that when I think about new series or new films, I always come to the idea of the heroic rite of passage for the adolescent female as a reoccurring theme. And, the hilarious thing about *Firefly* was I thought it was not going to be that, I'm done with that ... and then

River came along and turned into a superhero. [*Laughs*] I guess it's just a tic with me.[8]

Whedon's Equality Now speech is his fullest explanation of his signature obsession with empowered women. With disarming irony, he offers an ever-expanding response ("when you're asked something 500 times, you really start to think about the answer") to the ad-nauseam press junket query: "why do you always write these strong women characters?": because of his "extraordinary, inspirational, tough, cool, sexy, funny" mother and "smarter," "stronger" and "occasionally taller" wife; because of his father and stepfather, "who understood that recognizing somebody else's power does not diminish your own"; because "these stories give people strength" – "not just women; it's men"; because "they're hot." Ultimately, the question is misdirected – "why aren't you asking a hundred other guys why they don't write strong women characters?" – and ridiculous:

> Because equality is not a concept. It's not something we should be striving for. It's a necessity. Equality is like gravity. We need it to stand on this earth as men and women. And the misogyny that is in every culture is not a true part of the human condition. It is life out of balance, and that imbalance is sucking something out of the soul of every man and woman who is confronted with it.

Fight Scenes. In a deliciously self-referential moment in "Lessons" (*BtVS*S 7.1 – written by Joss Whedon) Buffy trains little sister Dawn by practising on an about-to-be-reborn vampire. But Dawn has been watching the show in which she is a character and comments metatextually: "But he's new. He doesn't know his strength. H-he might not know all those fancy martial arts skills they inevitably seem to pick up."

Fight scenes are of course a staple of the Whedonverses, in which the white hats must constantly engage in hand-to-hand (or sword-to-sword, axe-to-axe) battles with vampires, demons, gods, operatives, or Reavers. Many of the best of them were directed by Whedon. That showdown at the end of "When She Was Bad," when Buffy kills the remaining members of the order of Aurelius and "grind[s her] enemies into talcum powder with a sledgehammer"; the knock-down and drag out – and kick to the groin – between Buffy and Angelus in "Innocence"; the sword fight between the same parties at the end of "Becoming," Part II; the battle to the death between Buffy and Faith in "Graduation Day," Part I; the pre-body-switch battle in the church between Faith-in-Buffy and Buffy-in-Faith at the end of "Who Are You"; Buffy's final "split" with Caleb in

"Chosen" – all were directed by Whedon with verve and alacrity; as were Angel's rumble with vampires in an alley, ending in a double-staking, in "City of" (*Angel* 1.1), River's martial arts exhibition in The Maidenhead and last stand against the Reavers in *Serenity*; Thor versus Iron Man versus Captain America and Thor versus The Hulk on the Helicarrier in *The Avengers*.

Genre-Hybridity (Turning on a Dime). Whedon had his work on *Astonishing X-Men* in mind when he told *Marvel Spotlight* "Being able to turn on a dime – that's sort of the benchmark of everything that I do; the funny in the middle of the scary, the happy in the middle of the sad, etc. [...]. I definitely like a lot of humor and a lot of humanity in the middle of dire peril. Those are the two things that interest me; jokes and dire peril."

In his conversation with James Longworth (*JWC* 149), he offers a further explanation of this signature predilection. Humour, he is convinced "hit[s] ten times as hard [...] in the middle of something dramatic. That to me is the essence of what I'm interested in. It's something you see in the Hong Kong films that [Quentin] Tarantino has followed. You don't *know* what kind of scene you're in. Something can be very funny and then suddenly very terrifying – very exciting, and suddenly very ridiculous [...]. Ultimately, while humor is definitely the voice that I'm the most comfortable with, drama is the structure that will always attract me."

One of the reasons the first film made from a Joss Whedon screenplay failed was because *Buffy the Vampire Slayer*'s director Fran Rubel Kuzui did not have the requisite sensibility to turn on a dime or navigate its genre hybridity (as media scholars now call it). (For more on *BtVS* the movie, see Chapter 5.) Whedon was thinking of the television version when he described the recombinant nature of what he sought to do:

We wanted to make that sort of short-attention-span, *The Simpsons* [FOX, 1989–], cull-from-every-genre all the time thing. You know, if we take this moment from *Nosferatu* [F.W. Murnau, 1922], and this moment from *Pretty in Pink* [Howard Deutch, 1986], that'll make this possible. A little *Jane Eyre* [Robert Stevenson, 1944] in there, and then a little *Lethal Weapon 4* [Richard Donner, 1998]. Not *3* [Richard Donner, 1992], but *4*. And I think this'll work. (*JWC* 32)

Spoken like a true film studies auteur.

Serenity, Whedon recognized (*Serenity* 25), was alternately romantic comedy (in the Mal/Inara scenes), zombie film (in the Reavers sequences), and siege movie-in-the-style-of-*Zulu* (Cy Endfield, 1963) (in the final sequence at Mr. Universe's), while still "sci-fi jollies" without "a Theremin playing" (*JWC* 115). Well aware of his multi-genre proclivity, Whedon was conscious too that it can be a liability: "Whenever I write anything, I want to stuff every genre in that I possibly can. And then people are like, 'Well, we don't know how to market that, and if we don't know how to market it [...]' [*Whispers.*] 'We're not going to make it' [...]" (*JWC* 149).

Still, Whedon recognizes genre's perks. For one thing, as he insists, "Genre helps me with structure, and structure helps me get through the day" (*JWC* 113), and without the existence of genres and their codes, he would have nothing to play off against: Angel's misguided leap into the driver's seat of the wrong convertible in the noirish "City of" (Angel 1.1 – co-written and directed by Whedon) could hardly be as funny to anyone who had never seen a Western (DVD commentary). *The Cabin in the Woods* and Marvel's *The Avengers* screen more richly for spectators familiar with (respectively) the horror and war film genres.

Giving the Devil His Due. "[W]hat some people consider 'sin,'" Whedon observes in the Serenity*: The Official Visual Companion* interview, "I consider human characteristics" (20).

David Simon, the prime mover behind HBO's brilliant *The Wire* (2002–8), announces in an official tie-in book that he has had it with simplistic distinctions between good guys and bad guys and gives us a big-city police drama that resolutely refuses to make them. Also on HBO David Milch's Western *Deadwood* likewise embraces "evil" men – especially its unforgettable Al Swearengen – in its dedication to (in the words of James McElroy) "demythologize an era and build a new myth from the gutter to the stars," "to embrace bad men and the price they paid to secretly define their time" (quoted in Lavery, ed., *Reading* Deadwood, 157). On Showtime *Dexter* offers us a new kind of hero, a Miami serial killer who slaughters only the truly evil. In *Battlestar Galactica* Ronald D. Moore made his villains, the speciecidal, monotheistically religious Cylons, just as interesting as the human characters.

Angelus, Caleb, D'Hoffryn, Dark Willow, Drusilla, Jubal Early, The First, The Gentlemen, Glory, Hamilton, Loki, The Master, The Mayor, Lindsay McDonald, Leilah Morgan, Niska, The Operative, Ethan Rayne, Saffron, Spike, Sweet, Mr. Trick, The Troika, Vamp Willow – these are all memorable Whedonian villains. "I can't write a character if I don't at some level understand where they're coming from and how they feel about the world [...]," Whedon has explained. "[I]f you don't love a character," Whedon is certain, "then you have no business writing them." And that includes bad guys: "I hate stock villains" (ET Online).

Whedon has shown an uncanny and disconcerting (as he admits) ability to ventriloquize his evil characters. First discovered when he wrote the "Innocence" scene in which Angelus is sexually cruel to Buffy after making love for the first time, Whedon would continue to demonstrate a real skill as the devil's mouthpiece.

Intertextuality. *Buffy the Vampire Slayer* certainly didn't invent the television use of clever references to other works of high and popular culture. *The Simpsons* had been doing it, as had others, since 1989, and the tendency to incorporate other "texts" into one's own had long been established as a distinguishing characteristic of the postmodern. *Buffy's* range – with allusions to and evocations of everything from *Apocalypse Now* to Bobba Fett, Buster Keaton, *Oedipus Rex,* Yoko Ono, Pink Floyd, *The Seventh Seal,* scrubbing bubbles, M. Night Shyamalan, *Thelma and Louise, Waiting for Godot, Walker, Texas Ranger,* Keith Olbermann, *Rescue Dawn* – was truly astonishing and became a Whedonian trademark of "Mr. Pop Culture Reference[s]" ("Pop Culture Q & A") television. *Angel* was less so, and *Firefly* and *Serenity,* set in another 'verse centuries in the future, were, of necessity and on purpose, not intertextual at all.

Killing Characters. In the original screenplay of *Speed,* an obnoxious lawyer character was summarily killed. When brought in as a script doctor on the project (see Chapter 6), Whedon would make the character more likeable, to the consternation of the studio: "Well, now we can't kill him," they complained. Whedon, of course, felt very differently: "Well, now you should [kill him] because now people will actually care when he dies." "[N]obody wants to kill a good guy," Whedon observes. "[I]t makes them twitchy, particularly on a series" (Bianculli).

Whedon would continue to kill and kill again ("Guns Don't Kill People. Joss Whedon […]"): Jenny Callendar, Joyce Summers, Buffy herself, Tara, Jonathan, Anya and Spike on *Buffy*; Doyle, Darla, Holtz, Leilah, Cordelia, Fred, Lindsay and Wesley on Angel; Wash and Book in *Serenity,* Penny on *Dr. Horrible,* Paul Ballard in *Dollhouse,* Giles in *Buffy* Season 8, everybody in *The Cabin in the Woods,* Agent Coulson in *The Avengers.* Not all these characters were heroes, of course, but we cared deeply when they died their signature deaths.

Language. That Whedon's work has inspired an Oxford University Press book on *Buffy's* language by a prominent lexicographer – Michael Adams's *Slayer Slang: A* Buffy the Vampire Slayer *Lexicon* (2003) – is a powerful testimony to its importance. In a preface to that book, Whedon collaborator, and former linguistics major, Jane Espenson tells us that Whedon's "idiolect"[9] is "an amplified version of his own speech. And it doesn't end with the fictional characters; the *Buffy* writers inevitably end up not only writing like Joss, but talking like him as well" (ix).

Though not, perhaps, as rich in language as *Buffy*, *Angel* would continue to basically speak Buffyspeak. *Firefly* and *Serenity*, however, would forge yet another Whedonian way of speaking. The "patois" (as Whedon accurately terms it[10]) spoken by the crew of the *Serenity* and others in the series and the movie is an amalgam of classic-Western-speech, a touch of Shakespeare, Irish, Victorian literature (Whedon has identified Dickens as a favourite writer), Chinese, of course, and, most surprisingly, Pennsylvania Dutch (Whedon acknowledges the strong influence of a book called *Tillie: A Mennonite Maid* [*Serenity* 8–10]).

Whedonian infatuation with language has an interesting, perhaps unexpected origin, as Whedon would explain to the *Sondheim Review*: "Growing up on show tunes [...] you become attuned to the rhythms of human speech. My writing isn't metric, but it is musical" (Schiff).

Losers. Buffy, Joyce Millman observed in *Salon* when the series was still on the air, "is an ode to misfits, a healing vision of the weird, the different and the marginalized finding their place in the world and, ultimately, saving it" (Millman, "The Death of Buffy's Mom"). As we have seen, Whedon himself once referred to his masterpiece as "a show by losers for losers" (quoted at http://www.crosswinds.net/~tlbin/cast/joss.html), a series which "reflect[ed] the imagination of the 'loser,' much like myself" (Ervin-Gore).

When Buffy is given the "Class Protector" award by her fellow seniors (*BtVS* "The Prom" 3.20), Jonathan Levinson, a loser himself, recalls the outsider status of the recipient (and by extension the entire Scooby Gang) in the Sunnydale social sphere (the words are not his): "We're not good friends. Most of us never found the time to get to know you, but that doesn't mean we haven't noticed [...]. But, whenever there was a problem or something creepy happened, you seemed to show up and stop it. Most of the people here have been saved by you, or helped by you at one time or another." The team at Angel Investigations, with its errant business cards and bad phone-answering technique, likewise seemed a low status operation. Only after AI defeats Jasmine, thereby ironically preventing world peace, does W&H proclaim them winners and offer them the Los Angeles office as a reward. The crew of the *Serenity*, captained by a defeated warrior in the struggle for independence, must likewise fly below the radar (literally) and exists outside normal society on the frontier of the cosmos, though these losers do succeed in delivering a mighty blow to the Alliance. *Dr. Horrible's* Billy aspires to be, and ironically succeeds in becoming, a super villain, but until then is in real life a paralysingly shy young man still "a few weeks away from a real, audible, connection" with the girl of his dreams.

Metaphor. Dr. Horrible explains to his beloved Penny (once they do connect) his views on the homeless: "they're a symptom. You're treating a symptom and the disease rages on, consumes the human race. The fish rots from the head as they say. So my thinking is why not cut off the head [...]." Penny, an advocate for the homeless, is shocked: "Of the human race?" she asks. "It's not a perfect metaphor," the Doctor responds. Whedon's metaphors more often do not go awry. "She's tore up plenty, but she'll fly true," Zoë tells Mal in the final sequence of *Serenity*. In the official companion book Whedon recalls Gina Torres's question about the "obvious" meaning of the line and the complete shock of Nathan Fillion (Mal) at the realization that its feminine pronoun referred to both the about-to-launch spaceship and the still grieving widow (Zoë's husband Wash [Alan Tudyk] had been killed in the successful struggle to broadcast the news of what happened on Miranda [*Serenity* 37].) Whedon seems to admit that he himself might not have realized the metaphorical meaning.

In the Whedonverses high school is a metaphorical hell. A girl whom nobody sees becomes literally a girl nobody sees. Lesbianism plays a metaphorical role – as witchcraft – before it arrives in the flesh. Angel is an alcoholic, only one "drink" away from falling off the wagon. Willow's abuse of magic becomes (heavy-handedly) a kind of drug addiction. The monk who explains Dawn's real nature just before he dies ("No Place Like Home," *BtVS* 5.5) announces with his almost last breath: "My journey's done, I think," to which the Slayer replies: "Don't get *metaphory* on me. We're going." The Whedonian is metaphory to the hilt.

The Naughty. In "Restless" (written and directed by Joss Whedon), as Buffy and Willow crawl through the curtains of the latter's dreamspace, the Slayer scolds her friend: "Well, you must have *done* something." Willow will have none of such an accusation: "No. I never do anything. I'm very seldom naughty."

In Australia, where I journeyed on a *Buffy* speaking tour in the summer of 2003, *Buffy the Vampire Slayer* aired at 10.30 at night. David Franken, the television executive who booked *BtVS* down under, knew from the moment he saw the pilot that it was an adult show, not meant for the children. In the USA, ever-confused on what constitutes mature viewing, the WB warned that its then signature show *might not* be suitable for younger viewers. *Buffy was* an adult show. Supremely intelligent, rife with allusion, "punderful," poignant, exciting, complex. Despite Willow's dream insistence to *Buffy* in "Restless," true for herself of course, although there was that time she tried to seduce Oz with the aid of Barry White, and, of course she nearly destroyed the world and would have except for a memory of broken yellow crayons ..., *Buffy the Vampire Slayer* was, in fact quite naughty, indeed all of Whedon's work, is quite wicked in fact.[11]

In "Amends" (3.10), Buffy finds her mother putting up the family Christmas tree. When Joyce asks for quite natural decorating advice – "So, angel's on top again?" – Buffy, her mind on a different kind of Angel, is startled by the question and suggests going with a star instead.

In "The Freshman" (4.1), the first episode of *Buffy's* college years, Willow enthuses about the academic possibilities of university life:

It's just in High School, knowledge was pretty much frowned upon. You really had to work to learn anything. But here, the energy, the collective intelligence, it's like this force, this penetrating force, and I can just feel my mind opening up – you know? – and letting this place thrust into and spurt knowledge into ... that sentence ended up in a different place than it started out in.

In Season 4's Emmy-nominated "Hush" (4.10), Xander mistakes Buffy's pantomimed staking of The Gentlemen until she adds an actual stake to the demonstration. Later, Anya shows her appreciation for Xander's "bravery" against Spike by inserting her right index finger in and out of the circle formed by her left thumb and index finger.

In "Who Are You" (4.16), Faith (in Buffy's body) deduces, in conversation with Tara, that Willow is now gay,

So Willow's not driving stick anymore. Who would have thought? I guess you never really know someone until you've been inside their skin.[12]

In the same episode, Faith-in-Buffy encounters the Vampire Spike, whom she has never met, who picks a verbal fight with his nemesis – and loses badly:

Spike: You know why I really hate you, Summers?
Faith: (*cheerfully*) 'Cause I'm a stuck-up tight-ass with no sense of fun?
Spike: Well ... Yeah, that covers a lot of it.
Faith: 'Cause I could do anything I want, and instead I choose to pout

and whine and feel the burden of Slayerness? I mean, I could be rich. I could be famous. I could have anything. Anyone. Even you, Spike. I could ride you at a gallop until your legs buckled and your eyes rolled up. I've got muscles you've never even dreamed of. I could squeeze you until you pop like warm champagne and you'd beg me to hurt you just a little bit more. And you know why I don't? Because it's wrong.

In the same season's "Restless" (4.22), Xander and Oz talk of their witch friend and her new love Tara:

Xander: So whatcha been doin'? Doing spells? (*to Oz*) She does spells with Tara.
Oz: Yeah, I heard about that.
Willow: (*anxious*) I'm gonna be late. (*walks off*)
Xander: Sometimes I think about two women doing a spell … and then I do a spell by myself. (*Oz looks at him. Xander looks at Oz, then quickly away.*)

In "Family" (5.6) Spike baits the Slayer to "Come and get it," and she responds "I'm coming right now" – all of which turns out to be the vampire's fantasizing while he has sex with Harmony.

In "The Gift" (5.22), Spike answers Xander's question why dark rituals always involve blood:

'Cause it's always gotta be blood. Blood is life, lackbrain. Why do you think we eat it? It's what keeps you going, makes you warm, *makes you hard*, makes you other than dead.

In the famous musical episode of *Buffy*, Season 6's "Once More with Feeling" (6.7), Tara levitates from her bed in response to Willow's out-of-frame ministrations as she sings "You make me complete. You make me com…"

In the teaser of "Chosen" (7.22), the final, 144th episode of *Buffy*, the Slayer and Caleb, The First's chief minion, do battle, a clash continued from "End of Days" the previous week. Facing Buffy as she wields her magic scythe, he taunts her that "she doesn't have the …" to battle him (the last word inaudible/censored). She responds by slicing him in two – from the groin up. "Who does these days," she quips in classic Slayer style, referring, of course, to the "balls" Caleb had been unable to pronounce. "I've always been amazed with how Buffy fought," Xander observes in "Anne" (3.1), "but … in a way, I feel like we took her punning for granted."

Moments later in "Chosen," Buffy tries to explain to Angel her growth – and her unfinishedness – with a baking metaphor:

> Because – OK, I'm cookie dough. I'm not done baking. I'm not finished becoming whoever the hell it is I'm gonna turn out to be. I make it through this, and the next thing, and the next thing, and maybe one day I turn around and realize I'm ready. I'm cookies. And then, you know, if I want someone to eat – (*eyes go wide as she catches herself*) or enjoy warm, delicious cookie me, then … that's fine. That'll be then. When I'm done.

In the same episode, Willow worries aloud about the "Beaucoup d'mojo" she is being asked to perform (transferring the power of the Slayer to all potential slayers everywhere), and 16-year-old Dawn is a bit slow to fathom her metaphor:

> Willow: Whoa, hey! Not to poop on the party here but I'm the guy who's going to have to pull this thing off …. This goes beyond anything I've ever done. It's a total loss of control and not in a nice, wholesome, "my girlfriend has a pierced tongue" kind of way.
> Buffy: I wouldn't ask if I didn't think you could do it.
> Willow: I'm not sure that I'm stable enough ….
> Dawn: (*realizes*) Oh! Pierced tongue!

In the first episode of *Angel* ("City of," 1.1), Doyle refers to newly employed Cordelia as a "stiffener."

In "Waiting in the Wings," Cordelia and Angel, under the spell of the magic theatre, kiss and almost make love. When Cordelia comments that "it's a good thing it wears off right away," Angel readily agrees, while at the same time removing his tux jacket and strategically placing it over his genitals.

In "Spin the Bottle," a Season 4 episode of *Angel* (4.6) in which Lorne's magic spell goes awry and causes all the members of Angel Investigations to revert to their teen selves, we find this exchange between Cordelia and Wesley as he introduces himself:

> Wesley: It's Wesley, thank you. Wyndham-Pryce. (*grabs his lapels, puffs up with pride*) I am from the Watcher's Academy in southern Hampshire. In fact, I happen to be head boy.

Cordelia: Gee, I wonder how you earned that nickname.
Wesley: A lot of effort, I don't mind saying.

Later in the same episode, wooden stakes, fitted before Wesley and the others lose their memory, inadvertently, embarrassingly erupt from his sleeves.

In "Serenity," *Firefly's* intended first episode, Jayne, after being castigated by Mal for his remark that Kaylee wishes Simon was a gynaecologist, responds "Just because Kaylee gets herself all lubed up over ..." before the Captain silences him and banishes him from the table.

In "Our Mrs. Reynolds," after Jayne seeks to trade Vera, his prized weapon, for Mal's unsought "bride" Saffron, the Captain rejects his offer and sends him to his room with "Go play with your rainstick." Moments later Mal tells "a naked and all articulate" Saffron that "it's been a while ... a long damn while since anybody but me took a hold a' my plow."

In *Serenity*, Kaylee utters a similar complaint – that it has been a year since she has had anything "twixt her nethers weren't run on batteries."

In *Dr. Horrible's Sing-Along Blog*, Captain Hammer sings of his "love" for new girlfriend Penny:

> This is so nice
> I just might sleep with the same girl twice
> They say it's better the second time
> They say you get to do the weird stuff

From left of the frame his stalkerish fans, two females, one male, pop in to announce, hopefully, "We'd do the weird stuff."

A viewer with a dirty mind might be tempted to find something naughty in these scenes. Every one of them was written and directed by the very often naughty Joss Whedon.

One-ers. In a comprehensive interview in *The* Serenity *Official Visual Companion*, Whedon speaks of the first scene onboard the spaceship, which introduces major cast members in a "one-er," a continuous, no-cuts tracking shot:

> I deliberately went through every room in the ship and met everybody in one shot not to show-off camerawork [...] but because what I wanted was a sense of community and continuity and a sense of safety, and to give things not a theatrical but kind of a humanistic feel. (*Serenity* 27)

Such a complex shot, as he goes on to explain, is not as impossible-to-pull-off as it may seem: for when the director is the writer, each line of dialogue, each movement of the camera and all the blocking can be built in from inception.

Whedon makes the same point with regard to his television one-ers – that astonishing shot at the beginning of "Conviction" (*Angel* 5.1), for example, in which Whedon takes the viewer on a guided tour of the new Wolfram and Hart set, introducing/reintroducing each key character, all the while shooting only the right side of Alexis Denisof's (Wesley's) face[13] – a mere 27 takes were required to complete it! A TV director, Whedon explains, who is also a showrunner need not seek major coverage of each and every scene; he knows the shape and purpose of his one-ers and need not fear that, in post-production, the editor will be stuck without the necessary close-ups to assemble a scene.

One of Whedon's directorial signatures, one-ers simply reflect his desire to "use the frame for as long as it can be used" (DVD Commentary to "Innocence"). From "Prophecy Girl" on, long takes are a Whedon staple. I have already commented on the one-er that follows Xander simultaneously through his dreamscape and the Buffy set in "Restless." In "The Body," "Once More with Feeling," "Chosen," on *Angel* and on *Firefly*, Whedon continues to favour the long take. One shot in "The Body," stretching from Buffy's attempted CPR of her mother to a shot of a hyper-real telephone as she prepares to call Giles, lasts three minutes and twenty-seven seconds. The brilliant "Objects in Space" begins with a one-er following River's psychic meander through *Serenity* and ends with a *tour de force* long take that reveals the *Serenity's* crew for the first time as one, united. (Like the shot that follows Xander in "Restless," Whedon's "tenth character" – aka "my spaceship" – one-ers are likewise, tours of the set. [See Wilcox and Cochran 7].)

One-ers also appeal to Whedon's love of a moving camera. As he says in one of his enthralling pre-production "Mee-mos" for *Serenity* ("Frames/Lens/Perspective"), "A master that works for a long while – in different ways – is way more interesting to me than lots of close-ups. *I want everything in motion*, the *Serenity* crew, the camera, the story – so when it stops – say, to look out at Inara overlooking the mountains – we feel the stillness, we drink it" (*Serenity* 19; my italics).

In explaining the aesthetic of the above-mentioned one-er at the beginning of *Serenity* the movie, Whedon cites an unusual but revealing inspiration:

> *Mr. Rogers* [PBS, 1968–2001] is very popular with younger kids, because he does no cutting – he takes you from place to place with

him everywhere he goes, and that's one of the reasons why it's so soothing. Well, not that I need to soothe the audience, and not that they're little children, but I think something can be said for long takes, when people are watching people in a space that they understand, even subconsciously, it's actually there and people are actually interacting in that time and space.

(Serenity 27)

The first half of film's first century, recall, saw a clash between equally certain advocates for Eisensteinian montage and the long take, between those who, like the Russian filmmaker and theorist, believed that the essence of the cinema was to be found in the cut and those like the French critic André Bazin who put their faith in the "democratic" nature of what the camera can reveal without manipulation. It was a debate Whedon and Michael "Shoot to the Edit" Bay – must certainly have learned about as film studies majors at Wesleyan (see Chapter 3). Whedon would stand with democracy – and Mr. Rogers.

Redemption. "Redemption," Whedon readily acknowledges (*New York Times*), is "one of the most important themes in my work," and the seed crystal for this thematic signature was, of course, the character of Angel. Both on *Buffy* and later on his own show, Angel's story "about addiction and how you get through that and come out the other side, how you redeem yourself from a terrible life" is central to Whedon.

Why? Whedon himself is puzzled: "I'm pretty much an average guy, yet I have an enormous burden of guilt. I'm not sure why. I'm a WASP, so it's not Jewish or Catholic guilt; it's just there. Ultimately, the concept of somebody who needed to be redeemed is more interesting to me. I think it does make a character more textured than one who doesn't."[14]

Religion in Narrative. In the first *Onion AV Club* interview (*JWC* 28), Whedon responds to Tasha Robinson's question about fan idolization of his work. With typical modesty he insists he is "not a rock star" and it is not him they "worship": "It's about the show, and I feel the same way about it […]. There's nothing creepy about it. I feel like *there's a religion in narrative*, and I feel the same way they do. I feel like we're both paying homage to something else; they're not paying homage to me"[15] (my italics).

The Whedonian is likewise a homage to story, to the atheist Whedon's religion in narrative. He is never more passionate or eloquent than when he speaks of story, as he does here with James Longworth concerning story's primal origins:

[U]ltimately, stories come from violence, they come from sex. They come from death. They come from the dark places that everybody has to go to, kind of wants to, or doesn't, but needs to deal with.[16] If you raise a kid to think everything is sunshine and flowers, they're going to get into the real world and die. And ultimately, to access these base emotions, to go to these strange places, to deal with sexuality, to deal with horror and death, is what people need and it's the reason that we tell these stories.

(JWC 57)

Another voice in a tradition as old as Aristotle's "Poetics," Whedon identifies narrative, including his television storytelling, as an effort to "encapsulate these things [violence, sex, death], to inoculate ourselves against them, so that when we're confronted by the genuine horror that is day-to-day life we don't go insane."

If "stories are sacred," if "creating narrative is a basic human function," that does not mean that the storyteller should moralize. Instead, narrative, Whedon is convinced, has "a responsibility to be irresponsible" – "to be anything other than a polemic," to "fulfill that human need for scary stuff, and sexy stuff, and racy stuff, and wrong stuff, and disturbing stuff."

On the DVD commentary to "Chosen," *Buffy the Vampire Slayer's* 144th and final episode, Joss Whedon confesses how, at the end of 2002–3, a production year in which he had been David Kelleying his way through three series, showrunning *Buffy*, *Angel* and *Firefly*, he was completely worn out when the time came to direct the action and special effects extravaganza of The First's defeat, the closing of the Hellmouth, the destruction of Sunnydale, and a final epic smile. With no time or strength for his usual reimagining from the bottom up of the end, he resorted, he admits, far too much to "over over two shot," the "gold standard of boring television." "Chosen," of course, is anything but boring or dull or unimaginative, but it is not Whedon at his prime. Nor is the attitude, the sense of exhaustion, at all Whedonesque.

Again and again on the DVD commentaries to these exemplary episodes we find him talking about his love for his work. "I've never had more fun in my life," he says on the "Restless" commentary, and he will, earlier and later, say much the same thing about "Hush," "Once More with Feeling," "Waiting in the Wings," "Objects in Space." We shouldn't be surprised. What emerges in a creative portrait of the imagination of Joss Whedon is a man who knows very well what he's doing and loves doing it. Which is why we love it too.

EPILOGUE

"You think you know, what you are, what's to come. You haven't even begun"

In which predictions are made about the future achievements of Joss Whedon.

For the creative person, *carpe diem* has a special meaning: since he is trying to do something that has never been done before, he must look for the rare opportunity and then seize it. To recognize what is rare, one must have the kind of knowledge of the world that is gained only by moving about in it.

(Howard Gruber, *Darwin on Man* 252)

Although we think of the creative person as highly task-oriented rather than ego-oriented, it is also true that the set of tasks taken as a whole constitutes a large part of the ego: to be oneself one must do these things; to do these things one must be oneself.

(Howard Gruber, "The Evolving System at Work," 13)

Joy can co-exist with frustration in a creative person.

(Howard Gruber, "The Evolving System at Work," 7)

ooooooooooo

My personal hope is that [Whedon after *The Avengers*] lets *a hundred (or maybe a dozen) Whedons bloom*. Let's hope he repays the loyalty of his fans by opening the doors of the entertainment kingdom to the kind of writers and creators who might not get a crack at the big time without his backing. Nobody's done more than Whedon to create and inspire a generation of TV writers; many of the best scribes working today got their start on Whedonverse programs and most of the rest were powerfully influenced by his shows. I hope he throws his weight behind those writers' most impassioned passion projects [...], backs those writers' pitches, gets their shows on the air and brings more fine entertainment products to the Web.

(Maureen Ryan, *'Avengers'* Fans: Thank TV For That Awesome Movie [And What Joss Should Do Next]" (my italics)

In an earlier chapter, you will recall, we visited, with the aid of Michael Davis, the *Captain Kangaroo* writer's room in the middle of the 1960s, about the time Joss Whedon was born, and here, at the end, it is worth stepping inside once again. "Through good days and bad, the hand-selected team [Bob] Keeshan [Captain Kangaroo] assembled brought out the best in him," Davis observes, with Norton Wright as his guide. "Bob wanted to be more than what he was, but he didn't have the talent [...]. His potential was modest," Wright would recall. But everyone in the room, according to Wright, had ambitions:

> Our writers were from terrific schools, and they knew the Broadway stage, from Neil Simon to Gower Champion. They all harbored the desire to do infinitely more than what they were doing at *Captain Kangaroo* but they, like me had fallen into a tender trap. It was a consistent job with health and pension benefits and decent salary. (Davis 57)

And so no one – not Bob Keeshan, not Norton Wright, not *Captain Kangaroo* writer Tom Whedon – ended up doing "infinitely more." But Whedon's son did, imaginatively escaping all the "tender traps," to become ... the creator of the Whedonverses.

There is so much left for Joss Whedon to do: "I really need to learn to play a musical instrument," Whedon responded when asked about his future plans. "I would also love to produce something for Broadway. I'd also like to explore making a musical motion picture, and I even have some ideas about writing a ballet. Then again, I wouldn't mind taking a couple of years off and teaching. There is also that pesky science-fiction novel that one wants to have written. So, there is very little that I don't wish to be doing in the future. I am sort of a wannabe everything" (Priggé 201). Take note that Whedon offered this to-do list seven years prior to Marvel's *The Avengers*.

Any *Buffy* devotee will recognize the quote in the title of this epilogue: Tara utters these words to Buffy in the Slayer's "Restless" dream; later, as a voice-over, they are the post-dream last words of the episode and the season. In the first episode of Season 5, "Buffy vs. Dracula," the Count enunciates them yet again to Buffy. Earlier I suggested they had come "to speak not to just the destiny of Buffy the Vampire Slayer but of *Buffy the Vampire Slayer*" and wondered if "over a decade later, the admonition seems even more relevant, with 'you' becoming not Buffy or *Buffy* but Joss Whedon himself." It is time now, as these pages come to an end, to do some speculating, to wonder "where do we go from here" – to conjecture where the maker of the Whedonverses might take us.

As I mentioned earlier, Whedon would skip presenting a panel at Comic-Con in 2006: "I had nothing to talk about," he would tell *Entertainment Weekly*. "I went from running three shows to making a movie [*Serenity*] to kind of coming to a screeching halt in terms of what I was putting out to the public – except for comic books." He had no desire to become "that guy who's like, [*in a desperate voice*] 'Hey! You want your picture taken with me? I'm that guy who did *Buffy*. Remember?' You suddenly start to feel like Sam Rockwell in *Galaxy Quest*" (Gopalan).

Writing in 2006 in *Cinematical* – after Comic-Con but before Whedon had withdrawn from Wonder Woman – Mark Beall contemplated the careers of George Lucas and Whedon. While admitting he has never been a big fan of his work, Beall still praises Whedon's "boundless energy and enthusiasm," his importance "to the [geek] community," his wonderful relationship with his fans. He was nevertheless willing to contemplate the possibility that Whedon has "burned himself out early, or was perhaps even overrated from the beginning" (Beall).[1]

In 2007 and 2008, however, Whedon would be back at Comic-Con again with news of a variety of projects: the long-talked about *Ripper* project, which would bring Giles to life as a BBC TV movie; *Goners*, still in development;[2] *The Cabin in the Woods*, co-authored with Drew Goddard; more *Buffy*, *Angel* and *Serenity*, *Dr. Horrible* and *Dollhouse*. Marvel's *The Avengers*, however, was not yet on the horizon.

Interviews with Whedon during his supposed "dark period"[3] at the end of the last decade showed him to be much more retrospectful and philosophical than at any time since his career began. In a meditative and quite poignant second conversation with Tasha Robinson (2007 – included in *JWC* 143–61), for example, Whedon's response to a query about whether he had ever considered giving up on the movies – he answers, "Yes, yes" – becomes a revealing trip down memory lane:

> When I was a script doctor, I was wealthy and miserable. I never had less fun succeeding at a job in my life. Then I got to do TV, and for the first time in my life, people just let me do the thing. That was amazing. Then, when I made *Serenity*, they let me do the thing. They helped me, they guided me through it. It was my first movie, and the people at Universal were amazingly supportive at the same time as being instructive, but at

Figure 12:
Joss Whedon
introduces *Much
Ado About Nothing*
at the Toronto
International Film
Festival (September
2012). Photo by
Nikki Stafford

the end of the day, I did my thing. Once you've done that, it's hard to go back to the other, to not being able to do your thing. To putting up with, "Gee, these guys had a bad weekend because of such and such," or "Now they're looking at this actress," whatever it is.

Which, oddly enough, leads him to the subject of rage.

After "the appalling things that happened to *Firefly*," the temptation presented itself to "just live inside [his] rage," and he tried that, though eventually realizing rage "ain't that tasty." Nietzsche thought the highest wisdom was to be found in *amor fati*, in loving your fate, in the ultimate acceptance of everything that transpires in a life as being for a purpose and ultimately irrevocable. Only in his forties, Whedon looks back in wonder at his good fortune and seems ready to declare *amor fati*:

> I've had more luck than any 10 guys I know. I've been able to tell my story more than a few times, and that's the greatest gift. If I'm never given that gift again, I still will have had it, and I'm grateful for that. My gratitude has finally exceeded my rage by a good, long margin, and when I wake up in the morning with my work and my family, gratitude is the thing that guides me, not rage. (148)

Compare Whedon's stance at 44 to that of David Chase, 20 years his senior, creator of *The Sopranos*, often acclaimed as the greatest television series ever made, who admits in an interview that, even after making *The*

Sopranos, his life continues to be governed by rage: "I'm still … too angry. I … shouldn't be this angry. I shouldn't be this volatile for my age and for the … for, basically what's been a really great life. I have a great family. I have a great career. And I … you know, and what am I so pissed off about?" (Lawson 220).

To be an artist requires learning to walk "the finest line you ever have to walk," Whedon suggests in the "Pop Culture Q & A" (September 2005): "you spend your entire artistic life trying to get to a place where you have absolute control over your work and can say exactly what you're trying to say the way you want to say it" (*JWC* 124). To reach such a mountaintop, however, as any visitor to the Whedonverses knows full well, requires a price: "you have to get through so much oppression and nonsense and pain" – and substantial hair loss: the "eccentric wannabe auteur with bright red hair down to his waist" (*JWC* 66) has become a man with "forehead … like, huge, like SCARY, like I think I can see Cary Grant and Eva Marie Saint hanging off it" (*Dr. Horrible* Letter).[4] And once attained, a liability immediately appears: "you're *instantly* in danger of becoming hermetically sealed and cut off from anyone around you." The artist must continue to struggle to "be in the world" – "listening" to trusted collaborators, "learning" from experience, "not just sort of swimming around in your power" (*JWC* 124).

Whedon's own dream as an artist is not so much to make one of those highly personal works that, as he observes, sometime turn out to be a disappointment: he wants instead to maintain a reciprocal, imaginative "connection with the audience": "The way I work is through the audience going, 'That's me! I'm doing that! I feel that!' And so if I lose that, then I'm useless" (*JWC* 125). "That's who I am. I'm the fan that got the closest." With Marvel's *The Avengers*, it seems clear, his achievement was reaching a previously unimaginable audience while still maintaining connection.

But even if he does continue to succeed at that kind of magical transubstantiation, making his imagination ours, Whedon realizes, with tremendous maturity, that too could result in his eventual redundancy:

I think at some point I may become useless, anyway: The things I have to say will no longer be things that people need to hear – either because I've accomplished what I set out to accomplish and created a new genre paradigm with characters – where people go, "Okay – now we accept the strong women, and the morals click, and you're just sort of doing this over and over again." I might become the old guy. But I hope that if I do, I become the old guy who … realizes it.

Unlike, say, George Lucas.[5]

Asked by MSN what he would like to see as an epitaph, Whedon had a long-in-preparation response: "You know, I've been thinking about this since I was, like, 11, which is not surprising for me. And it's changed a lot. Right now? I would want it to say that I was still learning."[6]

Or perhaps, given a long life, it might look something like this:

Figure 13: He Saved
Our Imaginations
a Lot

APPENDIX A

Joss Whedon Filmography

Ep. #	Episode Title	Film/Series	Writer(s)	Director	Air/Release Date
2.2	Little Sister	*Roseanne*	Joss Whedon	John Pasquin	9/19/1989
2.5	House of Grown Ups	*Roseanne*	Whedon	Pasquin	10/10/1989
2.10	Brain-Dead Poets Society	*Roseanne*	Whedon	Pasquin	11/28/1989
2.13	Chicken Hearts	*Roseanne*	Whedon	Pasquin	12/19/1989
1.3	The Plague	*Parenthood*	Whedon	Alan Myerson	9/29/1990
1.8	Small Surprises	*Parenthood*	Whedon	Matia Karrell	11/3/1990
1.12	Fun for Kids	*Parenthood*	Whedon	Alan Arkush	8/11/1991
NA	NA	*Buffy the Vampire Slayer*	Whedon	Fran Rubel Kuzui	7/31/1992
NA	NA	*Toy Story*	Whedon (et al.)	John Lasseter	11/22/1995
1.1	Welcome to the Hellmouth	*BtVS*S	Whedon	Charles Martin Smith	03/10/97
1.2	The Harvest	*BtVS*S	Whedon	John T. Kretschmer	03/10/97
1.12	Prophecy Girl	*BtVS*S	Whedon	Joss Whedon	06/02/97
2.1	When She Was Bad	*BtVS*S	Whedon	Whedon	09/15/97
2.7	Lie to Me	*BtVS*S	Whedon	Whedon	11/03/1997
NA	NA	*Alien Resurrection*	Whedon	Jean-Pierre Jeunet	11/26/1997
2.14	Innocence	*BtVS*S	Whedon	Whedon	01/20/1998
2.21	Becoming, Pt. 1	*BtVS*S	Whedon	Whedon	05/12/1998
2.22	Becoming, Pt. 2	*BtVS*S	Whedon	Whedon	05/19/1998
3.1	Anne	*BtVS*S	Whedon	Whedon	09/29/1998
3.10	Amends	*BtVS*S	Whedon	Whedon	12/15/1998
3.16	Doppelgängland	*BtVS*S	Whedon	Whedon	02/23/1999
3.21	Graduation Day, Pt. 1	*BtVS*S	Whedon	Whedon	05/18/1999
3.22	Graduation Day, Pt. 2	*BtVS*S	Whedon	Whedon	07/13/1999
4.1	The Freshman	*BtVS*S	Whedon	Whedon	10/05/1999
4.10	Hush	*BtVS*S	Whedon	Whedon	11/03/1999
1.1	City of	*Angel*	Whedon, David Greenwalt	Whedon	05/10/1999

Ep. #	Episode Title	Film/Series	Writer(s)	Director	Air/Release Date
1.4	I Fall to Pieces	*Angel*	Whedon, Greenwalt	Vern Gillum	10/26/1999
4.16	Who Are You?	*BtVS*S	Whedon	Whedon	02/29/2000
4.22	Restless	*BtVS*S	Whedon	Whedon	05/23/2000
5.6	Family	*BtVS*S	Whedon	Whedon	11/07/2000
2.1	Judgment	*Angel*	Greenwalt, Whedon	Michael Lange	9/26/2000
NA	NA	*Titan A.E.*	Whedon and Ben Edlund	Don Bluth and Gary Goldman	6/16/2000
5.16	The Body	*BtVS*S	Whedon	Whedon	02/27/2001
5.22	The Gift	*BtVS*S	Whedon	Whedon	05/22/2001
6.7	Once More, with Feeling	*BtVS*S	Whedon	Whedon	11/06/2001
2.13	Happy Anniversary	*Angel*	David Greenwalt, Whedon	Bill Norton	02/6/2001
7.1	Lessons	*BtVS*S	Whedon	David Solomon	9/24/2002
3.13	Waiting in the Wings	*Angel*	Whedon	Whedon	02/04/2002
4.6	Spin the Bottle	*Angel*	Whedon	Whedon	11/10/2002
1.1	The Train Job	*Firefly*	Whedon and Tim Minear	Whedon	9/20/2002
1.3	Our Mrs. Reynolds	*Firefly*	Whedon	Vondie Curtis Hall	10/4/2002
1.10	Objects in Space	*Firefly*	Whedon	Whedon	12/13/2002
1.11	Serenity, Pt. 1	*Firefly*	Whedon	Whedon	12/20/2002
1.12	Serenity, Pt. 2	*Firefly*	Whedon	Whedon	12/20/2002
1.15	The Message	*Firefly*	Whedon and Minear	Tim Minear	Unaired
7.22	Chosen	*BtVS*S	Whedon	Whedon	5/20/03
5.1	Conviction	*Angel*	Whedon	Whedon	10/1/03
5.15	A Hole in the World	*Angel*	Whedon	Whedon	2/24/04
5.22	Not Fade Away	*Angel*	Jeffrey Bell and Whedon	Jeffrey Bell	5/19/04
NA	NA	*Dr. Horrible's Sing-Along Blog*	Whedon, Maurissa Tancharoen, Jed Whedon, Zack Whedon	Whedon	7/15, 17, 19/2008
1.1	Ghost	*Dollhouse*	Whedon	Whedon	2/13/2009
1.6	Man on the Street	*Dollhouse*	Whedon	David Straiton	3/20/2009
1.13	Epitaph One	*Dollhouse*	Tancharoen and Jed Whedon (teleplay); Whedon (story)	Whedon	Unaired
2.1	Vows	*Dollhouse*	Whedon	Whedon	9/25/2009

Ep. #	Episode Title	Film/Series	Writer(s)	Director	Air/Release Date
2.13	Epitaph Two: Return	*Dollhouse*	Maurissa Tancharoen, Jed Whedon and Andrew Chambliss	Solomon	1/29/2010
NA	NA	*The Cabin in the Woods*	Whedon and Drew Goddard	Drew Goddard	4/13/2012
NA	NA	Marvel's *The Avengers*	Whedon and Zak Penn	Whedon	5/4/2012
NA	NA	*Much Ado About Nothing*	Whedon	Whedon	6/13/2013
NA	NA	*In Your Eyes*	Whedon	Brin Hill	Unknown

APPENDIX B

A Brief Joss Whedon Timeline

A full hypertext, realtime version of this timeline can be found at:
http://jossacreativeportrait.com

1904 John Ogden Whedon born
1932 Tom Whedon born
1936 Lee Stearns, Joss Whedon's mother, born
1964 Joss Whedon born
1973 Whedon's parents divorce
1979 Whedon accompanies his mother to England, where he becomes a
     student at Winchester College
1983 Whedon enrolls at Wesleyan University in Connecticut
1987 Whedon graduates from Wesleyan
1989 Whedon writes for *Roseanne* (1989–90)
1991 John Whedon dies
1992 Whedon's mother dies
1994 *Speed,* script-doctored by Whedon, is released; Whedon begins
     working on *Toy Story*
1995 Whedon weds Kai Cole
1997 *Alien Resurrection,* written by Whedon, is released; *Buffy the Vampire
     Slayer* (1997–2003) debuts on the WB
1999 *Angel* (1999–2004) debuts on the WB
2001 First issue of *Fray* published; *Buffy* moves to UPN
2002 *Firefly* debuts and is cancelled
2003 *Buffy* ends
2004 *Angel* ends; Whedon takes over *Astonishing X-Men*
2005 Whedon signs to direct Wonder Woman; *Serenity* premieres
2006 Whedon makes "Equality Now" Speech; *Buffy* Season 8 begins its
     run

2007 Whedon directs two episodes of *The Office*; Writers Strike begins; Whedon's authorship of *Runaways* begins

2008 *Dr. Horrible's Sing-Along Blog* airs on the Internet

2009 *Dollhouse* (2009–10) debuts; *The Cabin in the Woods* filmed

2010 *Dollhouse* is cancelled

2011 *Much Ado About Nothing* and Marvel's *The Avengers* filmed

2012 *The Cabin in the Woods* and Marvel's *The Avengers* released

2013 *Much Ado About Nothing* released; Marvel's *Agents of S.H.I.E.L.D.* debuts on ABC in the US and Channel 4 in the UK

APPENDIX C

The School of Whedon

Part of Joss Whedon's genius is his ability to bring out the best in those he works with. I would posit this as a necessity for a great television artist. It struck me only recently one of the great themes of the show – the importance of community, trust, friendship – is found not only in the episodes but in their creation [...]. Joss Whedon in effect created a school of writers (cf. a school of painters) who grew more and more sharply skillful with Whedon's support.

(Rhonda V. Wilcox, *Why* Buffy *Matters*, 6)

The "school of Whedon" of which pre-eminent Whedonverses scholar Rhonda Wilcox speaks could be said to include every significant collaborator – the writers, directors, cast and crew, illustrators – of his television series (*Buffy, Angel, Firefly, Dollhouse*) his web series *Dr. Horrible*, his movies (*Serenity, The Cabin in the Woods*, Marvel's *The Avengers*), his comic books (*Fray, The Amazing X-Men, The Runaways, Buffy* Season 8), his productions for Bellwether (*Much Ado About Nothing, The Wastelanders, In Your Eyes*).

Go to http://jossacreativeportrait.com

You will find there a real-time comprehensive directory of the members of the SoW. Each individual's page includes a thumbnail sketch, a photo (if available), and significant links (e.g. IMDb, Wikipedia, etc.).

NOTES

Prologue – Michael Bay versus Joss Whedon

1 I am indebted to the invaluable Buffyverse Data Base for most of my dialogue quotations.

2 At the 2004 Slayage Conference on the Whedonverses, Stacey Abbott delivered a Mr. Pointy Award-winning keynote entitled "'Cavemen vs Astronauts – weapons to be determined': Angel, Spike and the Buddy Genre." My debt to her in this prologue is, I trust, obvious. The talk appears in her *Angel* monograph in the TV Milestones series.

3 Asked for his "marching orders" (with the T-shirt in mind), Whedon replied "I'm thinking that I'd like them to sit … and possibly roll over" (*JWC* 124).

4 In *Dr. Horrible's Sing-Along Blog*, Whedon would seem to be sending up such obsessions in Captain's Hammer's stalkers' proud display of their hero's laundry receipt.

5 For more on critical/academic assessment of the Whedonverses, see my essay "'I Wrote My Thesis on You': *Buffy* Studies as an Academic Cult." Hornick's comprehensive "Buffyology: An Academic Buffy Studies & Whedonverses Bibliography," Wilcox's "In the Demon Section of the Card Catalog," and Macnaughtan's *The Buffyverse Catalog*. A Survey in *Slate* (Lametti et al.) recently confirmed the pre-eminence of *Buffy the Vampire Slayer* as a scholarly topic.

6 We should take note of the caution Whedon adds to this statement: "Of course, if they're dressing up like Willow and staying in their basement for nine months at a time, that's not good." And elsewhere he does somewhat amend (sardonically) his "get a life" stance:

> Hey, I've been outside. There's bugs. I'm in LA now, but there's weather occasionally. We're on cloud watch today, but yes, everybody should have a life but these shows are designed for exactly that. I never put on a costume the way Tim Minear did to go to conventions and stuff, but I also didn't know they existed when I was little. These shows are designed to be in people's lives, in their fiction, in their dreams, in their porn, in everything. (Topel, CHUD Interview)

7 See Constance Havens's *Joss Whedon* for an interview with Basinger (14–16).

8 Whedon, too, has praised Bay. Speaking of his time at Wesleyan in an interview with IGN-Film Force, he observed: "Actually, I'm a fan of Michael's. Best eyes in the business."

9   "It makes perfect sense that Michael Bay would own a dog like Mason," Hochman observes. "The colossal English mastiff, easily 200 pounds, galumphs around the 34-year-old filmmaker's Brentwood bachelor pad with all the reserve of a Clydesdale on Viagra. Everything about Mason is gigantic: his branch of a tail, his Pavarotti-esque woof, his Jacuzzi-size doggy dish. There is no escaping it: This dog is bigger than your dog. This is the biggest dog in Los Angeles. Let's get real, this is the biggest dog on the planet!"

10 In conversation, Basinger notes that Bay, wanting to establish conceptual templates for this "shoot for the edit" style, does contribute heavily to the development of his scripts.

11 See my essay "*My So-Called Life* Meets *The X-Files.*"

12 With a laugh, Whedon told Dark Horse comics that *Buffy* "reflects the imagination of the 'loser,' much like myself" (Ervin-Gore).

13 Totals for *Cabin* and *Avengers* as reported on Box Office Mojo, 1 December 2012.

14 I refer here to the original, etymological meaning of the word "poet" (*Oxford American Dictionary*): ORIGIN Middle English: from Old French *poete*, via Latin from Greek *poētēs*, variant of *poiētēs* '*maker, poet,*' from *poiein* '*create.*'

Introduction – From the Mind of Joss Whedon

1   Although Havens's "biography" does offer some valuable insights (the interview with Jeanine Basinger, for example, is most welcome), it is, as a piece of scholarship, inexcusably rushed, unreliable and dishonest. Any attentive reader can spot scores of errors both careless (Joss [*sic* – Joe] Reinkemeyer) and ungrammatical ("Essential to Joss's concept for *Buffy* was to take all of the misery of his high school years and put them [*sic*] into the series" [33]) and will no doubt wonder, too, why no documentation of sources is provided. Quotation after quotation, most from Whedon's many interviews (important sources for this book as well), fill Havens's pages – all uncredited, creating the erroneous impression that the book is the author's continuous conversation with its subject.

2   Udovitch's piece was published in the 11 May 2000 issue of the magazine, but we know from several references (she refers in the article to Gellar's on-set visible scar, acquired in Buffy's flight from Adam in "The Yoko Factor" [4.20]; she watches the filming of a scene in which Buffy regrets having studied French instead of Sumerian) that her visit took place during the filming of "Primeval" (4.21), the next to the last episode of Season 4.

3   We should not find such rapid production in the world of television that surprising. In an interview with ET Online, Whedon had confessed that "When we fall behind, which tends to happen, I've been known to write a 'Buffy,' start to finish, in three days."

4   During the filming of Fellini's masterpiece, the Italian director had also deflected the concerns of everyone from his producer to his star, Marcello Mastroianni, as to whether or not "the maestro" actually knew what *8½* was about. Fellini would, of course, incorporate these doubts into the film itself, making it in large part a movie about the inability of Guido Anselmi (Mastroianni – Fellini's alter ego) to make a movie.

5   Another example: in the scene at The Bronze in Giles's dream, we find the following exchange:

> Willow: Something is trying to kill us. It's like some primal ... some animal force.
> Giles: That used to be us.
> Xander: Don't get linear on me now, man.

Of course there seems little danger of "Restless" itself becoming linear, even in straight-arrow Giles's dream segment.

6   In the first episode of Season 5, "Buffy vs. Dracula," written by Marti Noxon, Dracula, seeking to convince Buffy that her power is very near his own, intones the same line to her.

7   At the time of writing, the trailer remains viewable on YouTube at http://youtube.com/watch?v=0BvP99-Ci6k.

8   Xander in "Primeval" (*BtVS*S 4.21): "So no problem, all we need is combo Buffy – her with Slayer strength, Giles's multi-lingual know how, and Willow's witchy power."

9   Gruber's own *magnum opus* was a study of Darwin – *Darwin on Man* (1981).

10 For more on Gruber, see my essay "Creative Work: The Method of Howard Gruber," from which much of my overview here is drawn.

11 Truffaut was interested most of all in the contribution of film directors to the visual style, especially the *mise-en-scène*, of a movie; he chafed at the idea that the director's role was "merely custodial"; he embraced the writings of Alexandre Astruc, whose essay on "The Camera Pen" (1948) had argued that in the hands of a true stylist filmmaking could be as precise as articulate and precise as literature.

    Truffaut's motives were clear: he was critical of what he took to be a too great emphasis among his contemporaries on the screenwriter in the assessment of film; he attacked well-written, "well-made," literary films and their "tradition of quality" (in which excellence was almost entirely understood in literary terms, with the director considered merely "the gentleman who adds the pictures" [Innsdorf 21]).

12 First, television was thought of as a producer's medium: talk of Steven Bochco's *Hill Street Blues* (NBC, 1981–7) became a critical commonplace. Soon after, both industry and fans found themselves all a-buzz over movie auteur David Lynch's role in the creation and directing of *Twin Peaks* (ABC, 1990–1). By the end of the century, David Kelley (*Picket Fences*, CBS, 1992–6), David Milch (*NYPD Blue*, ABC, 1993–2002), Joshua Brand and John Falsey (*St. Elsewhere*, NBC, 1982–8; *Northern Exposure*, ABC, 1990–5) were, if not household words, at least known television authors.

13 For more on new television auteurs, see my "The Imagination Will be Televised."

14 Some of Gray's original talk now appears in *Show Sold Separately* 111–13.

Chapter 1 – Television Son

1   We owe this acronym to the IGN-Film Force interview, coined in their extensive and probing interview with Whedon.

2   Mike Davis describes *Upstairs at the Downstairs* as "a hip performance space on Fifty-sixth Street that was a breeding ground for actors and comedians in the late 1950s and '60s" (58).

3   According to Wikipedia, *The Electric Company* began to include "[s]hort pieces that featured the Marvel Comics character Spider-Man (which was provided to [Children's Television Workshop] free of charge) and cast members from the show. Stories involved the web-masked superhero (Danny Seagren) foiling mischievous characters involved in petty criminal activities (such as burglary or assault). Interestingly, Spider-Man spoke only in cartoon word balloons appearing over his head, which were accompanied by electronic punctuation sounds for emphasis when they appeared on-screen. Also, unlike in the pages of Marvel Comics, he was never seen out of costume as his alter-ego, Peter Parker. [...] The segment's theme song also claimed, 'Spider-Man, where are you coming from? Spider-Man, nobody knows who you are.'"

4   Asked by Jossisahottie.com to name his favourite *Golden Girl*, Whedon didn't hesitate for a moment: "Bea, dude! Bea!" (*JWC* 39).

5   The prediction was not entirely correct: "I have two older brothers, two younger half-brothers, and a stepsister, and all of them actually have real jobs," Whedon admits. "I fear them." (Priggé 51)

6   Interestingly, in the *Fresh Air* interview his attitude about television escalates into "total snob."

7   For example, Whedon would tell UndergroundOnline: "I don't watch TV. [...] It's not because of any prejudice against television. It just that you can either watch TV or you can make TV."

Chapter 2 – Fan Boy

1   When the interviewer chides Whedon – "But you were writing to yourself, so it really didn't accomplish much, did it?" – his reply is classic Whedon: "Yeah, you point that out now."

2   "While DC used sci-fi to exalt the virtues of scientific progress and the certainty of peace through technology," Wright shows, "Marvel spoke to the anxieties of the atomic age" (202).

3   Cage was a technological enhanced criminal-cum-supersoldier-cum-superhero who became a fifth wheel to The Fantastic Four.

4   Almost all the facts and every unidentified quotation in this discussion of Whedon's time at Winchester are indebted to the IGN-Film Force interview with Whedon.

5   Whedon is still astonished that he was even admitted: "I bizarrely managed to get into the single best school in the country, through no merit of my own. I really don't know how that happened. I was lazy, I was terrible."

6   Whether Part I or Part II, I do not know. *Henry V*, quoted in "The Gift" (*BtVS*S 5.22), Whedon did not read until much later (IGN-Film Force).

7   Asked "Is *Hamlet* mad?" (*JWC* 37), Whedon has a semi-definitive answer: "If the person playing him gets there, yes." Elsewhere he debunks "'the entire play takes place in Hamlet's imagination' theory," while simultaneously denying that the play was the inspiration for "Normal Again" (*BtVS* 6.17), the episode in which

an under-demonic-influence Buffy finds herself in an insane asylum hallucinating that she is the chosen one) (*New York Times*)

8   Whedon's description of quintessentially British "A Levels" must be quoted:

> You spend the last two years of high school studying for those three tests, and you choose your three subjects. It's very odd, but it's also great because I didn't have to take math or science. […] that's why my wife does the bills. […] When the bills come and I go, "What's a decimal?" So we'd have class for an hour and twenty minutes, like in college, and then there'd be three more hours until dinner, and we'd just stay. We'd just stay and keep talking. Some of them were doing it because they were desperate to get good grades, they wanted to get into Oxford or Cambridge. One of them mentioned to me, "You know, Joss, you're not taking the A levels, you don't have to stay." "Dude, where else would I be?" It was amazing. Four hours at a stretch, great scholars and a great teacher completely prying open the text of *Hamlet*. I mean, what more fun can there be? Spoken like a man who never had sex in high school. (IGN-Film Force)

9   Wilcox notes that River in the series and Whedon at the time of the epiphany are the same age ("I Do not Hold to That" 158).

10 Born in 1905, Sartre died in April of the same year as Whedon's epiphany.

Chapter 3 – Film Studies Major

1   "It's not like anybody was begging for me. I was clearly a ne'er-do-well. And, in fact, when we got into Wesleyan, in our packet of information, I had no grades. I had a lot of reports that said, 'He seems to be intelligent, but I wouldn't say he applies himself terribly much'" (IGN-Film Force).

2   "Wesleyan just kind of … we clicked. There was something about it. I am well aware, and was at the time, that it may have been the weather. It may just have been a nice day" (IGN-Film Force).

3   In correspondence, Slotkin offers the following brief history of Wesleyan's film programme:

> When Joss was here, Film was administratively a subfield of Art – in practice, a collaboration between Jeanine Basinger and an Art professor, and myself and Joe Reed out of English/American Studies. Joss did substantial coursework in both American Studies and Film. In the early 1990s we were able to get Film separated from Art, as an interdisciplinary program (which unlike a [department] cannot hire its own faculty), combining the work of volunteer faculty from American Studies, German and Anthropology (documentary) – with Basinger as the center holding it together. We also had visiting profs to do film-making courses. Since 1999 Film has been a dept, and hired its own faculty. Its basis (and orientation) is now more in the formal analysis of film (plus history of the medium), less in the American culture-studies vein. There are now two full-time Film profs in addition to Basinger, plus long-term adjuncts teaching film making – and we have a state of the art facility.

4 "Anybody can tell you where to point a camera – and quite frankly, nobody can tell you how. You can either do that or you can't," Whedon would comment. "Learning what a gaffer is, or how to load your own film is great – I actually had to load my own film during my thesis film once, because my crew was too stoned. They just said, 'We're really too stoned to change it'" (IGN-Film Force).

5 I refer, of course, to Jeanine Basinger's keynote – "Joss Whedon, Film Major: A+ All the Way" – at the third Slayage Conference, June 2008.

6 Asked to rate Wesleyan as a "contact school," Whedon would reply:

> It was, in a low-key way, and now it's gotten bigger. I was hired as a research assistant by a grad, and that was set up by Jeanine. In my time here, I think I've hired at least five – some of whom were hired by others who I didn't know were Jeanine students, or Wesleyan students, until after they were here. We have, every year, the Wesleyan get-together – and every year, an astonishing number of people who are working heavily in the film industry and bright new people coming up. A lot of the people who are ten years behind me are doing really well, and it grows.

Asked if there was a Wesleyan "palpable vibe," he said:

> You know, yes and no. There's a lot of different kinds. I mean, Michael Bay and I both came out of the same year, or we were maybe a year apart. Michael Bay, Jon Turteltaub and me. I wouldn't say that we're all brothers under the skin, artistically.

7 "I think that that was just a phase," Whedon acknowledges. "Those kids seem to have gone away."

8 I draw here largely on Loewenstein's "Basinger's Students Make Their Mark" article in *Variety*.

9 The quotes, all in Loewenstein, are from Gordon Crawford, Brad Fuller and Stephen Schiff respectively.

10 For more on this generational clash, see my essay "'Like Light': The Movie Theory of W.R. Robinson."

11 In the IGN-Film Force interview we catch a glimpse of Whedon's acceptance of the mostly non-theoretical Basinger approach. In answering a question about his minor in women's studies at Wesleyan, Whedon replies (after first clarifying that he did not pursue such a minor) that

> when you're dealing with feminism you're dealing with a lot of people who understand feminism better than they understand film, and again you pose something and that doesn't just go. [...] the point is, *you can have an agenda as long as you let the film come to you* and take that out of you. I know a guy who could not get through a paper without talking through Freudian theories of infantile sexuality. And his lecture on *The Wild Bunch*, in terms of Freudian theories of infantile sexuality, was actually fascinating. *Because he loved The Wild Bunch, he understood the movie, and then he let it speak to him. He didn't try and like shove in a theory* (my italics).

12 Unlike Basinger, who has remained a Whedon confidante for over a quarter of a century, Slotkin has interacted with Whedon only "[o]ccasionally" since his days at Wesleyan. "We tend to meet when he comes to Middletown, and at the annual party in LA for Wesleyan's film alums (I've only gone to it twice)."

13 Slotkin has also authored highly praised novels, including *Abe,* about the youth of the 16th President of the United States, which Whedon named as the "book you recommend everybody should read" – though he does offer the caution that "it's very much an American thing" (*JWC* 36).

14 All the quotations from Slotkin in this section are from his generous and informative April 2008 response to a series of questions I asked about Whedon and Wesleyan.

15 In Whedon's essay "My Five Favorite Batman Movies," Michael Mann's adaptation of Cooper's *Last of the Mohicans* (1992) comes in at number three.

16 George Lucas, who has openly acknowledged the effect of *The Hero with a Thousand Faces* on *Star Wars,* is yet another Campbell-influenced filmmaker.

17 With great embarrassment Whedon points out a few moments – the scene in "The Harvest," for example, in which Angel is clearly standing in sunlight – in which *Buffy* unintentionally violates its own rules.

18 Kubrick would be on Whedon's mind as well in recollecting the filming of *The Cabin in the Woods* (directed by Drew Goddard): "We had been in the woods – we actually shot the cabin stuff first – and then to bring them to this stark, white Kubrick-esque place was so startling" (CW: *OVC* 36). Whedon is probably thinking of the Ludovico labs in *A Clockwork Orange* (1971) or perhaps the space station in *2001* (1968).

19 Whedon laments to Jim Kozak that "the animated musical died with Howard Ashman" (*JWC* 92).

20 Franklin Pangborn (1889–1958) was a great American character actor, who usually played fussy or officious characters in films like W.C. Fields's *The Bank Dick* (1940) and Preston Sturges' *Sullivan's Travels* (1941).

21 "An all-time favorite movie? For a long time it was a dead heat between *The Bad and the Beautiful* and *Once Upon a Time in the West,* but at the end of the day, my favorite movie is still *The Matrix*" (Topel, CHUD Interview).

22 Whedon would, of course, cast his fellow Wesleyanite as Hadley in *The Cabin in the Woods.*

23 The daughter of Martin Scorsese and Julia Cameron.

Chapter 4 – Television Writer

1 Jeanine Basinger helped him secure the position ("Joss Whedon, A+ Film Major").

2 For more on the temptations of money in television screenwriting, see Stepakoff's *Billion-Dollar Kiss,* especially the chapters "How'd You Like to Make Ten Grand" (27–51) and "Green Envelopes" (52–73).

3 Would-be writers write 'spec' scripts in the hope of convincing agents, and subsequently showrunners, that they would be welcome additions to a television show's writing staff. Stepakoff provides a fascinating discussion of the ins and outs of the spec script (76–8), in which he reaches the conclusion which appears as an epigraph to this chapter.

4   Tom Whedon read his son's early work but, according to Joss, didn't critique it: "He just loved them. I was shocked. [...] I valued his approbation enormously. Didn't expect it. That gave me the courage to go on" (IGN-Film Force).

5   "You know," Whedon recalls, "I remember one of my father's friends saying, 'Have they let you start to write a script yet?' I was like, 'Yeah, I'm on my fourth'" (IGN-Film Force).

6   Interestingly, on the Season 2 *Roseanne* DVD collection, we can watch a lovey-dovey 10th anniversary reunion of the cast and an extended interview with John Goodman in which nary a negative word is said about the atmosphere on the show.

7   Meanwhile the "bad Roseanne" was, Whedon reminds, doing morale-crushing things like telling David Letterman that "I hate the writers. I'm going to fire them all" (IGN-Film Force). "I was just devastated."

8   Whedon told IGN-Film Force that he wrote six *Roseannes*; the other two might have been either "Somebody Stole My Gal" (2.4) or "Born to Be Wild" (2.16) or "Hair" (2.17) – each an episode anecdotally reported as being Whedon-authored.

9   All of my comments on Whedon's *Roseanne* episodes make the assumption, admittedly far from certain given the ruthless rewriting for which the series was famous, that he wrote the lines and created the situations in the televised version.

10 One season later, a young writer named Amy Sherman-Palladino and partner Jennifer Heath began writing for *Roseanne*, eventually being responsible for over a dozen episodes from 1990 to 1994 – Sherman-Palladino would stay on with the show even after Heath left. She would, of course, go on to create another long-running WB series, *Gilmore Girls* (2000–7), establishing *Roseanne* as an important seedbed for future writers and showrunners. See my essay "'Impossible Girl'."

11 I have not been able to see any of Whedon's *Parenthood* episodes.

12 In 2010, *Parenthood* would be rebooted, this time more successfully, by *Friday Night Lights* mastermind Jason Katims. In the fall of 2012, the new *Parenthood* would begin its third season.

Chapter 5 – *Buffy* Goes to the Movies

1   Alfred Wegener (1880–1930) was a German meteorologist who first hypothesized the theory of continental drift; Gregor Mendel (1822–84) was, of course, the German-Czech pioneer of genetic theory. Both died unaware of their posthumous influence and fame.

2   Whedon's memory of the film in question was a bit off. In the same interview he would correct the title to *Attack of the Killer Bimbos*, but the name of the film was actually *Assault of the Killer Bimbos* (Anita Rosenberg, 1988).

3   Whedon is, of course, evoking Buffy from an episode he himself wrote ("Anne" 3.1): Buffy: Hey, Ken [a Hell demon], wanna see my impression of Gandhi?" (*crushes his skull with a club*). Lily: Gandhi? Buffy: Well, you know, if he was really pissed off."

4   Rubens, Whedon recalls, "was my beacon of hope in that whole experience," "a delight to be around, trying to make it [the movie] better. He actually said to me, 'I'm a little worried about this line, and I want to change it. I realize that it'll

change this other thing, so if that's a problem. . . ..' I'm like, 'Did I just hear an actor say that?'"

5   Ironically, Sutherland had played a Fellini-like filmmaker in Paul Mazursky's *Alex in Wonderland* (1970).

Chapter 6 – Script Doctor/Screenwriter

1   "The Last Sundown," *Buffy the Vampire Slayer:* The Complete Seventh Season on DVD (Disc 6).
2   Whedon acknowledges as well that though "Gypsy curse" might be a bit of a cliché, he decided to go with "the classics" instead of, say, "Danish curse."
3   The Writers Guild of America objected to Mankiewicz's "creative consultant" credit.
4   Saralegui's career as a film producer and occasional writer has not been stellar. In the past decade, he has had a series of forgettable films – *Red Planet* (Antony Hoffman, 2000), *Queen of the Damned* (Michael Rymer, 2002), *The Time Machine* (Simon Wells, 2002), *Showtime* (Tom Dey, 2002), *The Big Bounce* (George Armitage, 2004) – all of which have met with critical disdain and middling box office success.
5   By far the best source on Whedon's script doctoring is Jim Kozak's interview ("*Serenity* Now") in *In Focus* magazine, now reprinted in *JWC* (85–106).
6   The IMDB reports that Keanu Reeves signed on to play Jack only after Whedon was brought in, but that timeline seems unlikely.
7   My discussion of Whedon's involvement in *Toy Story* draws heavily on his interview with Kozak (*JWC* 92–3). All quotations come from that interview unless otherwise specified.
8   In the *In Focus* interview, Whedon would appear to acknowledge being somewhat disappointed he was not included in the DVD discussion.
9   *Toy Story* would be released Thanksgiving weekend the following year, 22 November 1995.
10 Surely I am not the only one hearing an echo of the following exchanges from "Becoming, Part I" (*BtVS* S 2.21) in these words:

> Buffy: Oh, I'll fight him if I have to. But if I don't get there in time, or if I lose, then Willow might be our only hope.
> Willow: I don't wanna be our only hope! Uh, I crumble under pressure. Let's have another hope.

11 "That sort of movie fell by the wayside while I was there. I watched as the musical numbers became more and more beautifully animated and more and more disposable musically."
12 Whedon recalls, "Then they said, 'No, wait, we want to do "My Fair Lady" with *Marco Polo*.' Which I not only wrote a script for, I actually wrote the lyrics for three songs that [veteran stage composer] Robert Lindsey Nassif wrote the music to" (*JWC* 92).
13 The references are, of course, to two other monumental flops of recent memory *Ishtar* (Elaine May, 1987) and *Heaven's Gate* (Michael Cimino, 1980).

14 Mayflower reports in his script review in November 2001 that Andy Tennant was to rewrite and direct *Afterlife*. I can find no evidence that the project is still active.

15 *Alien* (Ridley Scott, 1979), *Aliens* (James Cameron, 1986), and *Alien³* (David Fincher, 1992). Subsequent films have included *AVP: Alien vs. Predator* (Paul W.S. Anderson, 2004), *AVPR: Alien vs. Predator Requiem* (Colin and Greg Strause, 2007), and *Prometheus* (Ridley Scott, 2012).

16 After one or two visits to the set, Whedon recalls, "I literally didn't see any of it again until I saw the director's cut, during which I actually cried. [...] It was a single manly tear rolling down my cheek. About an hour into the movie, I just started to cry. I said, 'I can't believe this.' I was heartbroken" (Robinson, *Onion AV Club*, 2001)

17 AICN spared no invective in its description of the Alien queen/Ripley spawn of the film's climax: "Is the creature THAT BAD? YES, YES YES YES YES YES. That creature is (excuse my French, technically I think it's German) fucking awful, a total rotting piece of shit. Why am I cussing? Because there are simply no other words ... well perhaps stupid doo doo head would apply to the designer. It is horrible. BAD, terrible, awful. Nasty, bad, puke. How this ever got off the page and on to the screen is beyond me." Whedon would agree: "I don't remember writing, 'A withered, granny-lookin' Pumpkinhead-kinda-thing makes out with Ripley.' Pretty sure that stage direction never existed in any of my drafts" (*JWC* 94).

Chapter 7 – *Buffy* Does Television

1 The exhaustion may have started much earlier. When IGN-Film Force asked "Was there a sense of burnout towards the end, as far as everyone looking on to what the future was going to hold?" Whedon's answer was perhaps more candid than he intended: "Yeah, that started around Season 3. So it was sort of like, 'We're still here, guys. I know you guys are doing movies, it's very exciting [...] Oh, so it's *Dangerous Liaisons*, but with kids [*Cruel Intentions* (Roger Kumbel, 1999)] – that's going to be fun. We still have to make the show. Is anybody with me?'"

2 David Greenwalt has offered a somewhat different account of *Buffy's* origin. In the Greenwalt version, the idea of adapting *Buffy* for television was there from the beginning, proposed, again with no success, by Berman back when the movie script was written and, again, when the film was released. Berman was not to be denied three times, however: When, in the mid-1990s, she again pitched the idea, "Finally, they [Fox? the WB?] said, 'Well, if you can get Joss Whedon (but you never will) we might consider it.' So she went and got Joss, who said – and this is the revenge of the writer – 'I want to see this thing done correctly.' So anyway, they decided to make this little show" ("David Greenwalt," 149).

3 For Kuzui's own somewhat self-congratulatory version of the birth of *BtVS*, see *The Watchers Guide* I, 246–7. Gail Berman substantially confirms Kuzui's basic outline (249).

4 Whedon told Longworth (*JWC* 49–50) that it was Harbert who said, "This is an hour. You have too much. With all the action and suspense you want to create in

a half hour, you're never going to get a chance to get into the character, and that's what's interesting and that's what you're interested in."

5   Matthew Pateman offers an exhaustive, brilliant meditation on the meaning of Whedon's title (1–12).

6   Or perhaps "Martha the Immortal Waitress," as he tells IGN-Film Force.

7   Asked by IGN-Film Force if the original pilot – "the presentation" – would ever be included on a DVD set, Whedon's answer was an adamant, and then profane (with a touch of New York street slang), "no":

> IGNFF: Is the presentation ever going to make it to DVD?
> Whedon: Not while there is strength in these bones.
> IGNFF: Well, I mean, it's one of the most heavily bootlegged things on the Internet …
> Whedon: Yeah. It sucks on ass.
> IGNFF: Yeah, it does, but it's sort of that archival, historical perspective …
> Whedon: Yeah, I've got your historical perspective … (IGN-Film Force)

8   In the prolific horror writing of the American H.P. Lovecraft (1890–1937), the world was once inhabited by demonic "old ones" who eventually lost their hold upon our reality but continue to haunt our nightmares and enter our world through Hellmouthy intersticies. Whedon's most Lovecraftian episode is clearly "A Hole in the World" (*Angel* 5.15). *The Cabin in the Woods* would, of course, revisit the Lovecraft mythos.

9   This chapter draws on my entry on *BtVS* in *50 Key Television Programmes*.

10 For more on Whedon's DVD commentaries, see my "Emotional Resonance and Rocket Launchers."

11 In "Buffy vs. Dracula" (5.1), of course, *Buffy* does offer us bat transformations.

12 Whedon's discussion of the industry's attitude about writers becoming directors is revealing:

> Part of the reason I made [...] *Buffy* is because as a writer – even a successful one – in Hollywood, when you say you want to direct movies, they're appalled. They look like, "Do you kill babies?" I mean, they're just shocked. "What? You want to what?" "I'm a storyteller. I want to tell stories. I want to direct." "Uh, I don't get it. You want to what?"

He goes on to make comments of great relevance to any showdown between cavemen and astronauts: "people actually said to me, 'Well, if you'd directed a video,' – like, say, Michael Bay – 'I'm like, just once, somebody please say to a video director, 'Well, if you'd written a script. If you just knew how to tell a story.' I mean, the percentage of video directors who have actually told stories" (Robinson, *Onion AV Club* 2001).

Chapter 8 – Creator of *Angel* and *Firefly*

1   As Whedon explained to Salon.com, the relationship between Angel and Buffy is very much like *Cheers*' Sam and Diane:

That's why we had Angel go bad when he and Buffy got together. Because – and I've gotten into so much trouble for this phrase – what people want is not what they need. In narrative, nobody wants to see fat, married Romeo and Juliet, even if fat, married Romeo and Juliet happen to be [Dashiell Hammett's detective couple] Nick and Nora Charles and they're really cool and having a great time in their lovely relationship and really care about each other and have nice, well-adjusted children. Guess what? People don't want to see it. (*JWC* 73)

2   Whedon acknowledges that Angel was not his only option in pursuing a spin-off: "I've always been of the opinion that any one of these guys could sustain their own show. I think they're that good. I think they're that interesting. And I think they're that pretty. But Angel became the logical choice for a few reasons, and that was clear early on" (*JWC* 9).

3   In his conversation with Longworth, Whedon is surprisingly candid about his weariness with the teen drama:

Sometimes I'm like, "Oh my God, I just want to work with Abe Vigoda. Get me away from these fucking teenagers." [...] Especially because at the WB there's a rotation of actors you just go, "Oh my God, I'm so sick of this world." But then, I *tend* toward stories about adolescents. I tend toward young-adult fiction, toward that moment in life. I'm interested in that. Yeah, I definitely want to tell other stories. I want to tell stories about grown-ups, and, to an extent that's what *Angel* is. (*JWC* 59)

4   Joyce Millman's description of Angel is close to definitive and deserves quoting in full:

Angel often wears the dazed look of a lost lamb. He's bewildered by modern life, and he's as penurious and cranky as you'd expect from a 240-year-old (celibate) man. Yet he tries endearingly to fit in with humans; his halting attempts at small talk look more like he's pleading for mercy, and he's the worst dancer in the world. But for all the fun the show pokes at Angel's un-hipness, the overall tone is melancholic. Angel wants forgiveness, but knows he doesn't deserve it. He longs to be human again, but he's resigned to his eternal fate. He is an exquisitely tragic hero, part dark avenger, part world-weary gumshoe. Angel may hunt malevolent creatures, but the monster he fears most is the one inside himself. ("Angel," *Essential Cult Television Reader* 30)

5   See Janet Halfyard, "The Dark Avenger: *Angel* and the Cinematic Superhero" in Abbott, *Reading* Angel (149–62).

6   *The New Oxford Dictionary* defines chiaroscuro as "an effect of contrasted light and shadow created by light falling unevenly or from a particular direction on something."

7   Asked what he would have to offer "different from the norm" if forced to do an *Angel* clip show, Whedon replied, "It would only be the clips of Wesley falling

over" (*JWC* 367). For more on *Angel's* humour, see Abbott's "Nobody Scream, or Touch My Arms" in *Reading* Angel (Abbott's title is the source of my allusion to "comic stylings") and Wilcox and Lavery 227–8.

8   "Like most 12-steppers," Millman observes, thinking of David Greenwalt's observation that Angel is like a recovering alcoholic, "he has given himself over to a higher power" – the Powers That Be (Millman, *"Angel," Essential Cult Television Reader* 30).

9   Asked by Edward Gross (at the end of *Buffy* Season 4/*Angel* Season 1) why he only directs episodes he has written, Whedon replies:

> It's easier to write an episode than direct it. Well, not easier, but Scheduling-wise, I usually direct an episode when there is something I desperately want to say – where there's a moment that I want to capture, an idea I want to try out. To create something, that means actually writing it. I may actually direct a couple of episodes that I don't write next year, just because of my time being as it is. By and large, the only time I've done it is when I've co-written with David Greenwalt. The bottom line is that I like to create. To me, the writing is the most important thing, and if I'm going to take the time to direct something and it really pulls a lot out of my schedule, usually I want it to be something of my own. At the same time, it would certainly be interesting to direct somebody else's script.

10 "There are only twenty-four hours in a day," Whedon would tell Underground Online, "and raising a child certainly eats into that. I have been spending an enormous amount of time with this tiny boy that I'm in love with. That's my son by the way. I don't want that to come out wrong" (Sullivan).

11 This intentionally Slayer Speakish term is my own coinage. See "Apocalyptic Apocalypses: The Narrative Eschatology of *Buffy the Vampire Slayer*" (paragraphs 6–7, 16).

12 Whedon seems to have forgotten that Season 3 of *Angel* had a cliffhanger ending, with Connor deep-sixing Angel on the floor of the Pacific at the close of "Tomorrow" (3.22).

13 "I never would have killed Wesley if we hadn't been cancelled," Whedon admitted to the *Onion AV Club* (*JWC* 144).

14 For an excellent discussion of "Not Fade Away" see Roz Kaveney's "A Sense of the Ending: Schrödinger's *Angel*," in which she suggests that the episode's final scene is a variation of the famous thought experiment by a quantum physicist that left an imaginary cat both alive and dead if Heisenberg's uncertainty principle (suggesting that light may be both a wave and a particle) is correct.

15 Asked by Longworth which of his "children" – *Buffy* or *Angel* – he liked best, Whedon replied by extending the metaphor with parental wisdom: "It's basically like saying, 'Girls, girls, you're *both* pretty'" (*JWC* 59).

16 In the second volume of Firefly: *The Official Companion*, Whedon recalls being especially worried about the network's response to the very-Western "Heart of Gold" episode (174). The series would be cancelled before it aired.

17 The theft of Minear after a promise not to do so to David Greenwalt apparently caused more than a little tension between Whedon and *Angel's* co-showrunner (Firefly: *The Official Companion* I 8). Greenwalt would leave *Angel* at season's end.

18 See Heather Ash's "The Next Generation: *Battlestar Galactica* Creator Ron Moore Reimagines Deep Space" (41–50) and "Cutting Corners: Keeping Science Fiction Real" (71–3) in Porter, Lavery and Robson's *Finding* Battlestar Galactica.

19 Jeff Jensen reported in *Entertainment Weekly* that Whedon had "promised the Fox execs that *Firefly* would have humor, action, and F/X aplenty, while zeroing in on existential angst and those quiet, human moments […] like urinating." "One of the first things I thought was, I'm gonna have a ship with a toilet," says Whedon. "I wanted a ship that felt lived-in" ("Galaxy Quest").

20 Given that a certain Firefly-class space ship is clearly visible over Caprica in a scene in the *Battlestar* miniseries, the reimagined Battlestarverse and the Whedonverses must intersect at some level. Asked by *GeekMonthly* about his current TV watching and video game obsessions, Whedon replies: "I get addicted to things. So I don't have video games. If I had a video game console in my house, I would never work again. So I have to dose myself. I mean, obviously I watch *Battlestar*, but that's like air."

21 *Alien*, Whedon observed, "gave a real sense of, 'We live here. And this is where we eat, and this is where we sleep, and we climb up from here to here, and the vents run here" (*JWC* 144).

Chapter 9 – Creator of *Serenity*

1 These mee-mos also bring the funny. Talking in "Joss on Light" about some development in cinematography, Whedon observes that the reference "makes me sound all know-about-lightingy" and will certainly help earn him respect (*Serenity* 23).

2 On his DVD commentary, Whedon makes reference to the "Greedo effect" in his characterization of Mal: Lucas's preposterous recutting of the Cantina scene in *Star Wars: A New Hope* so that Han Solo shoots Greedo the Bounty Hunter in self-defence. A popular anti-revisionary Lucas T-shirt reads "Han Shot First." Whedon was determined to depart from *Star Wars* as an ancestor text in other ways. He wanted his ending, for example, to be "messier" than "If we hit this porthole [*sic*] in the Death Star, everything will be fine!" (*JWC* 110).

3 Whedon sarcastically claims he had been seriously considering the Oliver Stone approach (in *Alexander the Great* [2004]) for establishing the film's backstory: having Anthony Hopkins talk for 20 minutes.

4 Abbott notes that "[t]he tagline 'Can't Stop the Signal' refers both to the truth about the Alliance and the truth about *Firefly*, and also serves to vindicate the Browncoats – on and off screen – for their persistence in fighting a seemingly 'unwinnable' war" (237–8).

Chapter 10 – Visiting the *Dollhouse*

1 See "The Genius of Joss Whedon," my "Afterword" to *Fighting the Forces* (251–6).

2 The title of James Longworth's interview with Whedon. See *JWC* 42–63.

3 Rogers offers a memorable depiction of Whedon's *Dollhouse* defensiveness during a sitdown:

You know you've offended Joss Whedon when he stops talking in Whedonisms. Usually the writer-director is funny, wry, and acutely self-aware – just like the characters he creates for his shows and movies. [...] He'll order a chardonnay at lunch and slouch sideways in a booth, riffing on geek tropes from *Star Trek* to *Twilight Zone*.

But suggest that his TV show *Dollhouse* was really just about a pretty girl in a dominatrix outfit getting beaten up every week and Whedon transfigures into Buffy's erudite, ever-so-slightly supercilious mentor, Giles – if you could imagine Giles in a hoodie. The words get longer, the references more arcane. He sits up and leans over his plate of scallops, elbows on the table. The professor has arrived, and class is in session. (174)

Chapter 11 – Not Making Wonder Woman

1   Whedon, of course, denies that money was/is a lure: "It's the exact same job," he insists, no matter what the film's budget (*JWC* 146)

2   "Basically I'm never satisfied with where I am. I always want to be doing more: I always want to be doing the next thing," Whedon would tell James Longworth (*JWC* 52). Interestingly, Whedon has Ripley tell Call in *Alien Resurrection* that the scientists are keeping her alive because she is the "latest thing."

3   See Whedon's unorthodox essay "My Five Favorite Batman Movies."

4   Whedon had brought to the table an idea for a smaller, more personal Batman film; "the machine" (Whedon's phrase – see the epigraph to this chapter), however, was looking for a big movie to relaunch a franchise.

5   By comparison, both of Singer's X-Men films earned back at least twice their production cost in the USA alone.

6   "You know, his parents were killed, he lives in Gotham and he dresses like a bat! Game over, man. The fact that they made four bad Batman movies is kind of a testament to the triumph of the human spirit, because it's, like, almost impossible" (Matheson).

7   The words are Neil Gaiman's in his dialogue with Whedon for *Time Magazine*.

8   Admittedly Whedon's previously quoted admission to *Time Magazine* – "In my head, it's the finest film ever not typed yet" – could be taken as a too-clever-by-half admission that he had not actually written the script. His description of his method to Jim Kozak –

> The way I work, I'm like a vulture. I circle and circle and then I dive. I usually don't actually write anything until I know exactly how it's going to turn out. I don't "let the computer take me away." I'm an absolute Nazi about structure. I make outlines. I make charts and graphs with colors. (*JWC* 97)

– likewise allows him a measure of wiggle room, though it does smack of rationalization.

9   *Slither*, of course, starred Whedon's own Nathan Fillion, *Buffy's* Caleb, *Firefly/Serenity's* Mal and *Dr. Horrible's* Captain Hammer.

Chapter 12 – Networks of Enterprise

1 Our models were David E. Kelley, Aaron Sorkin (*West Wing*) and Tom Fontana (*Oz*).

2 Am I the only one who hears a kind of odd echo in the exchange between Mal and the captain of another pirate ship (who has tried to rob him and leave him for dead) in *Firefly's* "Out of Gas"?:

> Mal (to Captain): Take your people and go.
> Captain: You would have done the same.
> Mal: We can already see I haven't. Now get the hell off my ship.

3 My catalogue here is almost entirely dependent on admissions made in DVD commentaries and is admittedly incomplete. Unless otherwise indicated, the source is the author of the screenplay in question.

4 Sean Connery, of course, played James Bond in such iconic films as *Doctor No* (Terence Young, 1962) and *Goldfinger* (Guy Hamilton, 1964), whereas Lazenby was a disastrous, completely forgettable Bond in *On Her Majesty's Secret Service* (Peter R. Hunt, 1969).

5 What Espenson came up with – "No one else exists either. Buffy is all of us. We think. Therefore, she is." – seems a bit more Cartesian than Nietzschean, but it still brings the funny.

6 See Justine Larbalestier's "*Buffy's* Mary Sue is Jonathan: *Buffy* Acknowledges the Fans" in *Fighting the Forces* (227–38).

7 On the DVD commentary Goddard introduces the episode as being one where he will frequently admit his non-authorship, and indeed he will in the course of it acknowledge not only Joss but Marti Noxon and Jane Espenson as the real source of some of its best moments.

8 Minear explains that his contribution was in return for a promise to show up at Whedon's house for one of his Shakespeare readings.

9 The actor who played Doyle, Glenn Quinn, had himself died of a drug overdose in 2002.

10 J.J. Abrams, Harold Ramis, Jason Reitman and Amy Heckerling have all directed for the show.

11 Whedon writes,

> At the center of it all is Veronica herself. Bell is most remarkable not for what she brings (warmth, intelligence, and big funny) but for what she leaves out. For all the pathos of her arc, she never begs for our affection. There is a distance to her, a hole in the center of Veronica's persona. Bell constantly conveys it without even seeming to be aware of it. It's a star turn with zero pyrotechnics, and apart from the occasionally awkward voice-over, it's a teeny bit flawless.
>
> Season 1 works as mystery, comedy, and romantic drama, often simultaneously. But what elevates it is that in a TV-scape creepily obsessed with crime-solving, *VM* actually asks why. It knows we need our dose of solution as a panacea against the uncontrollable chaos of life's real mysteries. And it shows, feelingly, that having the answers is never enough.

12 Unless otherwise indicated, all future references in this section are to The Cabin in the Woods *Visual Companion*.

13 It should be noted that it seems clear from their "In the Woods" colloquy that Goddard was not as disillusioned as his mentor with the state of the genre.

14 The original 2011 posters for *Cabin* (eventually replaced in the "Cabin as a Rubik's Cube" rollout) emphasize this aspect, each proclaiming one of the idiocies of contemporary horror: "IF YOU HEAR A STRANGER OUTSIDE ... HAVE SEX"; "IF AN OLD MAN TELLS YOU NOT TO GO THERE ... MAKE FUN OF HIM"; "IF SOMETHING IS CHASING YOU ... SPLIT UP."

15 One of the lessons learned was the difference between a TV producer and his movie counterpart:

> A television show is the producer's set. A movie is the director's set. And I wanted to be respectful of that. So if there was something that I felt we needed, Drew and I would always talk about it. When it came to schedules and stuff, that was really my purview. I couldn't make things miraculously work the way I wanted them to and we had a pace at which we moved, and it never changed. (*CWOVC* 25–6)

16 For the record, Whedon's inherited comic book superhero flaws, according to Kaveney, include "an unexamined use of default clichés," an "overfond-ness for storylines that return to a status quo ante," cutting his heroes "too much moral slack," "excessive use of the reset button" and "an occasionally cavalier attitude to continuity" (203, 212–13, 219).

17 Kaveney provides a valuable discussion of Whedon's involvement with Kitty Pryde, comparing her with Willow instead of Buffy. See "Gifted and Dangerous" (210–11).

18 Long a harsh critic of movies made from superhero comics – his objections "not just as a comic-book geek, but as a storyteller" – Whedon is heartened by the fact that, post-*Spider-man* (Sam Raimi, 2002), the genre is "getting a tiny bit better" (Grossman), increasingly in the hands of people who actually grew up loving them instead of "ninety-year-old bald tailors with cigars, going, the kids love this!" (Grossman). As Whedon tells Tasha Robinson, "I think we're out of the time when it was a bunch of old men in suits, going [*Old-timey businessman voice.*] 'Kids like the comic books. He's bitten by a spider. Does it have to be a spider? Nobody likes spiders, they don't test well'" (*JWC* 157). Directing Marvel's *The Avengers* would, of course, allow him to make his own mighty contribution.

19 Although the first six issues of *Fray* appeared regularly beginning in 2001, the last two were delayed when Whedon found himself making *Firefly* in order to fulfill his development deal with Fox, and artist Karl Moline likewise began working on other projects for another comic book company. "It is much to my lasting shame," Whedon would tell Underground Online, "that it took so long" (Sullivan).

20 Whedon tells Brian Ash that *Fray*'s artist Karl Moline "looked a lot at the movies *Blade Runner* [Ridley Scott, 1982] and *Fifth Element* [Luc Besson, 1997] because those are both urbanization gone mad" (*JWC* 19).

21 As K. Dale Koontz has shown in a perceptive chapter of *Faith and Choice in the Works of Joss Whedon, Fray* is another version of the hero's journey as outlined by Joseph Campbell (and learned at the feet of Richard Slotkin at Wesleyan):

> Those who walk the path of Campbell's hero's journey must achieve a certain balance between the spiritual and the material, which Whedon's Fray has succeeded in doing. While she continues to live with one foot in her old world of thieving, Fray has the other planted firmly in a better world, one in which humanity has a defender – a Slayer. By taking the hero's journey, Fray has achieved freedom from the fear of death which, for her, equals the freedom to live without either anticipating the future or regretting the past. (63)

22 In writing *Alien Resurrection,* of course, Whedon had likewise joined a series – a cinematic one – in progress.

23 "[Y]ou can't pick up an *X-Men* because you have to have read the 19 before the issue you pick up to understand what's happening" (Ervin-Gore).

24 For Whedon's and editor Mike Martz's accounts of how he came to do *Astonishing* see "The Spolight Interview with Joss Whedon" and "Inside Joss Whedon's X-Men" respectively.

25 Kaveney notes that one of the things "Whedon learned from Claremont in particular and comics in general is that death really does not have to be permanent when you are dealing with superheroes" (215).

26 *BtVS*S fanfic writers, determined not to let their inspiration go quietly into that good night, had been talking about doing a Season 8 even before the series had actually ended in May 2003.

27 In *Joss Whedon: The Complete Companion,* Jack Milson offers a good "Whedon 101" overview of *Sugarshock!*

28 In *Dr. Horrible's Sing-Along Blog: The Book,* we learn that both Moist and Bad Horse – originally pitched for *Angel* – were Edlundian ideas (10)

Chapter 13 – Marvel's *The Avengers*

1 The official coffee table book, *The Art of Marvel*'s Avengers offers a detailed and exquisite insider's look at how Whedon and his team created the film's *mise-en-scène,* aka "everything that's in the frame."

2 According to Rogers, in March 2010 Whedon sat down with Marvel executive Kevin Feige "intending simply to give his take on the script. What Whedon heard himself saying about it surprised even him. 'I don't think you have anything,' he said. 'You need to pretend this draft never happened'" (196).

3 An ulterior motive also comes to mind, as Rogers notes (196): Marvel has a reputation for frugality and tends to hire lower-priced directing talent.

4 As Whedon told O'Hehir ("Interview"), unlike his earlier challenge as a writer and director, *Serenity,* a film that presented a supreme challenge because of the requirement to "target [a relatively small] fan base" while necessarily establishing the characters for a larger audience, his Marvel movie came with a pre-existing

boost: "with *Avengers*," "particularly Iron Man right now, because of the movies, Captain America, too, and the Hulk because of the TV show, everyone's got their own juice." ·

5 Ensley Guffey's discerning piece on *The Avengers* in the forthcoming *The Joss Whedon Reader* offers a valuable reading of the film as a war movie.

6 "On my deathbed," Miller would go on to say, "I very well may look back on my life's brightest moments and have to decide if the birth of my first child should be above or below watching Hulk go completely apeshit in *The Avengers*."

Chapter 14 – Joss Whedon, Auteur

1 Whedon makes the same observation to James Longworth (*JWC* 48).

2 In a featurette on the Season 7 DVD, Whedon catalogues his own ten favourite episodes of *Buffy:* (10) "Prophecy Girl"; (9) "Conversations with Dead People"; (8) "Restless"; (7) "Becoming" (Part II); (6) "The Wish" (5) "Döppelgangland"; (4) "The Body"; (3) "Hush"; (2) "Once More with Feeling"; (1) "Innocence."

3 Others have attempted to identify the Whedon DNA. Here, for example, is Adam Rogers's breakdown of "The Whedon Way" (175):

- Girl with superpowers
- Great (dead) secondary characters
- Snappy dialogue
- Musical numbers
- Deep nerd-outs
- Angsty bad guys
- Totally self-aware self-awareness

4 We should note, however, that Whedon can, when necessary, ventriloquize the religious. In *The Avengers*, when Black Widow warns Steve Rogers about the wisdom of taking on Thor, we get the following exchange as Captain America prepares to parachute out of the jet that carries him:

Black Widow: These men come from legend. They're basically gods.
Captain America: Ma'am, there's only one God, and I'm pretty sure he doesn't look like that.

5 In "Gingerbread," written by St. John and Espenson, we find it once again, coming from the mouth of Xander: "No one else is seeing *the funny* here?"

6 A good example of Whedon's jocular approach to science is the name he gives the substance Dr. Horrible needs to make his freeze ray work: "wonderflonium." In turn, his writing staff used the word "phlebotinum" to refer to any mystical/ magical contrivance needed for the plot.

7 The absence of Buffy's father, for example, was motivated by time constraints: "you have to deal with that character; how he's dealing with his ex-wife's death for example. We have so many characters to service it made things simpler to use the short hand of, 'he's just not there'" (*New York Times*).

8   Compare his admission in the official *Serenity* companion: "[A]pparently I can't write anything without an adolescent girl with superpowers, and I just have to accept that about myself and be at peace" (*Serenity* 16).

9   "Idiolect" refers to "the speech habits peculiar to a particular person" (*Oxford American Dictionary*).

10 *The Oxford American Dictionary* defines "patois" as "the dialect of the common people of a region, differing in various respects from the standard language of the rest of the country: *the nurse talked to me in a patois that even Italians would have had difficulty in understanding.*

11 *Buffy* didn't inspire as much condemnation, as, say, its contemporaries the Harry Potter books. Almost always flying below the cultural radar, it was consistently snubbed at the Emmys, and it rarely angered or offended those it should have, though L. Brent Bozell's always zealous Media Research Center did once name it "the most dangerous show on television" towards the end of its run.

   Buffy did not always slip by the censors. In England, as Viv Burr details in an excellent essay in *Slayage*, the BBC, it seems, often aired edited versions of Buffy in its regular 6.45 slot, excising sexual *and* violent moments, while broadcasting uncensored episodes late night on Friday. In the process, as Burr shows, moral complexities were frequently left on the cutting room floor.

12 Whedon had *Firefly* in mind when he admitted, "I've always had it easy with language, because I'll always throw in a word that's not *quite* the word we're not supposed to use, but clearly means it" (Firefly: *The Official Companion* II 9).

13 As we learn on the DVD commentary, Denisof had been stricken by Bell's Palsy on the left side of his face.

14 Whedon cannot speak of the autobiographical source of his obsession with redemption without bringing the funny: "I think the mistakes I've made in my own life have plagued me, but they're pretty boring mistakes: I committed a series of grisly murders in the eighties and I think I once owned a Wilson-Phillips Album."

15 The equation of religion and story may have a family origin. Whedon recalls that the "best piece of advice" given by his sitcom writer father was, "If you have a good story, you don't need jokes. If you don't have a good story, no amount of jokes can save you." What did Whedon take away from that advice? "[T]hat tenet of '*the story is god*' is the most important thing I could have learned" (Robinson, *Onion AV Club* 2001; my italics).

16 It seems likely that Whedon has read Bruno Bettelheim's *The Uses of Enchantment* (1989), the basic thesis of which is similar to his argument here.

Epilogue

1   While acknowledging that Lucas "has a stronger geek pedigree" (an assertion he takes as incontestable), he is likewise certain (and who would argue with him on this?) that the *Star Wars* creator "has taken the most popular sci-fi movie franchise in history into a straight free fall."

2   Whedon is anxious to correct the rumour that *Goners* interfered with his work on *Wonder Woman:*

Not while I was doing *Wonder Woman*. And [Warner Bros.] knew that. I sold *Goners* to Universal with the understanding that *Wonder Woman* was happening [first]. If *Goners* had completely unveiled itself in a perfect structure and the way it needed to be, I would have sat down and written it and maybe it would've gone first. But I really kept *Goners* at bay because of *Wonder Woman*. There's also a lot of ... there's personal stuff that I'm not interested in talking about that was difficult. And then there's also wonderful stuff that was difficult, which was my children. I had to create a system whereby I could get a full day's work [done] and still be the father that I want to be. (Gopalan)

3 In a post-*Avengers* letter to his fans, Whedon dismissed the notion: "A lot of stories have come out about my 'dark years', and how I'm 'unrecognized' [...] I love these stories, because they make me seem super-important, but I have never felt the darkness (and I'm ALL about my darkness) that they described" ("Purple").

4 Whedon is alluding, of course, to the final scene in Hitchcock's *North by Northwest* (1959).

5 There is another way in which Whedon's career could end prematurely. The great German poet Rilke was once asked if he would undergo the then new technique of psychoanalysis. His answer? "I'm sure [psychotherapists] would remove my devils, but I fear they would offend my angels" (quoted in Cage 127), and without both there could be no art. In a 2003 interview with MSN, we find the following exchange, in which Whedon contemplates a strikingly similar scenario:

> MSN: I'm assuming you exorcised some bad high school experience *Buffy*. What personal demons are you still hoping to work out through your work, and in what medium will you tackle those?
> JW: Well, you know, I have a shrink now, so I won't be making any more TV.
> MSN: No, you can't do that! Get rid of him!
> JW: Yes! Make me worse. I need material.
> MSN: You have fans, damn it!
> JW: They expect pain and I want to give it to them!

6 In her keynote at the *Slayage* Conference on the Whedonverses 3, Basinger revealed that Whedon has offered an alternative epitaph. Since he never had the opportunity to take Basinger's "Four Directors" course at Wesleyan – a seminar devoted to Hitchcock, Preminger, Minnelli and von Sternberg – he wants that failure epitaphly memorialized: "He never got to take the Four Directors class."

BIBLIOGRAPHY

The following bibliography is comprised of print, Internet, and DVD resources which were instrumental in writing this book. Readers will also want to consult two comprehensive and indispensable Whedonverses bibliographies, the first an Internet resource, the second a book:

Hornick, Alysa. "Buffyology: An Academic Studies & Whedonverses Bibliography." Available at http://www.alysa316.com/Buffyology.
Macnaughton, Don. *The Buffyverse Catalog: A Complete Guide to* Buffy the Vampire Slayer *and* Angel *in Print, Film, Television, Comics, Games, and Other Media, 1992–2010.* Jefferson, NC: McFarland, 2011.

Abbott, Stacey, Angel. *Television Milestones.* Detroit: Wayne State University Press, 2008.
———. "'Can't Stop the Signal': The Resurrection/Regeneration of *Serenity*." In Wilcox and Cochran, 227–38.
———. "Kicking Ass and Singing 'Mandy': A Vampire in LA." In *Reading* Angel, ed. Stacey Abbott, 1–13.
———. "'Nobody Scream … or Touch My Arms': The Comic Stylings of Wesley Wyndham-Pryce." In *Reading* Angel, ed. Stacey Abbott, 189–203.
———. "'We'll Follow *Angel* to Hell … or Another Network.' The Fan Response to the End of *Angel.*" In *Reading* Angel, ed. Stacey Abbott, 230–3.
Abbott, Stacey, ed. *Reading Angel: The TV Spinoff with a Soul.* Reading Contemporary Television. London: I.B.Tauris, 2005.
Adams, Michael. *Slayer Slang: A Buffy the Vampire Slayer Lexicon.* New York: Oxford University Press, 2003.
Altman, Rick. "Television/Sound." *Studies in Entertainment: Critical Approaches to Mass Culture,* ed. Tania Modleski, 39–54. Bloomington: Indiana University Press, 1986.
Anders, Charlie Jane. "Several Reasons Why *Avengers* Kicks Ass (That You Haven't Already Heard)." *io9,* 4 May 2012. Available at http://io9.com/5907585/several-reasons-why-avengers-kicks-ass-that-you-havent-already-heard. (Accessed 4 May 2012.)
Armstrong, Kelly, Dave Ross and George Freeman. *Angel: Aftermath. Angel.* Vol. 5. San Diego: IDW, 2009.
Auerbach, Nina. *Our Vampires, Ourselves.* Chicago: University of Chicago Press, 1995.
"*Avengers*: Joss Whedon Talks Sequel, Buffy and X-Men Parallels." *Los Angeles Times,* 15 May 2012. Available at http://herocomplex.latimes.com/2012/05/15/avengers-joss-whedon-talks-sequel-buffy-and-x-men-parallels/. (Accessed 27 May 2012.)

Banfield, Stephen. *Sondheim's Broadway Musicals*. Ann Arbor: University of Michigan Press, 1993.

Barfield, Owen. *Speaker's Meaning*. San Rafael, CA: The Barfield Press, 1967.

Basinger, Jeanine. *Anthony Mann*. Boston: Twayne, 1979.

———. *The World War II Combat Film: Anatomy of a Genre*. New York Columbia University Press, 1986.

———. *A Woman's View: How Hollywood Spoke to Women, 1930–1960*. New York: Knopf, 1993.

———. *American Cinema: One Hundred Years of Filmmaking*. New York: Rizzoli, 1999.

———. *Silent Stars*. New York: Knopf, 1999.

———. "The Lure of the Gilded Cage: *All I Desire* and *There's Always Tomorrow*." *Bright Lights Film Journal* Issue 48 (May 2005). Available at http://www.brightlightfilm.com/48/sirklure.htm. (Accessed 10 June 2005.)

———. "Joss Whedon, A+ Film Major." Keynote Address, The *Slayage* Conference on the Whedonverses (3). Henderson State University, Arkadelphia, Arkansas, USA (5–8 June 2008).

Battis, Jes. *Blood Relations: Chosen Families in* Buffy the Vampire Slayer *and* Angel. Jefferson, NC: McFarland, 2005.

Bazin, Andre. *What Is Cinema?* Vols 1 and 2, ed. and trans. Hugh Gray. Berkeley: University of California Press, 1971.

Beall, Mark. "Geek Beat: Redemption." *Cinematical*. Available at http://www.cinematical.com/2006/10/10/mark-bealls-geek-beat-redemption/. (Accessed 2 April 2008.)

Bell, Jeffrey. "The Magic Bullet" Commentary. Angel: *Season Four on DVD*, Disc 5.

———. "Not Fade Away" Commentary. Angel: *Season Five on DVD*, Disc 6.

Bercovici, Jeff. "*Avengers* Director Joss Whedon on Trying to Be More Like Buffy." *Forbes*, 3 May 2012. Available at http://www.forbes.com/sites/jeffbercovici/2012/05/03/avengers-director-joss-whedon-on-trying-to-be-more-like-buffy/print/. (Accessed 13 April 2008.)

———. "Why *Avengers* Director Joss Whedon Is Going Small for His Next Act." *Forbes*, 4 May 2012. Available at http://www.forbes.com/sites/jeffbercovici/2012/05/04/why-avengers-director-joss-whedon-is-going-small-for-his-next-act/. (Accessed 10 May 2012.)

Bernardin, Marc. "Tara, Wesley and 13 Other Joss Whedon Deaths that Broke Our Hearts." *Blastr*, 7 May 2012. Available at http://blastr.com/2012/05/15-most-heartbreaking-jos.php. (Accessed 9 May 2012.)

Bernstein, Abbe, et al. Firefly: *The Official Companion*. Vol. 1. London: Titan Books, 2006.

———. Firefly: *The Official Companion*. Vol. 2. London: Titan Books, 2007.

Bettelheim, Bruno. *The Uses of Enchantment: The Meaning and Importance of Fairy Tales*. New York: Vintage, 1989.

Bianculli, David. "Fresh Air TV Critic David Bianculli Talks with JOSS WHEDON." *Fresh Air*, 9 May 2000. Available at http://whyy.org/cgi-bin/FAshowretrieve.cgi?2876. (Accessed 10 May 2000.) Reprinted in *Joss Whedon: Conversations*, 3–13.

Boreanaz, David, Brent Fletcher and Christian Kane. "Soul Purpose" Commentary. Angel: *Season Five*, Disc 3.

Breznican, Anthony. "Hero Worship." *Entertainment Weekly*, 4 May 2012. Available at http://www.ew.com/ew/article/0,,20587608,00.html. (Accessed 10 May 2012.)

Brownfield, Troy. "Brian Lynch on *Angel: After the Fall*." Newsarama.com. Originally available at http://forum.newsarama.com/showthread.php?t=123012&highlight=brian+lynch. (Accessed 2 December 2007.)

"'*Buffy* Studies': End of TV Series Clouds Future of Odd Academic Discipline." NPR Online. Available at http://www.npr.org/display_pages/features/feature_1262180.html. (Accessed 14 May 2003.)

"*Buffy the Vampire Slayer*: Television with a Bite." *A&E Biography* Featurette. Buffy the Vampire Slayer *The Complete Sixth Season on DVD*, Disc 6.

Burkhead, Cynthia. *Dreams in American Television Narratives: From* Buffy *to* Dallas. New York: Bloomsbury Academic, 2013.

Burr, Vivian. "*Buffy* and the BBC: Moral Questions and How to Avoid Them." *Slayage* 8 (March 2003). Available at http://slayageonline.com/PDF/burr.pdf. (Accessed 12 April 2007.)

Burt, Richard. *Unspeakable Shakespeares: Queer Theory and American Kiddie Culture.* New York: St. Martin's Press, 1998.

Byers, Michelle, and David Lavery, eds. *Dear Angela: Remembering* My So-Called Life. Lanham, MD: Lexington Books, 2006.

Cage, John. *Silence: Lectures and Writings.* Cambridge: MIT Press, 1961.

Caldwell, John Thornton. *Televisuality: Style, Crisis, and Authority in American Television.* New Brunswick: Rutgers University Press, 1995.

Campbell, Joseph. *The Hero with a Thousand Faces.* Bolingen Series XVII. Princeton: Princeton University Press, 1949.

Camus, Albert. *The Myth of Sisyphus and Other Essays*, trans. Justin O'Brien. New York: Vintage Books, 1955.

Carter, Bill. "The Unintended Career of TV's Prolific Writer; from Real Law Office to Two Fictional Ones." *New York Times*, 2 March 1998. Available at http://query.nytimes.com/gst/fullpage.html?res=9B0DE2DD1731F931A35750C0A96E958260&sec=&spon=&pagewanted=print. (Accessed 2 February 2007.)

———. *Desperate Networks.* New York: Broadway Books, 2006.

Chaw, Walter. "*The Dark Knight Rises*." *Film Freak Central* 19 July 2012. Available at http://www.filmfreakcentral.net/ffc/2012/12/the-dark-knight-rises.html. (Accessed 3 December 2012.)

———. "Marvel's *The* Avengers." *Film Freak Central* 3 May 2012. Available at http://www.filmfreakcentral.net/ffc/2012/05/the-avengers.html. (Accessed 11 May 2012.)

Collis, Clark. "The Year's Buzziest Fright Flick: Joss Whedon's Horror Movie Gives a Serious Case of *Cabin* Fever at the South by Southwest Festival." *Entertainment Weekly*, 30 March 2012. Available at http://www.ew.com/ew/article/0,,20582535,00.html. (Accessed 15 April 2012.)

Contner, James A., and David Fury. "Grave" Commentary. Buffy the Vampire Slayer*: The Complete Sixth Season on DVD*, Disk 6.

"Cult TV." *Talk of the Nation.* National Public Radio, 9 March 2004. Available at http://www.npr.org/templates/story/story.php?storyId=1753399. (Accessed 10 March 2004.)

Curtis, Bryan. "The Bad Boy of Summer: Michael Bay vs. His Critics." *Slate*, 15 June 2005. Available at http://www.slate.com/articles/news_and_politics/summer_movies/2005/06/the_bad_boy_of_summer.html. (Accessed 10 October 2007.)

Daniels, Les. *Wonder Woman: The Life and Times of the Amazon Princess*. San Francisco: Chronicle Books, 2000.

Dargis, Manohla. "Hot Properties." *The New York Times*, 30 December 2007. Available at http://www.nytimes.com/2007/12/30/books/review/Dargis-t.html. (Accessed 6 April 2008.)

"David Greenwalt" (interview). In *Writing Science Fiction and Fantasy Television*, ed. Joe Nazzaro, 148–61. London: Titan Books, 2002.

Davis, Michael. *Street Gang: The Complete History of* Sesame Street. New York: Viking, 2008.

Dawson, Angela. "Whedon Corrals Marvel Superheroes in *The Avengers*." *Business World* Online, 10 May 2012. Available at http://www.bworldonline.com/weekender/content.php?id=51507. (Accessed 10 May 2012.)

DeCandido, Keith R.A. "'The Train Job' Didn't Do the Job: Poor Opening Contributed to *Firefly's* Doom." In Espenson, *Finding Serenity*, 55–61. Dallas: BenBella Books, 2004.

DeKnight, Steven. "Inside Out" Commentary. Angel: *Season Four on DVD*, Disc 5.

Dick, Bernard. *Anatomy of Film*. 3rd ed. New York: St. Martin's, 1998.

"*Dr. Horrible's Sing-along* Blog: The Script." In Whedon, et al., Dr. Horrible's Sing-along Blog: *The Book* 16–69.

"*Dr. Horrible* Sequel: Joss Whedon Updates on Second Neil Patrick Harris Film." *Huffington Post*, 19 November 2011. Available at http://www.huffingtonpost.com/2011/11/19/dr-horrible-sequel-joss-whedon_n_1102733.html. (Accessed 20 November 2011.)

Ebert, Roger. "*Alien Resurrection*." *Chicago Sun Times*, 26 November 1997. Available at http://rogerebert.suntimes.com/apps/pbcs.dll/article?AID=/19971126/REVIEWS/711260301/1023. (Accessed 22 March 2007.)

Edelstein, David. "'The Avengers': A Marvel-ous Whedonesque Ride." *Fresh Air* 3 May 2012. Available at http://www.npr.org/2012/05/03/151934102/the-avengers-a-marvel-ous-whedonesque-ride. (Accessed 22 May 2012.)

Eiseley, Loren. *The Man Who Saw Through Time*. New York: Scribner's, 1973.

Epstein, Daniel Robert. "Joss Whedon." Suicide Girls. Available at http://suicidegirls.com/interviews/Joss+Whedon/. (Accessed 15 October 2008.) Reprinted in Lavery and Burkhead, 129–37.

Erickson, Greg. "Humanity in a 'Place of Nothing': Morality, Religion, Atheism, and Possibility in *Firefly*." In Wilcox and Cochran, 167–79.

Ervin-Gore, Shauna. "Joss Whedon." darkhorse.com (2001). Available at http://www.darkhorse.com/news/interviews.php?id=737. (Accessed 15 October 2008.)

Espenson, Jane. "Earshot" Commentary. Buffy the Vampire Slayer: *The Complete Third Season on DVD*, Disk 5.

———. "Introduction." In *Finding* Serenity, ed. Espenson, 1–3.

———. "I Was Made to Love You" Commentary. Buffy the Vampire Slayer: *The Complete Fifth Season on DVD*, Disk 4.

———. "Superstar" Commentary. Buffy the Vampire Slayer: *The Complete Fourth Season on DVD*, Disk 5.

———. "Rm w/a Vu" Commentary. Angel: *Season One on DVD*, Disc 2.

Espenson, Jane, Drew Goddard, Nick Marck, Danny Strong and Tom Lenk. "Conversations with Dead People" Commentary. Buffy the Vampire Slayer: *The Complete Seventh Season on DVD*, Disk 2.

Espenson, Jane, ed. *Finding* Serenity: *Anti-Heroes, Lost Shepherds and Space Hookers in Joss Whedon's* Firefly. Dallas: BenBella Books, 2004.

———. *Inside Joss'* Dollhouse: *From Alpha to Rossum*. Dallas: BenBella Books, 2010.

ET Online 2000 Interview with Joss Whedon. Originally available at http://www.theslayershow.com/chat8.html. (Accessed 5 April 2002.)

Fanforum 2000 Interview with Joss Whedon. Originally available at http://www.fanforum.com/buffy/news/786.shtml. (Accessed 3 April 2002.)

"Filmmakers Reflect." *Toy Story* 10th Anniversary Edition. Disney-Pixar (2005).

Franich, Darren. "Joss Whedon to Direct *The Avengers*?: Existence of God No Longer in Doubt." *Entertainment Weekly*, 13 April 2010. Available at http://popwatch.ew.com/2010/04/13/joss-whedon-to-direct-the-avengers-existence-of-god-no-longer-in-doubt/. (Accessed 15 April 2010.)

Fritts, David. "Warrior Heroes: *Buffy the Vampire Slayer* and *Beowulf*." *Slayage* 17 (June 2005). Available at http://slayageonline.com/PDF/fritts.pdf. (Accessed 2 January 2007.)

Furey, Emmett. "Brian Lynch Talks *Angel: After the Fall*." Comic Book Resources. Available 11 June 2007 at http://www.comicbookresources.com/?page=article&id=11911. (Accessed 10 December 2007.)

Fury, David. "Helpless" Commentary. Buffy the Vampire Slayer: *The Complete Third Season on DVD*, Disk 4.

Fury, David, and Andy Hallett. "The House Always Wins" Commentary. Angel: *Season Four on DVD*, Disc 1.

Fury, David, and James A. Contner. "Primeval" Commentary. Buffy the Vampire Slayer: *The Complete Fourth Season on DVD*, Disk 6.

Fury, David, and David Grossman. "Real Me" Commentary. Buffy the Vampire Slayer: *The Complete Fifth Season on DVD*, Disk 1.

Fury, David, Christian Kane and Sarah Thompson. "You're Welcome" Commentary. Angel: *Season Five on DVD*, Disc 4.

Fury, David, Drew Goddard, D.B. Woodside and James Marsters. "Lies My Parents Told Me" Commentary. Buffy the Vampire Slayer: *The Complete Seventh Season on DVD*, Disk 5.

Gallagher, Diana G., and Paul Ruditis. *Angel: The Casefiles*. Vol. 2. New York: Simon Spotlight, 2004.

Gardner, Howard. "Breakaway Minds" (interview with Howard Gruber). *Psychology Today* (July 1981): 68–73.

———. *Frames of Mind: The Theory of Multiple Intelligences*. New York: Basic Books, 1985.

———. *Creating Minds: An Anatomy of Creativity Seen Through the Lives of Freud, Einstein, Picasso, Stravinsky, Eliot, Graham, and Gandhi*. New York: Basic Books, 1993.

Gellar, Sarah Michelle. "An Interview with Sarah Michelle Gellar." *Spectrum: The Magazine of Television, Film, and Comics!* (December 1999): 2–9.

"Genius." *Oxford English Dictionary* Online. 1989 Version.

Gershman, Michael. "Consequences" Commentary. Buffy the Vampire Slayer: *The Complete Third Season on DVD*, Disk 4.

Gilchrist, Josh. "*Avengers*' Writer-Director Joss Whedon on His 'Insanely Massive Ego.'" *The Hollywood Reporter*, 7 May 2012. Available at http://www.hollywoodreporter.com/heat-vision/avengers-writer-director-joss-whedon-marvel-321095. (Accessed 8 May 2012.)

Gillum, Vern, and Steven DeKnight. "Apocalypse, Nowish" Commentary. Angel: *Season Four on DVD*, Disc 2.

Ginn, Sherry. *Power and Control in the Television Worlds of Joss Whedon*. Jefferson, NC: McFarland, 2012.

Goddard, Drew, and David Solomon. "Selfless" Commentary. Buffy the Vampire Slayer: *The Complete Seventh Season on DVD*, Disk 2.

Goddard, Drew, and Nicholas Brendon. "Dirty Girls" Commentary. Buffy the Vampire Slayer: *The Complete Seventh Season on DVD*, Disk 5.

Greenberg, Drew. "Smashed" Commentary. Buffy the Vampire Slayer: *The Complete Sixth Season on DVD*, Disk 3.

Greenwalt, David. "Reptile Boy" Commentary. Buffy the Vampire Slayer: *The Complete Second Season on DVD*, Disk 2.

Golden, Christopher, and Nancy Holder. *Buffy the Vampire Slayer: The Watcher's Guide*. New York: Pocket Books, 1998.

———. *Sunnydale High Yearbook*. New York: Pocket Books, 1999.

Golden, Christopher, Stephen R. Bissette and Thomas E. Sniegoski. *Buffy the Vampire Slayer: The Monster Book*. New York: Pocket Books, 2000.

Gopalan, Nisha. "Whedon After 'Wonder'-land." *Entertainment Weekly*. Available at http://www.ew.com/ew/article/0,,20049318,00.html. (Accessed 15 November 2008.)

Gottfried, Martin. *Sondheim*. New York: H.N. Abrams, 1993.

Gray, Jonathan. "Resurrecting the Author: Joss Whedon's Place in *Buffy*'s Textual Universe." Paper given at Blood, Text, and Fears Conference, University of East Anglia, October 2003.

Gross, Edward. "Life in the Whedonverse: After Facing Repeated Frustrations in the Feature Film World, Joss Whedon Found Creative Happiness in a Universe of His Own Making." Available at http://www.vampiresandslayers.com/. (Accessed 25 November 2007.)

Grossman, Lev. "Interview: Neil Gaiman and Joss Whedon." *Time Magazine* 25 September 2005. Available at http://www.time.com/time/arts/article/0,8599, 1109313,00.html. (Accessed 28 September 2005.)

Gruber, Howard E. "Darwin's 'Tree of Nature' and Other Images of Wide Scope." In *On Aesthetics in Nature*, ed. Judith Wechsler, 121–40. Cambridge: MIT Press, 1978.

———. "'And the Bush Was not Consumed.' The Evolving Systems Approach to Creativity." In *Towards a Theory of Psychological Development*, ed. Sahan and Celia Modgli, 269–99. Windsor, UK: NFER, 1980.

———. "The Evolving Systems Approach to Creativity." In *Towards a Theory of Psychological Development*, ed. Sohan and Celia Modgil, 269–99. Windsor, UK: NFER, 1980.

———. "Cognitive Psychology, Scientific Creativity, and the Case Study Method." In *On Scientific Creativity*, ed. M.D. Graek, R.S. Cohen and G. Cimino, 295–322. Amsterdam: D. Reidel, 1980.

———. "On the Relation Between 'Aha Experiences' and the Construction of Ideas." *History of Science* 19 (1981): 41–59.

———. "History and Creative Work: From the Most Ordinary to the Most Exalted." *Journal of the History of the Behavioral Sciences* 19 (1983): 4–15.

———. "The Emergence of a Sense of Purpose." In *Beyond Formal Operations*, ed. M. Commons, 3–27. New York: Praeger, 1984.

———. "The Evolving Systems Approach to Creative Work." In Wallace and Gruber, *Creative People at Work: Twelve Case Studies*, 3–24.

———. "Foreword." In *Notebooks of the Mind: Explorations of Thinking*, by Nora John-Steiner, ix–xii. New York: Harper and Row, 1985.

———. "From Epistemic Subject to Unique Creative Person at Work." *Archives de Psychologie* 54 (1985): 167–85.

———. "Which Way Is Up? A Developmental Question." In *Adult Cognitive Development*, ed. R.A. Mines and K.S. Kitchener, 112–33. New York: Praeger, 1986.

Guffey, Ensley. "*The Avengers*." In Wilcox, et al., *A Joss Whedon Reader* (forthcoming).

Halfyard, Janet K. "The Dark Avenger: *Angel* and the Cinematic Superhero." In *Reading* Angel, ed. Stacey Abbott, 149–62.

Harris, Will. "Joss for a Minute: A Brief Chat with Joss Whedon." Available at http://www.bullz-eye.com/mguide/interviews/2005/joss_whedon.htm. (Accessed 15 April 2007.)

Hart, Hugh. "How Does Joss Whedon Rest Up? With a Whirlwhind Shoot for *Much Ado About Nothing*." *Wired*, 25 October 2011. Available at http://www.wired.com/underwire/2011/10/joss-whedon-much-ado-about-nothing/. (Accessed 15 December 2011.)

Havens, Candace. *Joss Whedon: The Genius Behind Buffy*. Dallas: BenBella Books, 2003.

Havrilesky, Heather. "Trapped in the *Dollhouse*." *Salon*, 12 February 2009. Available at http://www.salon.com/2009/02/12/dollhouse/. (Accessed 15 February 2009.)

Hein, Jon. *Jump the Shark*. New York: Plume Books, 2002.

Hibberd, James. "Joss Whedon Returns to Fox with New Series *Dollhouse*." TVweek.com. Available at http://www.tvweek.com/blogs/james-hibberd/2007/10/joss_whedon_returns_to_fox_wit.php. (Accessed 1 November 2007.)

Hills, Matt. *Fan Cultures*. London: Routledge, 2002.

Hills, Matt, with P.H. Barrett. *Darwin on Man: A Psychological Study of Scientific Creativity*. Chicago: University of Chicago Press, 1980.

Hills, Matt, and S.N. Davis. "Inching Our Way Up Mount Olympus: The Evolving Systems Approach to Creative Thinking." In *The Nature of Creativity*, ed. R.J. Sternberg, 243–69. New York: Cambridge University Press, 1988.

Hinson, Hal. "*Buffy the Vampire Slayer*." *Washington Post*, 31 July 1992. Available at http://www.washingtonpost.com/wp-srv/style/longterm/movies/videos/buffythevampireslayerpg13hinson_a0a790.htm. (Accessed 4 April 2007.)

Hochman, David. "Is Michael Bay the Devil?" *Entertainment Weekly*, 10 July 1998: 40.

Holder, Nancy. *Angel: The Casefiles*. Vol. 1. New York: Simon Spotlight, 2002.

———. *Queen of the Slayers*. New York: Simon Spotlight, 2005.

———. *Buffy: The Making of a Slayer*. London: Titan Books, 2012.

Holder, Nancy, with Jeff Mariotte and Maryelizabeth Hart. *Buffy the Vampire Slayer: The Watcher's Guide*. Vol. 2. New York: Pocket Books, 2000.

Howe, Desson. "*Buffy the Vampire Slayer*." *Washington Post*, 31 July 1992. Available at http://www.washingtonpost.com/wp-srv/style/longterm/movies/videos/buffythevampireslayerpg13howe_a0aee8.htm. (Accessed 4 April 2007.)

Hunter, Stephen. "*Alien Resurrection*: Birth of the Ooze." *Washington Post*, 28 November 1997. Available at http://www.washingtonpost.com/wp-srv/style/longterm/movies/videos/alienresurrectionhunter.htm. (Accessed 2 April 2007.)

IGN-Film Force Interview. "Featured Filmmaker: Joss Whedon: A Look at the Career of the *Buffy the Vampire Slayer* Creator." 2003. Available at http://www.ign.com/articles/2003/06/17/featured-filmmaker-joss-whedon. (Accessed 15 October 2008.)

Innsdorf, Annette. *François Truffaut*. New York: Touchstone, 1989.

"Into the Woods: Joss Whedon and Drew Goddard on the Making of the Film." In *The Cabin in the Woods: The Official Visual Companion*, 8–42.

Jacobs, A.J. "Interview with a Vampire Chronicler." *Entertainment Weekly*, 25 April 1997. Available at http://www.ew.com/ew/article/0,,287570,00.html. (Accessed 22 February 2002.)

Jenkins, Henry. *Textual Poachers: Television Fans and Participatory Culture*. New York: Routledge, 1992.

———. *Convergence Culture: Where Old and New Media Collide*. New York: New York University Press, 2008.

Jensen, Jeff. "*Dollhouse*: First Look at Joss Whedon's New Series." *Entertainment Weekly*. Available at http://www.ew.com/ew/article/0,,20200712,00.html. (Accessed 2 January 2008.)

———. "Galaxy Quest: *Buffy the Vampire Slayer* Mastermind Joss Whedon Launches an Intergalatic Western that Comes Complete with a Tight-Pants-Wearing Captain, A Space Hooker, and a Behind-the-Scenes Showdown." *Entertainment Weekly*, 13 September 2002: 96–9.

———. "The Goodbye Girl." *Entertainment Weekly*, 7 March 2003: 14–18, 21.

Jones, Gerard. *Men of Tomorrow: Geeks, Gangsters, and the Birth of the Comic Book*. New York: Basic Books, 2004.

"Joss Whedon – 'Angel' TV Series and Comic Book." Geekmonthly.com. Available at http://www.whedon.info/Joss-Whedon-Angel-Tv-Series-Comic.html. (Accessed 10 November 2007.)

"Joss Whedon Grocery List Garnering Huge Internet Buzz." Available at http://www.datelinehollywood.com/archives/2005/10/03/joss-whedon-grocery-list-garnering-huge-internet-buzz/. (Accessed 2 April 2007.)

"Joss Whedon to Take Over *Runaways*." Marvel.com. Available at http://marvel.com/news/comicstories.628. (Accessed 15 October 2006.)

"Joss Whedon-Official Handbook." *Marvel Spotlight: Joss Whedon/Michael Lark* (2006).

"Joss Whedon – The Pull List." *Marvel Spotlight: Joss Whedon/Michael Lark* (2006).

Jowett, Lorna. *Sex and the Slayer: A Gender Studies Primer of the* Buffy *Fan*. Middleton: Wesleyan University Press, 2005.

Kaveney, Roz, ed. *Reading the Vampire Slayer: The New, Revised, Unofficial Guide to* Buffy *and* Angel. 2nd ed. London and New York: Tauris Parke Paperbacks, 2004.

———. "A Sense of the Ending: Schrodinger's *Angel*." In *Reading* Angel, ed. Stacey Abbott, 57–72.

———. *Superheroes! Capes and Crusaders in Comics and Films*. London: I.B.Tauris, 2007.

———. "Writing the Vampire Slayer: Interviews with Jane Espenson and Steven S. DeKnight." In Kaveney, *Reading the Vampire Slayer*, 100–31.

Keats, John. *Selected Poetry and Letters*, ed. Richard Harter Fogle. New York: HRW, 1969.

Keller, Fred. "Over the Rainbow" Commentary. Angel: *Season Two on DVD*, Disc 6.

Kinsey, Tammy A. "Transitions and Time: The Cinematic Language of *Angel*." In *Reading* Angel, 44–56.

Kit, Boris. "Joss Whedon to Write and Direct *Avengers 2*." *Hollywood Reporter*, 7 August 2012. Available at http://www.hollywoodreporter.com/news/joss-whedon-avengers-sequel-359148. (Accessed 7 August 2012.)

Koontz, K. Dale. *Faith and Choice in the Work of Joss Whedon*. Jefferson, NC: McFarland, 2008.

Kott, Jan. *Shakespeare, Our Contemporary*. Trans. Boleslaw Taborski. Garden City, New York: Doubleday, 1964.

Kozak, Jim. "Serenity Now!" *In Focus*. Available at http://www.natoonline.org/infocus/05augustseptember/whedonuncut.htm. (Accessed 26 March 2008.) Reprinted in Lavery and Burkhead, 85–106.

Kristen. "Best News Ever! Joss Whedon Spills Exclusive Deets on His New Series." *EOnline*. Available at http://www.eonline.com/news/3956/best-news-ever-joss-whedon-spills-exclusive-deets-on-his-new-series. (Accessed 15 November 2007.)

Lametti, Daniel, Aisha Harris, Natasha Geiling and Natalie Matthews-Ramo. "Which Pop Culture Property Do Academics Study the Most?" *Slate*, 11 June 2012. Available at http://www.slate.com/blogs/browbeat/2012/06/11/pop_culture_studies_why_do_academics_study_buffy_the_vampire_slayer_more_than_the_wire_the_matrix_alien_and_the_simpsons_.html. (Accessed 12 June 2012.)

Larbalestier, Justine. "*Buffy's* Mary Sue Is Jonathan: *Buffy* Acknowledges the Fans." In Wilcox and Lavery, 227–38.

Laskas, Jeanne Marie. "Bay: The Hands-on Hotshot." *Esquire* July 2001. Available at http://www.esquire.com/features/the-screen/ESQ0701-JULY_BAY_rev_2. (Accessed 1 September 2007.)

Lavery, David. "Creative Work: On the Method of Howard Gruber." *The Journal of Humanistic Psychology* 33 (1993): 101–21.

———. "Like Light: The Movie Theory of W. R. Robinson." In *Seeing Beyond: Movies, Visions, and Values*, ed. Richard P. Sugg, 346–63. New York: Golden String Press, 2001.

———. Review Essay of *Buffy the Vampire Slayer: The Monster Book* by Golden, Bissette and Sniegoski, In *Buffy the Vampire Slayer: The Watcher's Guide*. Vol. 2, by Holder, Mariotte and Hart, and *The Sopranos: A Family History*, by Alan Rucker. *Television Quarterly* 31.4 (Winter 2001): 89–92.

———. "Afterword: The Genius of Joss Whedon." In *Fighting the Forces: What's at Stake in* Buffy the Vampire Slayer, ed. Rhonda V. Wilcox and David Lavery, 251–6. Lanham, MD: Rowman Littlefield, 2002.

———. "A Religion in Narrative: Joss Whedon and Television Creativity." *Slayage* 7 (December 2002). Available at http://slayageonline.com/PDF/lavery2.pdf. (Accessed 9 October 2007.)

———. "'Emotional Resonance and Rocket Launchers': Joss Whedon's Commentaries on the *Buffy the Vampire Slayer* DVDs." *Slayage* 6 (September 2002). Available at http://slayageonline.com/PDF/lavery.pdf. (Accessed 9 October 2007.)

———. "Apocalyptic Apocalypses: The Narrative Eschatology of *Buffy the Vampire*

Slayer." *Slayage* 9 (August 2003). Available at http://slayageonline.com/PDF/lavery3.pdf. (Accessed 5 April 2010.)

———. "*Buffy the Vampire Slayer.*" In *50 Key Television Programmes*, ed. Glen Creeber, 31–5. London: Arnold, 2004.

———. "'I Wrote My Thesis on You': *Buffy* Studies as an Academic Cult." *Slayage* 13–14 (October 2004). Available at http://slayageonline.com/PDF/lavery4.pdf. (Accessed 18 November 2007.)

———. "The Island's Greatest Mystery: Is *Lost* Science Fiction?" In *The Essential Science Fiction TV Reader*, ed. J.P. Telotte, 283–98. Lexington: University Press of Kentucky, 2008.

———. "The Imagination Will Be Televised: Showrunning and the Re-animation of Authorship in 21st Century American Television." In *Autorenserien: die Neuerfindung des Fernsehens* (*Auteur Series: The Rebirth of Television*), ed. Christoph Dreher, 63–112. Stuttgart: Merz & Solitude, 2010.

———. "Impossible Girl: Amy Sherman-Palladino and Television Creativity." In *Screwball Television: Critical Perspectives on* Gilmore Girls, ed. David Scott Diffrient, with David Lavery, 3–18. The Television Series. Syracuse: Syracuse University Press, 2010.

———. "*My So-Called Life* Meets *The X-Files*: Winnie Holzman's Influence on Joss Whedon." In Byers and Lavery, 211–16.

Lavery, David, ed. *Reading* Deadwood: *A Western to Swear By.* London: I.B.Tauris, 2006.

———. *The Essential Cult Television Reader.* Lexington: University Press of Kentucky, 2008.

Lavery, David, and Robert J. Thompson. "David Chase, *The Sopranos,* and Television Creativity." In *This Thing of Ours: Investigating* The Sopranos, 18–25. New York: Columbia University Press, 2002.

Lawson, Mark. "Mark Lawson Talks to David Chase." In *Quality TV: Contemporary American Television and Beyond*, 185–220. London: I.B.Tauris, 2007.

Lee, Patrick. "Joss Whedon Gets Big, Bad and Grown-up with *Angel.*" Interview. *Science Fiction Weekly* (1999). Reprinted in Lavery and Burkhead, 14–17.

Legel, Laremy. "Comic-Con: Exclusive Interview with Joss Whedon." (3 August 2007.) Available at http://www.ropeofsilicon.com/comic_con_exclusive_interview_with_joss_whedon/. (Accessed 15 October 2008.)

Leupp, Thomas. Interview with Joss Whedon. Available at JoBlo.com: http://www.joblo.com/index.php?id=5754>. (Accessed 15 October 2008.) Reprinted in *Joss Whedon Conversations*, 80–4.

Loeb, Jeph. "Citizen Joss." In Whedon, Moline and Owens. *Fray* n.p.

Longworth, James L., Jr. *TV Creators: Conversations with America's Top Producers of Television Drama.* Syracuse: Syracuse University Press, 2000.

———. *TV Creators: Conversations with America's Top Producers of Television Drama*, Volume 2. Syracuse: Syracuse University Press, 2002.

———. "Joss Whedon: Feminist" (interview). In *TV Creators*. Vol. 2, 197–220.

Lovecraft, H.P. *The Annotated H. P. Lovecraft*, ed. S.T. Joshi. New York: Dell, 1997.

Loewenstein, Lael. "Basinger's Students Make Their Mark: Wesleyan Maven Has Network of Devoted Grads." *Variety*, 27 March 2008. Available at http://www.variety.com/article/VR1117983035.html?categoryid=2870&cs=1&nid=2564. (Accessed 4 April 2008.)

Lynch, Brian. *Angel: Last Angel in Hell. Angel.* Vol. 6. San Diego: IDW, 2010.

Matheson, Whitney. "A Q&A with ... Joss Whedon." *Pop Candy* USA TODAY, 23 December 2005. Available at http://content.usatoday.com/communities/popcandy/post/2005/12/152533/1#.T75vxcmF9gw. (Accessed 15 October 2008.)

Mayflower, Darwin. "Script Review: *Suspension* and *Afterlife* by Joss Whedon." *Screenwriters Utopia*, 1 January 2001. Available at http://www.screenwritersutopia.com/modules.php?name=Content&pa=showpage&pid=2649. (Accessed 22 August 2007.)

McDuffee, Keith. "The Five: Worst Episodes of *Buffy* (or 'Bored Now')." TVSquad.com. Posted 31 October 2006. Available at http://www.tvsquad.com/2006/10/31/the-five-worst-episodes-of-buffy-or-bored-now/. (Accessed 10 January 2011.)

"Michael Bay Signs $50M Deal To Fuck Up *ThunderCats*." *The Onion*, 13 April 2009. Available at http://www.theonion.com/articles/michael-bay-signs-50m-deal-to-fuck-up-thundercats,2702/. (Accessed 17 April 2009.)

Miller, Frank, with Klaus Janson and Lynn Varley. *Batman: The Dark Knight Returns.* New York: Warner, 1986.

Miller, Joshua. "Review: *The Avengers*." CHUD, 29 April 2012. Available at http://www.chud.com/91485/review-the-avengers-joshs-take/. (Accessed 11 May 2011.)

Miller, Laura. "The Man Behind the Slayer." *Salon.* Available at http://www.salon.com/ent/tv/int/2003/05/20/whedon/index.html. (Accessed 15 October 2008.). Reprinted in Lavery and Burkhead, 71–9.

———. "Return of the Vagina Dentata from Outer Space: Sigourney Weaver Is in Fine Form in the Latest in the 'Alien' Series of Freudian-Toothed Slimefests, 'Alien Resurrection.'" *Salon* 26 (November 1997). Available at http://www.salon.com/ent/movies/1997/11/26alien.html?CP=SAL&DN=110. (Accessed 6 December 2007.)

Miller, Mark Crispin. "Hollywood the Ad." *Atlantic Monthly*, April 1990. Available at http://www.theatlantic.com/magazine/archive/1990/04/hollywood-the-ad/5005/ (Accessed 4 February 1996.)

Millman, Joyce. "*Angel*." In *The Essential Cult Television Reader*, ed. David Lavery, 28–35.

———. "The Death of Buffy's Mom." *Salon*, 12 March 2001. Available at http://www.salon.com/2001/03/12/buffy_mom/. (Accessed 1 April 2001.)

Milson, Jack. "Whedon 101: Sugarshock!" In *Money*, ed. *Joss Whedon*, 334–6.

Minear, Tim. "Are You Now or Have You Ever Been" Commentary. Angel: *Season Two on DVD*, Disc 1.

———. "Home" Commentary. Angel: *Season Four on DVD*, Disc 6.

Minear, Tim, and Jeffrey Bell. "Billy" Commentary. Angel: *Season Three on DVD*, Disc 2.

Minear, Tim, and Mere Smith. "Lullaby" Commentary. Angel: *Season One on DVD*" Commentary. Angel: *Season Three on DVD*, Disc 3.

Money, Mary Alice. "*Firefly's* 'Out of Gas': Genre Echoes and the Hero's Journey." In Wilcox and Cochran, 114–24.

———, ed. *Joss Whedon: The Complete Companion.* New York: Titan Books, 2012.

Morris, Gary, and Martuta Thesiger. Review of *A Woman's View: How Hollywood Spoke to Women 1930–1960. Bright Lights Film Journal* Issue 15 (November 1995). Available at http://www.brightlightsfilm.com/15/books.html. (Accessed 6 April 2008.)

Murray, Noel. "The Hollow Men." *Onion AV Club*, 15 January 2010. Available at http://www.avclub.com/articles/the-hollow-men,37159/. (Accessed 15 January 2010.)

Nelson, Robin. *State of Play: Contemporary "High-end" TV Drama*. Manchester: Manchester University Press, 2007.

Nguyen, Hanh. "Whedon Feeds 'Wonder Woman' Casting Rumors." Zap2It, 21 March 2005. Available at http://movies.zap2it.com/movies/news/story/0,1259,---25139,00.html. (Accessed 25 March 2005.)

Noxon, Marti. "What's My Line, Parts I & II" Commentary. Buffy the Vampire Slayer: *The Complete Second Season on DVD*, Disk 5.

Noxon, Marti, and David Fury. "Bargaining, Parts I & II" Commentary. Buffy the Vampire Slayer: *The Complete Sixth Season on DVD*, Disk 1.

Nussbaum, Emily. "Must See Metaphysics." *New York Times*, 22 September 2002. Reprinted in Lavery and Burkhead, 64–70.

———. "Sick of *Buffy* Cultists? You Ain't Seen Nothing Yet." *New York Times*, 8 June 2003.

O'Hara, Terrence, and Jeffrey Bell. "Orpheus" Commentary. Angel: *Season Four on DVD*, Disc 4.

O'Hehir, Andrew. "Interview: Joss Whedon on His Two Big Movies." *Salon*, 13 April 2012. Available at http://www.salon.com/2012/04/13/interview_joss_whedon_on_his_two_big_movies/singleton/. (Accessed 14 April 2012.)

———. "Pick of the Week: Joss Whedon's Horror Puzzler." *Salon*, 12 April 2012. Available at http://www.salon.com/2012/04/13/pick_of_the_week_joss_whedons_horror_puzzler/. (Accessed 13 April 2012.)

"Once More With Feeling" Script Book. New York: Simon Pulse, 2002.

"Origin Story: A *Doctor Horrible* Roundtable." In Whedon, et al., Dr. Horrible's Sing-along Blog: *The Book*, 8–15.

Ostow, Micol, and Steven Brezenoff. *The Quotable Slayer*. New York: Simon Pulse, 2003.

Pantozzi, Jill. "Joss Whedon and Warren Ellis Join for a Non-Sing-Along Web Series." *The Mary Sue*, 20 October 2011. Available at http://www.themarysue.com/joss-whedon-and-warren-ellis-join-for-web-series/. (Accessed 22 October 2011.)

Pateman, Matthew. *The Aesthetics of Culture in Buffy the Vampire Slayer*. Jefferson, NC: McFarland, 2005.

Perpetua, Matthew. "From *Buffy* to *The Avengers*: Joss Whedon's Best and Worst Projects." *Rolling Stone*, 2 May 2012. Available at http://www.rollingstone.com/movies/photos/from-buffy-to-the-avengers-joss-whedons-best-and-worst-projects-20120502#ixzz1vbgb54bh. (Accessed 10 May 2012.)

Petrie, Doug. "Fool for Love" Commentary. Buffy the Vampire Slayer: *The Complete Fifth Season on DVD*, Disk 2.

———. "The Initiative" Commentary. Buffy the Vampire Slayer: *The Complete Fourth Season on DVD*, Disk 2.

———. "This Year's Girl" Commentary. Buffy the Vampire Slayer: *The Complete Fourth Season on DVD*, Disk 4.

Phipps, Keith. "*The Avengers*." *Onion AV Club*, 2 May 2012. Available at http://www.avclub.com/articles/the-avengers,73396/. (Accessed 11 May 2012.)

Playdon, Zoe-Jane. "'The Outsiders' Society': Religious Imagery in *Buffy the Vampire Slayer*." *Slayage* 5 (May 2002). Available at http://slayageonline.com/PDF/playdon.pdf. (Accessed 18 October 2002.)

Pomerantz, Dorothy. "Joss Whedon May Not Be Getting $100 Million in Disney Deal, But He's Still Getting a Lot." *Forbes*.com, 9 May 2013. Available at http://www.forbes.com/sites/dorothypomerantz/2013/05/09/joss-whedon-may-not-be-getting-100-million-but-hes-still-getting-a-lot/. (Accessed 15 May 2013.)

Porter, Lynnette, David Lavery and Hillary Robson. *Finding* Battlestar Galactica: *An Unauthorized Guide*. Napierville, IL: Source Books, 2008.

Priggé, Steven. *Created By…. Inside the Minds of TV's Top Show Creators*. Los Angeles: Silman-James Press, 2005.

Puchko, Christy. "New Details on Joss Whedon's *In Your Eyes*, Plus Lead Announcements." Cinema Blend.com, 15 February 2012. Available at http://www.cinemablend.com/new/Details-Joss-Whedon-Your-Eyes-Plus-Lead-Announcements-29460.html. (Accessed 16 February 2012.)

Rambo, Elizabeth. "Banter, Battles, Betrayal, and 'Kissy th' face!': *Sugarshock!*'s Quintessential Whedonverse." Paper Presented at the *Slayage* Conference on the Whedonverses 5 (Vancouver, BC, July 2012).

Resnick, Laura. "That Angel Doesn't Live Here Anymore." In Yeffeth, *Five Seasons of Angel*, 15–22.

Ridley, John. "Three Writers Are Drawn by the Allure of Comics." *Morning Edition*. National Public Radio, 25 March 2006. Available at http://www.npr.org/templates/story/story.php?storyId=87867518. (Accessed 26 March 2006.)

Riess, Jana. *What Would Buffy Do? The Vampire Slayer as Spiritual Guide*. San Francisco: Jossey-Bass, 2004.

Robinson, Tasha. Interview with Joss Whedon. *Onion AV Club*, 5 September 2001. Available at http://www.avclub.com/articles/joss-whedon,13730/. (Accessed 25 October 2007.) Reprinted in *The Tenacity of the Cockroach: Conversations with Entertainment's Most Enduring Outsiders*, ed. Stephen Thompson, 369–77. New York: Three Rivers Press, 2002.

———. Interview with Joss Whedon. *Onion AV Club* 8 August 2007. Available at http://www.avclub.com/articles/joss-whedon,14136/. (Accessed 15 October 2007.)

Rodriguez, Rene. "*The Avengers*." *Miami Herald*, 4 May 2012. Available at http://www.miamiherald.com/2012/05/04/2781068/the-avengers-pg-13.html. (Accessed 11 May 2012.)

———. "The Mere Mention of His Name Is Enough to Make Movie Critics Hiss and Moan." *Miami Herald*. Available at http://michaelbay.com/articles/the-mere-mention-of-his-name-is-enough-to-make-movie-critics-hiss-and-groan/. (Accessed 11 November 2007.)

Rogers, Adam. "With *The Avengers* Joss Whedon Masters the Marvel Universe." *Wired*, May 2012: 170–5, 194, 196, 198–9.

Rosen, Lisa. "Family Tradition: With Hollywood Writers, the Apple Doesn't Fall Far from the Tree." *Written By* May 2007: 33–9. Reprinted in Lavery and Burkhead, 170–4.

Ruditis, Paul. *The Watcher's Guide*, Vol. 3. New York: Spotlight, 2004.

Rumi, Jalal Al-din. *Mystical Poems of Rumi*, trans. A.J. Arberry. Chicago: University of Chicago Press, 1968.

Ryan, Maureen. "*Avengers*' Fans: Thank TV for That Awesome Movie (And What Joss Should Do Next)." *Huffington Post*, 6 May 2012. Available at http://www.huffingtonpost.com/maureen-ryan/avengers-joss-whedon_b_1485356.html. (Accessed 22 May 2012.)

Sartre, Jean-Paul. *Nausea*, trans. Lloyd Alexander. New York: New Directions, 1964.

———. *Essays in Existentialism*, ed. Wade Baskin. New York: Citadel Press, 1965.

———. *Being and Nothingness*, trans. Hazel E. Barnes. New York: Washington Square Press, 1966.

Schatz, Thomas. *Hollywood Genres: Formulas, Filmmaking, and the Studio System*. New York: Random House, 1981.

Schiff, Len. "Joss Whedon: Absolute Admiration for Sondheim." *The Sondheim Review* 11.4 (Summer 2005). Available at http://www.sondheimreview.com/v11n4.htm#sample. (Accessed 9 September 2007.)

Schoolnik, Skip, David Fury, Juliet Landau and Steven DeKnight. "Destiny" Commentary. Angel: *Season Five on DVD*, Disc 2.

Schoolnik, Skip, Elizabeth Craft, Sarah Fain and Adam Baldwin. "Underneath" Commentary. Angel: *Season Five on DVD*, Disc 5.

Serenity: *The Official Visual Companion*. London: Titan Books, 2005.

Shaara, Michael. *The Killer Angels*. New York: Ballantine, 1974.

Siemann, Catherine. "Darkness Falls on the Endless Summer: Buffy as Gidget for the Fin de Siècle." In Wilcox and Lavery, 120–9.

Slotkin, Richard. *Abe: A Novel of the Young Lincoln*. New York: Holt, 2001.

———. "Creating Myths" (interview). *The Paula Gordon Show*. Available at http://paulagordon.com/shows/slotkin. (Accessed 11 November 2007.)

———. *Fatal Environment: The Myth of the Frontier in the Age of Industrialization, 1800–1890*. New York: HarperPerennial, 1986.

———. *Gunfighter Nation: The Myth of the Frontier in Twentieth Century America*. New York: HarperPerennial, 1992.

———. *Lost Battalions: The Great War and the Crisis of American Nationality*. New York: Holt, 2005.

———. *Regeneration Through Violence: The Mythology of the American Frontier, 1600–1860*. Middletown, CT: Wesleyan University Press, 1973.

Snyder, Daniel D. "Scarlett Johansson Has the Most Human Moment in *The Avengers*." *The Atlantic*, 7 May 2012. Available at http://www.theatlantic.com/entertainment/archive/2012/05/scarlett-johansson-has-the-most-human-moment-in-the-avengers/256822/. (Accessed 11/5/2012.)

Solomon, David, and Drew Greenberg. "The Killer in Me" Commentary. Buffy the Vampire Slayer: *The Complete Seventh Season on DVD*, Disk 4.

Sondheim, Stephen. *Four by Sondheim (A Little Night Music, Sweeney Todd, Sunday in the Park with George, A Funny Thing Happened on the Way to the Forum)*. New York: Applause Books, 2000.

South, James B., ed. Buffy the Vampire Slayer *and Philosophy: Fear and Trembling in Sunnydale*. Chicago: Open Court, 2003.

Spiegel, Danny. "Joss Whedon Q&A." Wizard Online. Available at http://www.wizarduniverse.com/021108whedon.html. (Accessed 8 April 2008.)

"Spotlight Interview with Joss Whedon." *Marvel Spotlight*: Joss Whedon/Michael Lark (2006).

Sragow, Michael. "Disney Got an Animation Genius When It Bought Pixar." *Baltimore Sun*, 27 January 2006. Available at http://articles.baltimoresun.com/2006-01-27/features/0601270097_1_john-lasseter-pixar-joe-ranft. (Accessed 10 October 2007.)

Stepakoff, Jeffrey. *Billion Dollar Kiss: The Story of a Television Writer in the Hollywood Gold Rush*. New York: Gotham Books, 2007.

Stevenson, Gregory. *Televised Morality: The Case of Buffy the Vampire Slayer*. Dallas: Hamilton Books, 2004.

Sullivan, Michael Patrick. Interview with Joss Whedon. Underground Online (2003). Available at http://www.whedon.info/Joss-Whedon-UnderGroundOnline-com. html. (Accessed 15 October 2008.)

Surell, Jason. *The Art of* The Avengers. New York: Marvel Worldwide, 2012.

Taylor, Charles. "*Bad Boys II*." *Salon*, 18 July 2003. Available at http://www.salon. com/2003/07/18/bad_boys_ii/. (Accessed 10 October 2007.)

Tales of the Slayers. Milwaukie, OR: Darkhorse Comics, 2001.

Tales of the Slayers. Vol. 2. New York: Simon Spotlight, 2003.

The Cabin in the Woods: *The Official Visual Companion*. New York: Titan Books, 2012.

"The Screenplay." In The Cabin in the Woods: *The Official Visual Companion*, 44–151.

Thompson, Robert J. *Television's Second Golden Age: From* Hill Street Blues *to* ER. London and New York: Continuum, 1996.

Tobias, Scott. "Epitaph Two: Return." *Onion TV Club*, 29 January 2010. Available at http://www.avclub.com/articles/epitaph-two-return,37694/. (Accessed 29 January 2010.)

Topel, Fred. Interview with Joss Whedon. C.H.U.D.com, 27 December 2004. Available at http://www.whedon.info/Joss-Whedon-Serenity-Movie-Chud.html. (Accessed 15 October 2008.)

Topping, Keith. *The Complete Slayer: An Unofficial and Unauthorized Guide to Every Episode of* Buffy the Vampire Slayer. London: Virgin, 2004.

Travers, Peter. "*Buffy the Vampire Slayer*." *Rolling Stone*. Available at http://www. rollingstone.com/reviews/movie/_/id/5947185/rid/5947186/. (Accessed 22 March 2007.)

Trechak, Brian. "Joss Whedon Producing Web Musical." Available at http://www. aoltv.com./2008/03/20/joss-whedon-poducing-web-musical/. (Accessed 4 April 2008.)

Tucker, Ken. "*Dollhouse* Becomes Pleasingly Complex, with More Info and Action." *Entertainment Weekly*, 21 March 2009. Available at http://watching-tv. ew.com/2009/03/21/dollhouse-joss-2/. (Accessed 22 March 2009.)

Tutuola, Amos. *The Palm-Wine Drinkard and My Life in the Bush of Ghosts*. New York: Grove Press, 1993.

TV Guide Guide to TV. New York: Barnes and Noble, 2005.

Udovitch, Mim. "What Makes Buffy Slay?" *Rolling Stone*, 11 May 2000: 60–2, 63–6.

VanDerWerff, Todd. "Dream On." *Onion TV Club*, 18 May 2010. Available at http:// www.avclub.com/articles/dream-on,41290/. (Accessed 19 May 2010.)

Vowell, Sarah. "Please, Sir, May I Have a Mother." *Salon*, 2 February 2000. Available at http://www.salon.com/2000/02/02/vowell_wb/. (Accessed 3 February 2000.)

Wallace, Doris B., and Howard E. Gruber, eds. *Creative People at Work*: Twelve Cognitive Case Studies. New York: Oxford University Press, 1989.

Watkins, Mary M. *Waking Dreams*. New York: Harper and Row, 1976.

Whedon, Joss. "Ace of Case." *Entertainment Weekly*, 27 March 2007. Available at http://www.ew.com/ew/article/0,,1114734,00.html. (Accessed 2 April 2007.)

———. Firefly: *A Celebration*. London: Titan Books, 2012.

————. "Afterword." The Cabin in the Woods: *The Official Visual Companion*, 172–3.

————. "The Body" Commentary. Buffy the Vampire Slayer: *The Complete Fifth Season on DVD*, Disk 5.

————. "Chosen" Commentary. Buffy the Vampire Slayer: *The Complete Seventh Season on DVD*, Disk 6.

————. "City of" Commentary. Angel: *Season 1 on DVD*, Disc 1.

————. "Conviction" Commentary. Angel: *Season Five on DVD*, Disc 1.

————. "Dear Fan Type."

————. "Foreword" to *Fray*.

————. "Hush" Commentary. Buffy the Vampire Slayer: *The Complete Fourth Season on DVD*, Disk 3.

————. "Innocence" Commentary. Buffy the Vampire Slayer: *The Complete Second Season on DVD*, Disk 4.

————. "Introduction." In *"Once More With Feeling" Script Book*. New York: Simon Pulse, 2002, ix.

————. "It's Shakespeare's Fault" (essay included in liner notes). *Buffy the Vampire Slayer – Once More with Feeling*. Rounder/Umgd, 2002.

————. "My Five Favorite Batman Movies." *Wizard* (September 2004): 50–1.

————. "Objects in Space." Firefly: *The Complete Series*, Disc 4.

————. "Equality Now Speech" ("On the Road to Equality"). 15 May 2006. Available at http://www.equalitynow.org/media/joss_whedon_accepts_equality_now_award. (Accessed 20 May 2006.)

————. "Once More with Feeling" Commentary. Buffy the Vampire Slayer: *The Complete Sixth Season on DVD*, Disk 2.

————. "The Purple." *Whedonesque*, 9 May 2012. Available at http://whedonesque.com/comments/28797. (Accessed 10 May 2012.)

————. "Reality TV" (essay included in liner notes). *My So-called Life: The Complete Series* (2007).

————. "Restless" Commentary. Buffy the Vampire Slayer: *The Complete Fourth Season on DVD*, Disk 6.

————. "Spin the Bottle" Commentary. Angel: *Season 3 on DVD*, Disc 2.

————. "Waiting in the Wings" Commentary. Angel: *Season Three on DVD*, Disc 4.

————. "Welcome to the Hellmouth" and "The Harvest" Commentary. Buffy the Vampire Slayer: *The Complete First Season on DVD*, Disk 1.

Whedon, Joss, et al. *Buffy the Vampire Slayer Season Eight*, Vol. 1: *The Long Way Home*. Milwaukie, OR: Dark Horse Books, 2007.

————. *Buffy the Vampire Slayer Season Eight*, Vol. 2: *No Future for You*. Milwaukie, OR: Dark Horse Books, 2008.

————. *Buffy the Vampire Slayer Season Eight*, Vol. 3: *Wolves at the Gate*. Milwaukie, OR: Dark Horse Books, 2008.

————. *Buffy the Vampire Slayer Season Eight*, Vol. 4: *Time of Your Life*. Milwaukie, OR: Dark Horse Books, 2009.

————. *Buffy the Vampire Slayer Season Eight*, Vol. 5: *Predators and Prey*. Milwaukie, OR: Dark Horse Books, 2009.

————. *Buffy the Vampire Slayer Season Eight*, Vol. 6: *Retreat*. Milwaukie, OR: Dark Horse Books, 2010.

————. *Buffy the Vampire Slayer Season Eight*, Vol. 7: *Twilight*. Milwaukie, OR: Dark Horse Books, 2010.

———. *Buffy the Vampire Slayer Season Eight*, Vol. 8: *Last Gleaming*. Milwaukie, OR: Dark Horse Books, 2011.

Whedon, Joss, Amy Acker and Alexis Denisof. "A Hole in the World" Commentary. Angel: *Season Five on DVD*, Disc 4.

Whedon, Joss, and Alexis Denisof. "Spin The Bottle" Commentary. Angel: *Season Four on DVD*, Disc 2.

Whedon, Joss, and Brian Lynch. *Fright Night. Angel: After the Fall*. Vol. 2. San Diego: IDW, 2009.

Whedon, Joss, and David Greenwalt. "City Of" Commentary. Angel: *Season One on DVD* Angel: *Season One on DVD*, Disc 1.

Whedon, Joss, and David Solomon. "Lessons" Commentary. Buffy the Vampire Slayer: *The Complete Seventh Season on DVD*, Disk 1.

Whedon, Joss, and John Cassaday. "Dangerous." In *Astonishing X-Men*. New York: Marvel, 2007.

Whedon, Joss, and John Cassaday. "Gifted." In *Astonishing X-Men*. New York: Marvel, 2006.

———. "Torn." *Astonishing X-Men*. New York: Marvel, 2007.

———. "Unstoppable." *Astonishing X-Men*. New York: Marvel, 2008.

Whedon, Joss, and Michael Ryan. *Runaways: Dead End Kids*. New York: Marvel Books, 2008.

Whedon, Joss, and Nathan Fillion. "Serenity" Commentary. Firefly: *The Complete Series*, Disc 1.

Whedon, Joss, and Tim Minear. "The Train Job" Commentary. Firefly: *The Complete Series*, Disc 1.

Whedon, Joss, Brett Matthews and Will Conrad. *Serenity: Those Left Behind*. Milwaukie, OR: Dark Horse Books, 2005.

———. *Serenity: Better Days*. Milwaukie, OR: Dark Horse Books, 2008.

Whedon, Joss, Brian Lynch and Franco Urru. *Angel: After the Fall*. Vol. 1. San Diego: IDW, 2008.

Whedon, Joss, Brian Lynch and Nick Runge. *Angel: After the Fall*. Vol. 3. San Diego: IDW, 2011.

Whedon, Joss, Brian Lynch, Stephen Mooney and Franco Urru. *Angel: After the Fall*. Vol. 4. San Diego: IDW, 2011.

Whedon, Joss, Karl Moline and Andy Owens. *Fray*. Milwaukie, OR: Darkhorse Comics, 2003.

Whedon, Joss, Marti Noxon and Seth Green. "'Wild at Heart' Commentary. Buffy the Vampire Slayer: *The Complete Fourth Season on DVD*, Disk 2.

Whedon, Joss, Maurissa Tancharoen, Jess Whedon and Zack Whedon. Dr. Horrible's Sing-Along Blog: *The Book*. New York: Titan Books, 2011.

"Whedon on *Horrible* Nomination." *io9* 19 July 2009. Available at http://io9.com/5317039/whedon-on-horrible-award-nomination. (Accessed 22 July 2009.)

"Wide Angle / Closeup: Director, Producer and Film Distributor Fran Rubel Kuzui." Available at http://members.aol.morgands1/closeup/text/kuzui.htm. (Accessed 15 October 2007.)

Wilcox, Rhonda V. "'I Do not Hold to That': Joss Whedon and Original Sin." In Wilcox and Cochran, 155–66.

———. "Introduction." In *Fighting the Forces: What's at Stake in* Buffy the Vampire Slayer, xvii–xxix. Lanham, MD: Rowman Littlefield, 2002.

————. *Why Buffy Matters: The Art of* Buffy the Vampire Slayer. London: I.B.Tauris, 2005.

————. "In the Demon Section of the Card Catalog: *Buffy* Studies and Television Studies." *Critical Studies in Television* 1.1 (Spring 2006). Available at http://cdn.cstonline.tv/assets/file/user_92/s6.pdf. (Accessed 15 August 2006.)

Wilcox, Rhonda V., and David Lavery. "Afterword: The Depths of *Angel* and the Birth of *Angel* Studies." In *Reading* Angel, ed. Stacey Abbott, 221–9. London: I.B.Tauris, 2005.

Wilcox, Rhonda V., and Tanya R. Cochran. "'Good Myth' – Joss Whedon's Further Worlds, and Episode Guide." In Wilcox and Cochran, 1–16.

Wilcox, Rhonda V., and David Lavery, eds. *Fighting the Forces: What's at Stake in* Buffy the Vampire Slayer. Lanham, MD: Rowman Littlefield, 2002.

Wilcox, Rhonda V., and Tanya Cochran, eds. *Investigating* Firefly *and* Serenity: *Science Fiction on the Frontier*. Investigating Cult TV. London: I.B.Tauris, 2008.

Wilcox, Rhonda V., Tanya R. Cochran, Cynthea Masson and David Lavery. *The Joss Whedon Reader* (forthcoming from Syracuse University Press, 2013).

Wright, Bradford W. *Comic Book Nation: The Transformation of Youth Culture in America*. Baltimore: Johns Hopkins University Press, 2001.

Yeffeth, Glenn, ed. *Five Seasons of* Angel. Dallas: BenBella Books, 2004.

————. *Seven Seasons of Buffy*. Dallas: BenBella Books, 2003.

Zakarin, Jordan. "Avengers' Damage to Manhattan Would Cost $160 Billion, Disaster Expert Estimates." *Hollywood Reporter*, 9 May 2012. Available at http://www.hollywoodreporter.com/news/avengers-damage-manhattan-would-cost-160-billion-322486. (Accessed 10 May 2012.)

————. "Exploring the Whedonverse: Inside the Cult Hero Fame of *Avengers'* Director Joss Whedon." 24 April 2012. Available at http://www.hollywoodreporter.com/news/joss-whedon-whedonverse-cult-hero-avengers-buffy-firefly-314554. (Accessed 25 April 2012.)

GENERAL FILMOGRAPHY

1900 (Bernardo Bertolucci, 1976)
2001: A Space Odyssey (Stanley Kubrick, 1968)
About a Boy (Chris and Paul Weitz, 2002)
Absence (Kevin Kolsch and Dennis Widmyer, 2009)
Age of Innocence, The (Martin Scorsese, 1993)
Agents of S.H.I.E.L.D. (ABC, 2013–)
Air Bud (Charles Martin Smith, 1997)
Air Force One (Wolfgang Petersen, 1997)
Alcoa Hour, The (NBC, 1955–7)
Alexander the Great (Oliver Stone, 2004)
Alias (ABC, 2001–5)
Alice (CBS, 1976–85)
Alien (Ridley Scott, 1979)
Aliens (James Cameron (1986)
Alien³ (David Fincher, 1992)
Alien: Resurrection (Jean-Pierre Jeunet, 1997)
All the President's Men (Alan J. Pakula, 1976)
American Pie (Paul Weitz, 1999)
Andy Griffith Show, The (CBS, 1960–8)
Angel (WB, 1999–2004)
Apocalypse Now (Francis Ford Coppola, 1979)
Armageddon (Michael Bay, 1998)
As Good as It Gets (James L. Brooks, 1997)
Assault of the Killer Bimbos (Anita Rosenberg, 1988)
Atlantis: The Lost Empire (Garry Trousdale and Kirk Wise, 2001)
AVP: Alien vs. Predator (Paul W.S. Anderson, 2004)
AVPR: Alien vs. Predator Requiem (Colin and Greg Strause, 2007)
Bad and the Beautiful, The (Vincente Minnelli, 1952)
Bad Boys (Michael Bay, 1995)
Bad Boys 2 (Michael Bay, 2003)
Band Wagon, The (Vincente Minnelli, 1953)
Bank Dick, The (Edward F. Cline, 1940)
Batman (Tim Burton, 1989)
Batman Begins (Christopher Nolan, 2005)
Battleship (Peter Berg, 2012)
Battlestar Galactica (Sci-Fi, 2004–8)
Beach Demons (Marc Longenecker, 2005)
Beautiful Mind, A (Ron Howard, 2001)

Benson (ABC, 1979–86)
Beverly Hills, 90210 (Fox, 1990–2000)
Big Bounce, The (George Armitage, 2004)
Black Hawk Down (Ridley Scott, 2001)
Blade (Stephen Norrington, 1998)
Blue Velvet (David Lynch, 1986)
Bonanza (NBC, 1959–73)
Boy Meets World (ABC, 1993–2000)
Brigadoon (Vincente Minnelli, 1954)
Bulworth (Warren Beatty, 1998)
Butch Cassidy and the Sundance Kid (George Roy Hill, 1969)
Cabin in the Woods, The (Drew Goddard, 2012)
Captain America: The First Avenger (Joe Johnston, 2011)
Captain America: The Winter Soldier (Anthony and Joe Russo, 2014)
Captain Kangaroo (CBS, 1955–84)
Cat People (Jacques Tourneur, 1942)
Catch Me If You Can (Steven Spielberg, 2002)
Charlie's Angels (ABC, 1976–81)
China Beach (ABC, 1988–91)
China Girl (Abel Ferrara, 1987)
Citizen Kane (Orson Welles, 1941)
City of Lost Children (Jean-Pierre Jeunet, 1995)
Close Encounters of the Third Kind (Steven Spielberg, 1977)
Cloverfield (Matthew Vaughan, 2008)
Cold Case (CBS, 2003–10)
Cool Runnings (Jon Turteltaub 1993)
Cosby Show (NBC, 1984–92)
Crimson Tide (Tony Scott, 1995)
Cruel Intentions (Roger Kumbel, 1999)
Curse of the Cat People (Robert Wise, 1944)
Dallas (CBS, 1978–91)
Dark Knight, The (Christopher Nolan, 2008)
Dark Knight Rises, The (Christopher Nolan, 2012)
Davy Crockett King of the Wild Frontier (Norman Foster, 1955)
Dawn of the Dead (George A. Romero, 1978)
Day of the Outlaw (André de Toth, 1959)
Dead Zone, The (David Cronenberg, 1983)
Deadwood (HBO, 2004–6)
Deep Rising (Stephen Sommers, 1998)
Delicatessen (Jean-Pierre Jeunet, 1991)
Descent, The (Neil Marshall, 2005)
Desperate Housewives (ABC, 2004–12)
Dexter (Showtime, 2006–13)
Dick Cavett Show, The (ABC, 1969–75)
Dick Van Dyke Show, The (CBS, 1961–6)
Die Hard (John McTiernan, 1988)
Dirty Dozen, The (Robert Aldrich, 1967)
Dirty Harry (Don Siegel, 1971)

Doctor No (Terence Young, 1962)
Doctor Who (BBC/Universal Television/BBC Wales, 1963–)
Dollhouse (Fox, 2009–10)
Don't Look Now (Nicholas Roeg, 1973)
Donna Reed Show, The (ABC, 1958–66)
Doogie Howser (ABC, 1989–93)
Dr. Horrible's Sing-Along Blog (Joss Whedon, 2008)
E.T. (Steven Spielberg, 1982)
Electric Company, The (PBS, 1971–7)
Eraserhead (David Lynch, 1977)
Everybody Loves Raymond (CBS, 1996–2005)
Evil Dead (Sam Raimi, 1981)
Evil Dead II (Sam Raimi, 1987)
Eye of the Needle (Richard Marquand, 1981)
Fantasy Island (ABC, 1977–84)
Fast Times at Ridgemont High (Amy Heckerling, 1982)
Felicity (WB, 1998–2002)
Fellini: I Am a Born Liar (Damian Pettigrew, 2002)
Fellini's Casanova (Federico Fellini, 1976)
Fifth Element (Luc Besson, 1997)
Firefly (Fox, 2002)
Friday Night Lights (NBC/Direct TV, 2006–11)
Galaxy Quest (Dean Parisot, 1999)
Gangs of New York, The (Martin Scorsese, 2002)
Getaway, The (Roger Donaldson, 1994)
Ghostbusters (Ivan Reitman, 1984)
Gilligan's Island (CBS, 1964–7)
Gilmore Girls, The (WB/CW, 2000–7)
Gladiator (Ridley Scott, 2000)
Glee (CW, 2009–)
Glitter (Vondie Curtis-Hall, 2001)
Godfather, The (Francis Ford Coppola, 1972)
Godfather III (Francis Ford Coppola, 1990)
Golden Girls, The (NBC, 1985–92)
Goldfinger (Guy Hamilton, 1964)
Gone with the Wind (Victor Fleming, 1939)
Great Gildersleeve (NBC, 1955–6)
Great Train Robbery, The (Edwin S. Porter, 1903)
Grimm (NBC, 2011–)
Halloween (John Carpenter, 1978)
Hamlet (Michael Almereyda, 2000)
Harry Potter and the Deathly Hallows, Part II (David Yates, 2011)
Heathers (Michael Lehmann, 1988)
Heaven's Gate (Michael Cimino, 1980)
Heroes (NBC, 2006–10)
Hill Street Blues (NBC, 1981–7)
Hook (Steven Spielberg, 1991)
Hostel (Eli Roth, 2005)

How I Met Your Mother (CBS, 2005–14)
Incredible Hulk, The (Louis Letterier, 2008)
Invasion of the Body Snatchers (Philip Kaufmann, 1978)
Iron Man (Jon Favreau, 2008)
Iron Man 2 (Jon Favreau, 2010)
Iron Man 3 (Shane Black, 2013)
Ishtar (Elaine May, 1987)
Island at the Top of the World, The (Robert Stevenson, 1974)
Island, The (Michael Bay, 2005)
It's a Living (ABC, 1980–2; Syndication, 1985–9)
It's Garry Shandling's Show (Showtime, 1986–90)
Jane Eyre (Robert Stevenson, 1944)
JFK (Oliver Stone, 1991)
John Carter (Andrew Stanton, 2012)
Johnny Guitar (Nicholas Ray, 1954)
Just in Time (ABC, 1988)
Justified (FX, 2010–)
Kill Bill (Quentin Tarrantino, 2003, 2004)
Klute (Alan J. Pakula, 1971)
Kraft Television Theater (NBC, 1947–58, ABC, 1953–5)
Last Action Hero (John McTiernan, 1993)
Leave It to Beaver (CBS/ABC 1957–63)
Léon: The Professional (Luc Besson, 1994)
Lethal Weapon 4 (Richard Donner, 1998)
Limey, The (Stephen Soderbergh, 1999)
Little Britain (BBC, 2003–2006)
Little Mermaid (Ron Clements, John Musker, 1989)
Lolita (Stanley Kubrick, 1962)
Lord of the Rings, The (Peter Jackson, 2001, 2002, 2003)
Lost (ABC, 2004–2010)
Lost Boys, The (Joel Schumacher, 1987)
Love for Lydia (ITV, 1979)
Lux Video Theatre (CBS, 1950–9)
M*A*S*H (CBS, 1972–83)
MacGyver (ABC, 1985–92)
Mad About You (NBC, 1992–9)
Mad Max (George Miller, 1979)
Mad Men (AMC, 2007–)
Magnolia (Paul Thomas Anderson, 1999)
Manchurian Candidate, The (John Frankenheimer, 1962)
Manhattan (Woody Allen, 1979)
Married … With Children (FOX, 1987–97)
Masterpiece Theatre (PBS, 1971–)
Matrix, The (The Wachowski Brothers, 1999)
McCabe and Mrs. Miller (Robert Altman, 1971)
Memento (Christopher Nolan, 2000)
Men in Black (Barry Sonnenfeld, 1997)
Minority Report (Steven Spielberg, 2002)

Minus Man (Hampton Fancer, 1999)
Misery (Rob Reiner, 1990)
Monty Python's The Meaning of Life (Terry Jones and Terry Gilliam, 1990)
Moulin Rouge (Baz Luhrmann, 2001)
Mr. Rogers (PBS, 1968–2001)
Much Ado About Nothing (Joss Whedon, 2013)
My So-Called Life (ABC, 1994–5)
National Treasure (John Turteltaub, 2004)
National Treasure: Book of Secrets (John Turteltaub, 2007)
New Adventures of Old Christine (CBS, 2006–2010)
Nickelodeon (Peter Bodganovich, 1976)
Night of the Demon (Jacques Tourneur, 1957)
Night of the Living Dead (George Romero 1968)
Nightmare on Elm Street (Wes Craven, 1984)
Nightmare on Elm Street 4: The Dream Master (Renny Harlin, 1988)
North by Northwest (1959)
Northern Exposure (ABC, 1990–5)
Nosferatu (F.W. Murnau, 1922)
Nothing in Common (Garry Marshall, 1986)
NYPD Blue (ABC, 1993–2005)
Office, The (NBC, 2005–13)
On Her Majesty's Secret Service (Peter R. Hunt, 1969)
Once Upon a Time in the West (Sergio Leone, 1968)
Ordinary People (Robert Redford, 1980)
Oz (HBO, 1997–2003)
Pain and Gain (Michael Bay, 2013)
Parenthood (NBC, 1990–1)
Parenthood (NBC, 2010–)
Parents (Bob Balaban, 1989)
Pearl Harbor (Michael Bay, 2001)
Pee-Wee's Playhouse (CBS, 1986–90)
Picket Fences (CBS, 1992–6)
Power Rangers (*Mighty Morphin Power Rangers*) (Fox/ABC, 1993–5)
Pretty in Pink (Howard Deutch, 1986)
Prisoner, The (ITV, 1967–8)
Prometheus (Ridley Scott, 2012)
Psycho (Alfred Hitchcock, 1960)
Pulp Fiction (Quentin Tarrantino, 1994)
Punch-Drunk Love (Paul Thomas Anderson, 2002)
Pushing Daisies (ABC, 2007–9)
Queen of the Damned (Michael Rymer, 2002)
Raiders of the Lost Ark (Steven Spielberg, 1981)
Reaper (The CW, 2007–9)
Red Planet (Antony Hoffman, 2000)
Rescue Dawn (Werner Herzog, 2006)
Rio Bravo (Howard Hawks, 1959)
Rock, The (Michael Bay, 1996)
Romeo and Juliet (Baz Luhrmann, 1998)

Ronin (John Frankenheimer, 1998)
Roots (ABC, 1977)
Roseanne (ABC, 1988–97)
Saving Private Ryan (Steven Spielberg, 1998)
Scream (Wes Craven, 1996)
Searchers, The (John Ford, 1956)
Seinfeld (NBC, 1990–8)
Serenity (Joss Whedon, 2005)
Seventh Seal, The (Ingmar Bergman, 1957)
Sex and the City (HBO, 1998–2006)
Shawshank Redemption, The (Frank Darabont, 1994)
Shield, The (FX, 2002–8)
Shining, The (Stanley Kubrick, 1980)
Showtime (Tom Dey, 2002)
Simpsons, The (Fox, 1989–)
Sin City (Robert Rodriguez and Frank Miller, 2005)
Six Feet Under (HBO, 2000–5)
Sixth Sense, The (M. Night Shyamalan, 1999)
Skyfall (Sam Mendes, 2012)
Slither (James Gunn, 2006)
Smallville (the WB/the CW, 2001–11)
Sopranos, The (HBO, 1999–2007)
South Park (Comedy Central, 1997–)
Speed (Jan DeBont, 1994)
Spider-Man (Sam Raimi, 2002)
Spider-Man 3 (Sam Raimi, 2007)
St. Elsewhere (NBC, 1982–8)
Stagecoach (John Ford, 1939)
Star Trek (NBC, 1966–9)
Star Trek: The Next Generation (Syndicated, 1987–94)
Star Wars I: *The Phantom Menace* (George Lucas, 1999)
Star Wars II: *Attack of the Clones* (George Lucas, 2002)
Star Wars III: *Revenge of the Sith* (George Lucas, 2005)
Star Wars IV: *A New Hope* (George Lucas, 1977)
Star Wars V: *The Empire Strikes Back* (Irvin Kershner, 1980)
Star Wars VI: *Return of the Jedi* (Richard Marquand, 1983)
Stargate SG-1 (Showtime/Sci-Fi, 1997–2007)
Stop Making Sense (Jonathan Demme, 1984)
Studio 60 on the Sunset Strip (NBC, 2006–7)
Sullivan's Travels (Preston Sturges, 1941)
Superman (Richard Donner, 1978)
Superman Returns (Bryan Singer, 2006)
Survivor (CBS, 2000–)
Sweeney Todd (Tim Burton, 2007)
Team America: World Police (Trey Parker, 2004)
Terminator: The Sarah Connor Chronicles (Fox, 2008–9)
Texas Chainsaw Massacre, The (Tobe Hooper, 1974)
Thelma and Louise (Ridley Scott, 1991)

Thor (Kenneth Branagh, 2011)
Thor: The Dark World (Alan Taylor, 2013)
Time Machine, The (Simon Wells, 2002)
Titan A.E. (Don Bluth and Gary Goldman, 2000)
Titanic (James Cameron, 1997)
Tokyo Pop (Fran Rubel Kuzui, 1988)
Tommy (Ken Russell, 1975)
Toy Story (John Lasseter, 1995)
Trainspotting (Danny Boyle, 1996)
Transformers (Michael Bay, 2007)
Transformers: Dark of the Moon (Michael Bay, 2009)
Transformers: Revenge of the Fallen (Michael Bay, 2011)
Trial, The (Orson Welles, 1962)
Twilight Zone (CBS, 1959–64)
Twin Peaks (ABC, 1990–1)
Twister (Jan DeBont, 1996)
Ugly Betty (ABC, 2006–10)
Upstairs, Downstairs (ITV, 1971–5)
Valley Girl (Martha Coolidge, 1983)
Veronica Mars (the WB, the CW, 2004–7)
Walker, Texas Ranger (CBS, 1993–2005)
Waterworld (Kevin Reynolds, 1995)
Way We Were, The (Sydney Pollack, 1973)
West Side Story (Robert Wise, 1991)
West Wing, The (NBC, 1999–2006)
Wild Bunch, The (Sam Peckinpah, 1969)
Will and Grace (NBC, 1998–2006)
Wire, The (HBO, 2002–8)
Wiseguy (CBS, 1987–90)
Wizard of Oz, The (Victor Fleming, 1939)
Wonder Years, The (ABC, 1988–93)
X-Files, The (Fox, 1993–2002)
X-Men (Bryan Singer, 2000)
X-Men 2 (Bryan Singer, 2003)
X-Men: The Last Stand (2006)
Zulu (Cy Endfield, 1964)

INDEX

For a more comprehensive index go to http://jossacreativeportrait.com.

Abbreviations: WAA Whedonverses actor/actress; WC Whedon Collaborator